涉外法治
人才培养
系列教材

总 主 编　石佑启
执行主编　韩永红

国际商法
理论与实务

INTERNATIONAL BUSINESS LAW
TEXT, CASES AND READINGS

韩永红 编著

法律出版社
LAW PRESS·CHINA
北京

图书在版编目（CIP）数据

国际商法：理论与实务：英文 / 韩永红编著．--
北京：法律出版社，2022
涉外法治人才培养系列教材 / 石佑启总主编
ISBN 978-7-5197-6991-8

Ⅰ．①国… Ⅱ．①韩… Ⅲ．①国际商法—教材 Ⅳ．
① D996.1

中国版本图书馆 CIP 数据核字（2022）第 145829 号

国际商法：理论与实务
GUOJI SHANGFA:LILUN YU SHIWU

韩永红 编著

策划编辑 朱 峰
责任编辑 韩泓宇
装帧设计 贾丹丹

出版发行 法律出版社
编辑统筹 辞书·融出版编辑部 法律翻译与出版研发中心
责任校对 马秋婧
责任印制 吕亚莉
经　　销 新华书店

开本 710 毫米 ×1000 毫米 1/16
印张 18 **字数** 466 千
版本 2022 年 10 月第 1 版
印次 2022 年 10 月第 1 次印刷
印刷 北京虎彩文化传播有限公司

地址：北京市丰台区莲花池西里 7 号（100073）
网址：www.lawpress.com.cn
投稿邮箱：info@lawpress.com.cn
举报盗版邮箱：jbwq@lawpress.com.cn
销售电话：010-83938349
客服电话：010-83938350
咨询电话：010-63939796

书号：ISBN 978-7-5197-6991-8
定价：68.00 元
凡购买本社图书，如有印装错误，我社负责退换。电话：010-83938349

总　序

面对世界百年未有之大变局，涉外法治人才培养已成为紧迫的国家战略。习近平总书记高度重视涉外法治建设和涉外法治人才培养工作。2019年2月25日，习近平总书记在中央全面依法治国委员会第二次全体会议上的讲话中指出：“要加快推进我国法域外适用的法律体系建设，加强涉外法治专业人才培养，积极发展涉外法律服务，强化企业合规意识，保障和服务高水平对外开放。”2020年11月16日至17日，中央全面依法治国工作会议在北京召开，首次提出并确立了习近平法治思想并将其明确为全面依法治国的指导思想。习近平总书记用“十一个坚持”系统阐述了新时代推进全面依法治国的重要思想和战略部署。习近平总书记指出：“要坚持统筹推进国内法治和涉外法治。”“要坚持建设德才兼备的高素质法治工作队伍。”培养高素质涉外法治人才是坚持统筹推进国内法治和涉外法治的题中之义。习近平法治思想为加强涉外法治人才培养指明了前进方向，提供了根本遵循。我国亟需培养一大批具有国际视野，通晓国际法律规则，能够有效参与国际法律事务，且善于维护国家利益的高素质国际化人才。

“致天下之治者在人才，成天下之才者在教化，教化之所本者在学校。”高校是涉外法治人才培养的主阵地，而高质量的教材则是高校构建涉外法治人才培养体系的重要支柱，也是新时期高质量推进涉外法治人才培养工作的重要保障。但目前我国涉外法治人才培养中的教材建设仍是突出的短板。一方面，外文原版教材在体例与内容上大多呈现“西方中心主义”，较少关注我国的立法、执法、司法进展及实践需求，存在“水土不服”的弊端；另一方面，国内虽已出版一些英文、汉英双语法学教材和法律英语教材，但面向的读者群各有不同，且未形成体系。因此，自主编写一套满足新时期涉外法治人才培养需要的系列教材实乃必要与适时之举。

广东外语外贸大学法学学科在设立之初即将涉外法治人才培养作为特色，已基本形成“法学＋外语”和“外语＋法学”两种涉外法治人才培养模式。2002—2007年，广东外语外贸大学曾陆续出版了“法律英语系列教材”（“十一五”国家规划教材）和“WTO法系列教材”，在全国产生了较好的影响。自2008年起，又陆续出版了《国际商法》《国际贸易法》等多部英文、汉英双语法学教材，现已多次印刷、再版，被全国百余所高校选用。在此基础上，为积极回应新时期国家涉外法治人才培养的需求，我们与法律出版社合作启动了“涉外法治人才培养系列教材”项目，组织了一批具有涉外法治人才培养经验的一线教师，展开教材编写工作，旨在为我国涉外法治人才培养贡献“广外力量”，共同推进我国涉外法治人才培养事业的发展。

“涉外法治人才培养系列教材”包含法律英语类教材和英文法学类教材两个子系列。其中，法律英语类教材包含《法律英语》《法律翻译》《法律英语辩论》《法律英语听说》，英文法学类教材包含《国际经济法》《国际商法：理论与实务》《国际商事仲裁》。这是一个开放的项目，两个子系列下会有更多的相关教材编写并出版。“涉外法治人才培养系列教材”注重满足我国高校涉外法治人才培养教学的实际需要。在体例上，“涉外法治人才培养系列教材”的编写兼采国内外同类教材的优点，编者本着便利于使用者的原则进行章节和栏目安排。该系列教材设置了英汉对照术语表、类型丰富的练习题、拓展性阅读资料等栏目，供读者根据自身情况选用。在内容上，“涉外法治人才培养系列教材”的编写兼顾理论性与实用性、全球性与地域性。该系列教材既注重对法律规则的讲解，也注重对案例的剖析；既注重对重要国际条约、国际惯例的阐释，也注重对主要国家国内法的介绍，尤其关注中国相应的立法、执法和司法实践。在语言上，“涉外法治人才培养系列教材”的编者用英文写作。该系列教材以英语为直接媒介，致力于高效地提升使用者的法律英语应用能力、法律知识获取能力和法律问题解决能力。

“涉外法治人才培养系列教材”的持续出版需要良好的组织协调工作，需要专业的出版服务，更需要高素质的编者。该系列教材的编者要具有全球视野、家国情怀，还要具有丰富的一线教学经验，法律专业与英语水平“两强”，对涉外法治人才培养怀有极大热情，舍得投入大量时间和精力。在此谨对各位编者的辛勤付出和敬业精神致以崇高敬意！对法律出版社高水准的编辑出版工作表示衷心感谢！

“涉外法治人才培养系列教材”的编写是一项探索性、挑战性的工作。虽然编者已努力为之，但鉴于个体认知的局限，以及编写工作的复杂性、任务的艰巨性，难免会有诸多疏漏与不足之处。恳请读者不吝指正，以便教材编写工作不断改进、编写质量不断提升。

石佑启

2022 年 8 月

Foreword

Given the fact that the world today is in the midst of a once-in-a-century transformation, the training of legal professionals for foreign-related legal affairs has become an urgent national strategy. Xi Jinping, General Secretary of the Central Committee of the Communist Party of China (CPC), attaches great importance to the development of foreign-related rule of law and the training of legal professionals for foreign-related legal affairs. At the second plenary meeting of the Commission for Overall Law-based Governance of the CPC Central Committee held on February 25, 2019, Xi Jinping stressed the necessity to facilitate the development of a legal system on extraterritorial application of Chinese laws, to improve the training of legal professionals for foreign-related legal affairs, to promote the development of foreign-related legal services and to strengthen enterprises' compliance so as to maintain and support China's high-level opening up. The Central Conference on Work Related to Overall Law-based Governance was held from November 16 to November 17, 2020, which first put forward Xi Jinping Thought on the Rule of Law and made it the guideline of overall law-based governance. Xi Jinping proposed "eleven points that we must continue to implement" to formulate the ideas and strategic plans concerning overall law-based governance in the new era. He pointed out that "we must take a coordinated approach to the rule of law at home and in matters involving foreign parties" and that "we must develop a force of high-caliber legal personnel with moral integrity and professional competence". The training of high-quality legal professionals for foreign-related legal affairs is indeed the key to a coordinated approach to promoting the rule of law at home and in matters involving foreign parties. Xi Jinping Thought on the Rule of Law serves as both a beacon and a fundamental guideline for strengthening the training of legal professionals for foreign-related legal affairs. Now, China is in urgent need to foster a constellation of talents who are internationally-minded and have a good command of multiple countries' laws, being capable of effectively participating in international legal affairs and safeguarding China's interests.

"The key to good governance lies in talents; the key to fostering talents lies in education; the key to education lies in schools." Therefore, universities are at the forefront of training legal professionals for foreign-related legal affairs, and high-quality textbooks are the mainstay of establishing a system for training such professionals, as well as the guarantee for effective training of such professionals in the new era. However, the existing textbooks are far from being satisfactory with regard to the training of legal professionals for foreign-related legal affairs. On the one hand, the original foreign textbooks are mostly West-centered in their organization and content, and they rarely focus on China's legislation, law enforcement, and practical needs, which may even lead to problems of poor adaptability. On the other hand, although some law textbooks in English have been published at home, they target different groups of readers and are not systematically published. Thus, it is actually a necessary and timely move to compile a new series of textbooks to meet the needs of training legal professionals for foreign-related legal affairs in the new era.

Guangdong University of Foreign Studies has the tradition of training legal professionals for foreign-related legal affairs since its discipline of law was established. For now, two basic modes for training such professionals have been established — the "Law + Foreign Language" mode and the "Foreign Language + Law" mode. From 2002 to 2007, Guangdong University of Foreign Studies published the legal English textbook series (Eleventh Five-Year National Plan Textbooks) and WTO law textbook series, which had a good influence across the country. Since 2008, Guangdong University of Foreign Studies has published some English or bilingual legal textbooks such as *International Business Law* and *International Trade Law* which have been repeatedly printed, republished and used as textbooks by over a hundred colleges and universities across China. On such basis, in order to proactively respond to China's need of the training of legal professionals for foreign-related legal affairs in the new era, we cooperate with Law Press·China to launch the Project of Textbook Series of Legal Professional Training for Foreign-Related Legal Affairs (the Textbook Series). We have organized a constellation of teachers who have experience of training legal professionals for foreign-related legal affairs to write textbooks, aiming to contribute "Guangwai's power" to the training of such professionals in China.

The Textbook Series includes two subseries: legal English textbooks and legal textbooks (English version). Legal English textbooks include *Legal English*, *Legal Translation*, *Legal English Debate*, and *Legal English Listening and Speaking*. Legal textbooks (English version) contain *International Economic Law*, *International Business Law: Text, Cases and Readings*, and *International Commercial Arbitration*. Since the project is inclusive, more textbooks in the two subseries will be compiled and published. The Textbook Series places a high value on the practical needs of China's universities pertaining to the training and education of legal professionals for foreign-related legal affairs. For example, in terms of the organization of the textbooks, the Textbook Series draws on the advantages of similar textbooks at home and abroad with chapters and content being well arranged for readers' convenience. In addition to the main text, English-Chinese bilingual glossaries, a variety of exercises and supplementary reading materials are included for learners to use flexibly. In terms of content, the Textbook Series gives consideration to both theory and practice, as well as global application and local application. To be more specific, the textbooks not only focus on the explanation of rules of law, but also attach importance to the dissection of cases; they not only lay emphasis on the interpretation of international treaties and international conventions, but also place a high value on the introduction to major countries' domestic law, especially China's relevant legislation, law enforcement and judicial practice. In terms of language, the textbooks are written in English. In the course of direct English learning, such textbooks are aimed at efficiently improving learners' proficiency in legal English, to acquire legal knowledge and to solve legal problems.

The continuous publication of the Textbook Series requires good organization and coordination, as well as professional publishing service. More important, it needs high-quality authors who are internationally-minded, patriotic, rich in teaching experience, adept at legal studies and foreign languages, keen on the training of legal professionals for foreign-related legal affairs and willing to devote much time and energy to the training of such professionals. I hereby would like to show my highest respect for authors of their dedication and commitment, and express my heartfelt thanks to Law Press·China for its excellent editing and publishing service.

The publication of the Textbook Series is an exploratory and challenging task. Although authors have paid great effort to complete it, given the fact that personal cognition is limited and that the task is complex and arduous, it seems inevitable that omissions and deficiencies may exist in the Textbook Series. Please contact us if any mistake is found therein and we are glad to correct such mistake so as to improve the quality of the Textbook Series.

Shi Youqi

August 2022

Preface

Facing great changes undergoing in the international relations and global governance, a demand for the foreign-related legal talents has become urgent in China. China needs to speed up the training of foreign-related legal talents with international vision, being familiar with international rules, being capable of participating in international legal affairs, being good at safeguarding national interests and promoting the reform of global governance rules. Responding to the needs of the times, writing and publishing a series of textbooks adaptable to the demand for the training of foreign-related legal talents is a significant project. It is also an important impetus for the author to write this textbook—*International Business Law: Text, Cases and Readings*. Moreover, the domestic and international legal environment in which international business transactions operate has witnessed new developments in recent years. For example, the Supreme People's Court of the People's Republic of China (PRC) has established the first and second international commercial courts in order to hear international commercial cases in a timely and fair manner, equally protect the legitimate rights and interests of Chinese and foreign parties, and create a stable, fair, transparent and convenient law-based business environment; on May 28, 2020, the Civil Code of PRC was adopted at the third session of the 13th National People's Congress and entered into force as of January 1, 2021; on September 12, 2019, the *United Nations Convention on International Settlement Agreements Resulting from Mediation* (also known as the Singapore Convention on Mediation) entered into force; *Convention on the Recognition and Enforcement of Foreign Judgments in Civil or Commercial Matters* was adopted on July 2, 2019 by the Hague Conference on Private International Law, aiming to promote efficiency by facilitating a uniform set of core rules for the recognition and enforcement of international judgments. In order to reflect these new developments, *International Business Law: Text, Cases and Readings* is intended to help the learners to understand and grasp the legal framework of international business transactions and improve their ability to solve legal problems arising from international business transactions.

In order to help learners to quickly understand this textbook, some related questions are briefly discussed as follows.

In terms of the structure, this textbook draws on the advantages of similar teaching materials at home and abroad, and organizes the structure according to the needs of English/bilingual teaching in colleges and universities of China. For example, there are different opinions on the definition and content of international business law. Scholars in civil law countries often take the domestic commercial legislation as the basis and include the regulations of commercial organizations, while those in common law countries tend to include all the legal issues involved in international business activities ranging from trade in goods and services to investment. The author hereof defines international business law in a more concise manner as the body of rules and norms that regulate the cross border transactions in goods and services between parties. On the basis of the definitions, following the theories underlying the international business law and the stages of international business activities, this textbook is divided into five parts: Part I The Environment of International Business， Part II Fundamentals of International Business Law, Part III Law of International Sale of Goods, Part IV Law of International Trade in Services, and Part V Law of International Commercial Disputes Resolution. Part III consists of three chapters: Chapter 1 Law of the Contract for International Sale of Goods, Chapter 2 Law of International Transport of Goods, and Chapter 3 Law and Banking Practice of International Payment. In addition to the texts, every part contains Learning Objectives, Cases, Exhibits, Chapter Summary and Exercises. "Learning Objectives" help readers to know the key points of this part or chapter, "Chapter Summary" is a wrapup of the main theories, rules and viewpoints discussed in this part or chapter, helping readers to review the main content. "Exercises" cover True or False Statements, Chapter Questions, Case Problems and Reading Materials, which are designed to be used by readers selectively.

In terms of the content, this textbook takes the theoretical, practical, global and local resources into account. It not only pays attention to important international treaties and international trade practices, but also keeps an eye on the influence of the national laws, especially the corresponding legislative and judicial practice in China. The author hopes to remind learners that international business law is not only international law but also domestic law. In learning international business law, learners should not only have a global vision, but also need to pay attention to local legal resources. In the course of discussing legal rules governing the international business transactions, this textbook clearly states the corresponding legal provisions and illustrates them with the assistance of exhibits, and various cases at home and abroad, so as to improve the practical characteristics of this coursebook. Bold letters are used to highlight the important content to remind learners of understanding and grasping.

In terms of the written language, this textbook tries to make the language rigorous, fluent and lively. The author believes that learning law in English should be committed to achieving at least three goals: the acquisition of legal knowledge, the improvement of legal English proficiency and the cultivation of legal thinking. And the acquisition of legal knowledge is the goal of the first level, improving learners' proficiency of legal English is the goal of the second level, and cultivating learners' logical and critical legal thinking is the goal of the third level. In order to cultivate learners' ability to think, analyze and solve legal problems directly in English, this textbook is written in English without any Chinese notes. This may bring challenges to a small number of readers, but may not result in learning difficulties. In most cases, the text of this book has fully explained the connotation of important legal rules and legal terms. At the same time, readers can refer to the List of Legal Terms in this book for comprehensive studying.

In the process of writing this textbook, the author has referred to a variety of relevant works, papers and electronic resources at home and abroad. The information of some works and papers can be found in the References of this book. The publication of this work has been generously funded by Guangdong University of Foreign Studies. And the trust and support from the Law Press·China and its editors have made the publication possible. The author would like to express her deep gratitude to them.

This textbook tries to avoid the "not acclimatized" problem of works on international business law written by foreign scholars, and is also committed to changing the rigid impression of local works. Of course, achievement of the goals is undoubtedly an arduous task. Although the author has made great efforts in writing, it is quite possible that there are still some mistakes and omissions. The author enjoys hearing comments, suggestions and criticisms on her work. All comments, suggestions and criticisms may be sent to the email address: unahan722@163.com. The author will consider them carefully and adopt them as many as she can in the following editions.

CONTENTS

Part I The Environment of International Business

Learning Objectives

(1) Understanding the influence of economic, political, legal and cultural forces on the development of international business and international business law
(2) Having a command of the general characteristics of world legal systems
(3) Knowing the fundamental concepts, characteristics, and sources of international law
(4) Realizing the role of international organizations in the development of international business and international business law

1 The Economic Environment of International Business

International business is the economic system of exchanging goods and services between individuals and businesses in multiple countries. International business is different from domestic business because the environment changes when transactions cross national borders. States generally have different economic environments, government systems, laws and regulations, currencies, taxes and duties as well as different cultures and practices. Typically, a company or an individual understands its domestic environment quite well, but is less familiar with the environment in other countries. Companies and individuals must invest more time and resources into understanding and dealing with the new environment.

1.1 Brief History of International Business

Today international business comprises a large and growing portion of the world's total business. As a matter of fact, international business is as old as the oldest civilization. Throughout the history of mankind, countries traded to obtain needed items from textiles to spices that were not readily available in their own countries. Asia, Middle East, Africa and Europe have been the major marketplaces of trade for hundreds of years. There was the most well-known ancient trade route—"Silk Road", which linked the market of ancient China with Middle East and Europe. Silk Road extends over 8,000 km (5,000 miles) on land and sea. Trade on the Silk Road was also a significant factor in the development of the civilizations of China, ancient Egypt, Mesopotamia, Persia, India and Rome, and helped to lay the foundations for the modern world. And by the sixteenth century, the first international sea trade route had been established by the Europeans. With the advent of great naval power, Portugal and Spain opened the Americas, India, and the Pacific to trade. They purchased textiles and porcelains from China with gold taken from Africa. For more than three hundreds of years, trade in cotton, corn, horses, weapons and even slaves thrived among Europe, America and Africa.

Much has changed in the field of international business since the end of World War II. The General Agreement on Tariffs and Trade (GATT) negotiation rounds resulted in trade liberalization, and this was continued with the formation of the World Trade Organization (WTO) in 1995. At the same time, worldwide capital movements were liberalized by most governments, particularly with the advent of electronic funds transfers. It was said the twentieth century was the century of emerging globalization. Although now there are some controversies between the so-called "globalization"and "deglobalization", nobody can deny the fact that the world is economically interdependent. Many economists and business experts believe that no trade can be purely domestic in such an economically interdependent world. No longer can an economic change in one country occur without causing reverberations throughout the world's markets. For example, the deterioration in trade relations between the United States and China may affect the manufacturing plants in Canada or Mexico. The Covid-19 affected the trade worldwide.

1.2 Economic Theories Underlying International Business

It is true that economics has had a strong influence on the shape and development of international business and the law governing international business. Indeed international business has been based on the perception that it is beneficial, that is, the gains to a country from trade outweigh the losses to the country, and the value is created through specialization and exchange in open markets. In the following, economic theories of absolute advantage, comparative advantage and competitive advantage underlying the international business will be briefly reviewed, not with a view to making contribution to the literature of economics, but providing readers for a better understanding of international business and international business law.

The core of absolute advantage theory states that nations should concentrate their efforts on producing those goods that they can make mostly efficiently, with a minimum of effort and waste. Any surplus of goods left over after domestic consumption is then traded for goods that another nation has produced under the same circumstances. Such theory was created by Adam Smith. The theory makes it clear that if Country A is more efficient or productive (whether measured in unit of labor cost, or dollars, or any other relevant commitment of resources) in a given industry, say steel, than Country B, and Country B is more efficient or productive in another industry, say textiles, and both Countries have need of the product of both industries. Country A should specialize in one and Country B in the other. Trades between the two Countries in two products will be beneficial (i.e. will conserve resources and create value) for both.

The theory of absolute advantage retained its validity for almost two centuries as the starting point for analysis of the gains from trade. The theory of absolute advantage was developed by David Ricardo, a nineteenth century British economist, into the theory of comparative advantage. The theory of comparative advantage states that a country can gain from trading goods even though it may not have an absolute advantage in producing those goods. This notion formed the basis for the theory of comparative advantage. Comparative advantage exists if the costs of production and price received for the goods allow the goods to be sold for a higher price in a foreign country than at home. When countries specialize in producing goods over which they have a comparative advantage, all countries will produce more and consume more, and wealth and employment will increase.

In 1990, as a modification of the earlier theories, Michael Porter proposed the theory of competitive advantage, advocating that a nation's advantage is determined by the ability of its companies to increase productivity and continuously innovate. It is often stressed that a nation's long-term competitiveness can best be achieved by encouraging a more attractive and competitive business environment. Some of the repeatedly proposed measures include reforms for improving conditions for the entry of new firms, improving the supply response of existing firms through privatization or foreign direct investment (FDI), improving labor productivity through improved education and training, and ensuring unit labor costs are in line with competitors and export market conditions. Thus, by improving the countries business environment, policymakers can open up new opportunities for existing and potential entrepreneurs, indirectly resulting in the increased competitiveness of companies.

In today's world, the politics of protectionism or free trade could turn an economic model inside out. But world trade has developed and become the major commercial activity that it is today based on these theories.

2 The Political Environment of International Business

The political environment is another important force that influences the international business. It refers to the type of government, the government relationship with business, and the political risk in a country. Doing business internationally thus implies dealing with different types of governments, relationships, and levels of risk.

Many different types of political systems are practicing in nations. Governments change in different ways, for example, by regular elections, occasional elections, death, or war. Government-business relationships also differ from country to country. Business may be viewed positively as the engine of growth, or may be viewed negatively as the exploiter of the workers, or somewhere in between as providing both benefits and drawbacks. Specific government-business relationships can also vary from positive to negative depending on the types of business operations involved and the relationship between the people of the host country and the people of the home country.

Almost all nations will regulate and control the goods or services passing through them. Nations regulate international business in many ways. The most common methods are **tariffs and non-tariff barriers**. Tariffs are import duties or taxes imposed on goods entering the customs territory of a nation. Tariffs are imposed for various reasons. They may include (1) collection of revenue, (2) the protection of domestic industries from foreign competition, (3) retaliation against another country or countries for imposing tariffs higher than agreed or for placing other unfair restrictions on their imports, or (4) to promote political or national security goals. For example, some tariffs provide incentives to import products from politically friendly countries and discourage the importing of products from unfriendly countries. Most tariff rates today are determined by agreements between nations.

Non-tariff barriers are all barriers to importing or exporting other than tariffs. They generally take the form of laws or administrative regulations that have the effect, directly or indirectly, of restricting access of foreign goods or services to a domestic market. Many laws and regulations in nations exist to protect the national economic and social well-being of a nation. These include health and safety regulations, environmental regulations, and industrial and agricultural standards, for example, virtually all nations require imported goods to be marked with the name of the foreign country of origin and labeled in their local language so that local consumers know what they are. Some nations may not permit the sale of certain genetically modified foods claiming the health and food safety concerns, while others permit. One nation may prohibit the sale of a certain pharmaceutical drug, even though it is considered safe and commonly sold in other countries. These laws and regulations are not necessarily enacted for the explicit purpose of restricting trade—for keeping out foreign goods and services that compete with local ones—but they may have that restricting effect.

One type of non-tariff barrier is the technical barrier to trade. These barriers take the form of technical regulations or standards that mandate how products are to be designed and how they will perform. Examples include safety standards for consumer products (such as infant cribs, car seats, etc.) and environmental standards for electrical goods. Non-tariff barriers are generally greater barriers to trade than tariffs, because non-tariff barriers can be disguised in detailed laws and regulations for claiming purposes of national security, public health and social well-being. Other obvious non-tariff barriers include quotas, embargoes, and boycotts. A quota is a restriction imposed by law on the numbers or quantities of goods, or of a particular type of good, allowed to be imported. Unlike tariffs, quotas are not internationally accepted as a lawful means of regulating trade except in some special cases. The term embargo is generally used when referring to a total or near-total ban on trade with a foreign country or countries. Embargoes can include restrictions on imports or exports, on financial transactions with the foreign country, or on travel between countries. Total or partial embargoes are often used as sanctions on countries that support terrorism, nuclear proliferation, or severe violations of human rights. The use of embargo is controversial in some circumstances. For example, the United States has maintained a near-total embargo on Cuba since the early 1960s. A boycott is a refusal to trade or do business with certain firms, usually from a particular country, on political or other grounds. Under certain circumstances, it can be illegal for a private firm or citizen to participate in a boycott.

In addition to tariffs and non-tariff barriers, nations may also impose **export controls**. An export control is a restriction on exports of goods, services, or technologies to a country or group of countries imposed for reasons of national security or foreign policy. Export controls in the United States are enforced through an export licensing system administered by the U.S. Department of Commerce. Licensing requirements can apply to exports of almost any type of goods or technologies, although advanced technology items that can contribute to the military capability of a foreign nation are most strictly regulated. In some cases, the mere sharing of technological or scientific information with a foreign national, without an export license, can be illegal. Before signing a contract for the sale of certain products or technical know-how to a foreign customer, U.S. exporters are generally advised to consider whether they will be able to obtain U.S. licensing for the shipment.

Tariffs, non-tariff barriers and export controls have a tremendous influence on how businesses make their trade and investment decisions. These decisions, in turn, are reflected in the patterns of world trade and the flows of investment capital. To conduct a business successfully in a foreign country, businesses need to have a good understanding of all these aspects of the political environment.

3 The Legal Environment of International Business

It is obvious that laws differ from country to country, and there are differences in the role of legislatures, the role of judges and the courts in applying and interpreting the law, and in legal procedures. These differences are rooted deeply in national culture, politics, economics, history and often are the result of centuries of gradual evolution, combined with rapid changes caused by wars, revolution, and political turmoil. No entity can neglect the differences when conducting international transactions in different countries.

3.1 Comparison of World Legal Systems

Though scholars have presented different opinions on the classification of world legal systems, the most widespread modern legal systems found in the world today can be briefly discribed as the common law, civil law, Islamic law, and mixed systems that incorporate characteristics of more than one.

3.1.1 The Civil Law System

The oldest and most influential of the legal system is the civil law system, which derived from ancient Roman law, including most of Eastern and Western Europe, Scandinavia, Latin America, Japan, and Russia. Mixed civil law systems include much of Africa (mixed with tribal law). This system is characterized by the use of detailed codes that establish both basic principles and detailed rules for regulating the conduct of individuals. And the grounds for deciding cases are found in these codes.

Prominent examples and models for much of the civil law world are the French Civil Code of 1804 and the German Civil Code of 1896. They were models for most contemporary civil codes in countries and regions such as Italy, Netherlands, Spain, Portugal, Switzerland, Japan, etc. China, except for China's Hong Kong Special Administrative Region (SAR) also has a tradition of codification in the law. The French Civil Code of 1804 is often referred to as the Code Napoleon, because of the extensive involvement of Napoleon (1769–1821) in its writing. Most scholars regard it as the first modern code. It incorporated the principal idea of the French Revolution, including the right to possess private property and the freedom to contract. The style and form of the French Civil Code of 1804 are easy to read, and understandable to everyone. The Code was intended to be a handbook for the citizen. The German Civil Code of 1896 was enacted almost a century later. Because Germany first had to unify itself and take shape as a nation, and the drafting project itself was enormous, taking more than 20 years to complete. The organization and form of the German Civil Code is incredibly precise and technical. Some special terminology was used, for example, the "real right". Legal concepts were defined and then used in the same way throughout the entire Code. Unlike the French Civil Code, the German Civil Code lacks the accessibility to the average people and is meant for the use of trained experts.

China can be described as a civil law country, but not as a result of received tradition, rather because its legal system is statute based. After decades of effort, *Civil Code of the People's Republic of China* (PRC) was adopted at the Third Session of the 13th National People's Congress on May 28, 2020. It took effect on January 1, 2021. In addition to Supplementary Provisions, it consists of seven books, namely, General Provisions, Property Rights, Contracts, Personal Rights, Marriage and Family, Succession, and Tort Liability, with a total of 1,260 articles. The Civil Code of PRC introduces significant changes to the existing civil legislation and judicial interpretation in the PRC. It abolished, amongst other laws, the General Provisions of the PRC Civil Law, the PRC Marriage Law, the PRC Guaranty Law, the PRC Contract Law, the PRC Property Law and the PRC Tort Liability Law. The Civil Code of PRC also responds to issues arising from the development of hi-tech and life sciences. For example, natural persons' voice is protected by the Code as a right of personality.

3.1.2 The Common Law System

The common law system is based on the system of judge-made rules that originated in medieval England around twelfth century and then was carried to the United States, Canada, Australia, India, etc. beginning in the seventeenth century. The common law's basis is court decisions, or precedent, which is also the principle factor distinguishing it from the civil law. That means the principles or rules of law on which a court rested a previous decision are authoritative in all future cases in which the facts are substantially the same. Of course, in common law countries, case decisions can always be overridden by statute, as long as the statute does not violate a constitutional doctrine.

The term of common law is used to describe the part of English law that is not based on statutes. In its narrow sense, it must be distinguished from the law that evolved out of equity. That is principles of justice providing parties with a remedy when none was available under common law. Until the nineteenth century, there continued to be a division between the courts of common law and courts of equity. The state of New York enacted a code of civil procedure in 1848 that merged them into one jurisdiction, and it was soon adopted by most of the American states and the American federal government. In England the courts of common law and courts of equity are merged through the Judicature Acts of 1873 and 1875. That means all the lawsuits including those based on common law and equity shall be tried in a single class of courts, using a single procedure.

Nowadays common law has developed to be a matrix of case law and statutes, and in case of discrepancy the statutes will prevail. It is concluded by some scholars that the civil law system and common law system are sharing more similarities.

Next, we use a chart to briefly compare the two legal systems: civil law system and common law system (See Exhibit I-1).

Exhibit I-1　General Characteristics of World Legal Systems

Characteristics	Civil Law	Common Law
basic source	codes	case law
reasoning	deductive	inductive
procedure	inquisitorial	adversarial
role of judge	fact finder	arbiter
use of previous court decisions	respected	required
skills of lawyers	interpretation of code law	using case precedents

3.1.3 Islamic Law

Over 20% of the world's population is Muslim, and they are mainly located in the Middle East, Northern Africa, and Central and Southeast Asia. The largest Muslim populations are in Pakistan, India, Bangladesh, Turkey, Iran, Afghanistan and Egypt. Islamic countries are undergoing tremendous social and political change. Some have adopted Western practices in business, society, and to a lesser extent, family life. Others have returned to strict Islamic principles. Some Islamic countries give limited rights to women; others abide by strict fundamentalist principles. For example, in Saudi Arabia unmarried women are the wards of their fathers, and widowed women are the wards of their sons.

Most Islamic countries today have modern legal systems, based on civil law or common law, mixed with principles of Islamic law. Islamic law is known as Sharia (or Shari'ah), meaning "divine law". It is derived from the Koran (Qur'an), and from the sunna. The Koran is the main religious book of the Islamic religion that expresses fundamental Islamic values. The sunna is the written record of the teachings and actions of the Prophet Muhammad. In addition, Islamic jurists and scholars qualified to interpret the scriptural sources have produced opinions known as fiqh. An understanding of the sharia requires reference to the fiqh for guidance. Islamic judges do not issue written opinions with the force of law, and they are not bound by the precedents of other courts. They are attempting to seek the truth, the divine word of God.

3.2 International Law and International Organizations

3.2.1 An Introduction to International Law

Traditionally, international law is defined as the body of rules and principles which are binding upon states in their relations with one another. Simply to put it, international law governs state-state relationships. A more contemporary definition: international law consists of rules and principles applicable to the conduct of states and of international organizations and with their relations inter se, as well as with some of their relationships with persons. States are not the only actors subject to international law. International organizations such as the United Nations (UN), the Association of Southeast Asian Nations (ASEAN) and the International Committee of the Red Cross also have international legal personality. International law is also applicable to genocide, war crimes and offenses against humanity committed by individuals in an official capacity.

International law has several characteristics that distinguish it from a country's domestic or municipal law. First, instead of being dictated by a legislative body, international law consists of rules that countries agree to be bound. It is lawmaking by consent. Indeed, international law exists because nations agree that it is in their best interests to cooperate and to conform to commonly accepted norms. Second, there is no global authority for enforcing international law. It is true that international courts and tribunals (such as the International Court of Justice or dispute bodies of the World Trade Organization) do issue judgments against nations. But nations must agree to be a party to these cases, and "hard" enforcement mechanisms as like in domestic courts do not really exist. International law has its enforcement mechanisms such as trade retaliation, the withholding of foreign aid or other assistance, the ceasing of diplamatic relationship, economic sanctions, and collective enforcement by the United Nations. The ultimate sanction against a country for violating international law is war, or the threat of it. In certain cases, where individuals are convicted of having committed international crimes, imprisonment and, in rare cases, the death penalty have been used.

The most frequently cited authority for the sources of international law is the Statute of the International Court of Justice, the judicial arm of the United Nations. It sets out both primary and secondary sources of international law. According to Article 38, the primary sources of international law are: (1) international treaties and conventions, (2) international custom or customary law, and (3) the general principles of law recognized by civilized nations. Secondary sources include the judicial decisions and teachings of the most highly qualified jurists of the various nations. Secondary sources provide evidence of what international law might be or how it should be interpreted. A treaty is a legally binding agreement between two or more nations. A treaty between two countries is said to be bilateral, and a treaty between three or more countries is multilateral. One of the most important principles of treaty law is *pacta sunt servanda* (meaning "the pact must be respected"). According to this principle, treaties are binding on the parties and must be performed by them in good faith. A convention is a legally binding multilateral treaty on matters of common concern, usually negotiated via conferences and open to adoption by many countries. Many conventions are negotiated under the auspices of the United Nations. International custom or customary law includes those commonly accepted rules of conduct that, through a consistent and long-standing practice, nations have followed out of a sense of binding obligation. Examples could include rules for the establishment of diplomatic missions, rules for the uniform prohibition against state-sponsored piracy on the high seas.

Scholars and practitioners often divide international law into two broad categories: public international law and private international law. Public international law regulates rights and obligations between states. Private International law defines rights and obligations between persons from different states. Public international law governs matters such as state territory, state succession, state responsibility, law of the sea, law of the outer space, international criminal law, international humanitarian law and International dispute settlement. Private international law might include rules of conflict of law for sales contracts, tortious liability, inheritance, marriage and divorce. Compared with public international law and private international law, international business law is a new branch of international law. The scope of international business law intersects with public international law and private international law. For the fundamentals of international business law, we will discuss in Part II.

3.2.2 The Role of International Organizations in International Business

According to the Charter of the United Nations, there are two kinds of international organizations: intergovernmental organizations (IGOs) and nongovernmental organizations (NGOs). IGOs are permanent organizations set up by two or more states to carry on activities of common interests. Their aims, functions, international personalities, rights and obligations of their members, internal structures, and etc. are set out in a "constitutional instrument" or charter, which is drafted and adopted by the organizations' member states. The United Nations is one typical IGO. NGOs, as their names indicate, are not established by states, but by the private persons or associations. They serve as coordinating agencies for private national groups in transnational affairs. There are a number of IGOs and NGOs that affect our study of international law and the development of international business law.

In the following, we will discuss some affiliated IGOs of the United Nations and IGOs that directly impact the development of international business and international business law, although there are many more worthy of mention.

◆ The United Nations Commission on International Trade Law (UNCITRAL)

The UNCITRAL was established by the United Nations General Assembly in 1966. It is the core legal body of the United Nations for international business transactions. It aims at creating greater harmonization of trade laws in different countries by drafting international conventions and model laws. It prepares conventions and model laws in a number of areas such as international commercial arbitration, electronic commerce, insolvency, international payments, sale of goods, transport law, procurement and infrastructure development. For example, the *United Nations Convention on Contracts for the International Sale of Goods* (CISG). These legal instruments are negotiated through an international process involving a variety of participants, including member states of UNCITRAL, nonmember states, invited intergovernmental and nongovernmental organizations.

◆ **The United Nations Conference on Trade and Development (UNCTAD)**

The UNCTAD was established in 1964 as an organ of the UN General Assembly intended to promote the interests of developing states in world trade. The UNCTAD serves as the focal point for the "integrated treatment" of trade and development, together with related issues in the areas of investment, finance, technology, enterprise development and sustainable development. In terms of structure, UNCTAD consists of the Conference, the Trade and Development Board (TDB) and subsidiary intergovernmental bodies, together with the secretariat. The Conference is UNCTAD's highest policymaking body and the forum where member states make assessments of current trade and development issues, discuss policy options and formulate global policy responses. It also formulates major policy guidelines and decides on the programs of work for the period before the next session. Currently, the Conference membership consists of 195 member states. The Trade and Development Board is the executive body of the Conference, taking action in implementing Conference decisions and ensuring the overall consistency of UNCTAD's activities with agreed priorities. Currently, there are three subsidiary intergovernmental bodies: (1) the Commission on Trade in Goods and Services, and Commodities; (2) the Commission on Investment, Technology, and Related Financial Issues; and (3) the Commission on Enterprise, Business Facilitation and Development.

◆ **World Trade Organization (WTO)**

Trade liberalization refers to the efforts of governments to reduce tariffs and non-tariff barriers to trade. In the twentieth century, important efforts have been made to liberalize trade by reducing tariffs and non-tariff barriers to trade. The *General Agreement on Tariffs and Trade* (GATT) was first signed in 1947, and continually expanded since that time, setting the rules for how nations will regulate international trade in goods and services. After eight rounds of negotiations, The Final Act Embodying the Results of the Uruguay Round of Multilateral Trade Negotiations was concluded and provided for the establishment of a World Trade Organization, which came into existence on January 1, 1995.

The WTO is a set of rules governing global trade, a forum for multinational trade negotiation, a tribunal for dispute settlement and an institution to review trade policies. Compared with the GATT, the WTO not only deals with trade in goods, but also trade in services and the protection of intellectual property rights. Moreover, the GATT had no formal institutional structure, while the WTO was created as an international organization to oversee all the Uruguay Round Agreements. The Final Act Embodying the Results of the Uruguay Round of Multilateral Trade Negotiations is made up of three parts. The first part, the formal Final Act itself, is a one-page "umbrella" that introduces the other parts. The second part of the Final Act is the WTO Agreement and its annexes. The 13 agreements on trade in goods (including GATT 1994), the *General Agreement on Trade in Services* (GATS), the *Agreement on Trade-Related Aspects of Intellectual Property Rights* (TRIPS), the *Understanding on Rules and Procedures Governing the Settlement of Disputes* (DSU), and the Trade Policy Review Mechanism (TPRM) are binding on all members of the WTO. The four plurilateral trade agreements (*Agreement on Trade in Civil Aviation*, *Agreement on Government Procurement*, *International Dairy Agreement* and *International Bovine Meat Agreement*)[①] are only binding on those members that have accepted them. The third and final parts consist of the Ministerial Declarations and Decisions.

Exhibit I-2

Outline of the Uruguay Round Final Act

I. FINAL ACT

II. AGREEMENT ESTABLISHING THE WORLD TRADE ORGANIZATION (WTO AGREEMENT)

Annex 1A: Agreements on Trade in Goods

1. General Agreement on Tariffs and Trade 1994
2. Agreement on Agriculture
3. Agreement on Sanitary and Phytosanitary Measures
4. Agreement on Textiles and Clothing
5. Agreement on Technical Barriers to Trade
6. Agreement on Trade-Related Investment Measures

① The latter two Agreements were terminated at the end of 1997.

7. Agreement on Implementation of Article VI [concerning antidumping]

8. Agreement on Implementation of Article VII [concerning customs valuation]

9. Agreement on Preshipment Inspection

10. Agreement on Rules of Origin

11. Agreement on Import Licensing Procedures

12. Agreement on Subsidies and Countervailing Measures

13. Agreement on Safeguards

Annex 1B: General Agreement on Trade in Services

Annex 1C: Agreement on Trade-Related Aspects of Intellectual Property Rights

Annex 2: Understanding on Rules and Procedures Governing the Settlement of Disputes

Annex 3: Trade Policy Review Mechanism

Annex 4: Plurilateral Trade Agreements

Annex 4(a): Agreement on Trade in Civil Aviation

Annex 4(b): Agreement on Government Procurement

Annex 4(c): International Dairy Agreement

Annex 4(d): International Bovine Meat Agreement

III. MINISTERIAL DECISIONS AND DECLARATIONS

The principles and rules established by the WTO have great influence on modern international business law.①

◆ The World Intellectual Property Organization (WIPO)

The WIPO was established in 1967. It is a specialized agency of the UN with 193 member states. Its role is to help foster and protect intellectual property rights in patents, industrial designs, trademarks, and copyrights. The WIPO administers a total of 24 intellectual property treaties. The WIPO Arbitration and Mediation Center offers alternative dispute resolution service, such as mediation and arbitration, to enable private individuals and corporations to settle their domestic or cross-border commercial disputes. The WIPO Arbitration and Mediation Center is also the global leader in the provision of domain name dispute resolution services. Many WIPO services to the public are fee-based and paid for by the people and companies who use them.

---

① As a negotiation result of the Doha Round, the *Trade Facilitation Agreement* (TFA) entered into force on February 22, 2017. It applies only to the WTO members that have accepted it.

◆ **International Chamber of Commerce (ICC)**

The ICC is the world business organization. It associates thousands of enterprises and business organizations from 110 countries. The ICC actively engages in drafting "private codifications" in trade law by harmonizing and standardizing international business practices. These "private codifications" are not legally binding. Their application depends on the recognition by the communities concerned. Thus in this way, the *Uniform Customs and Practice for Documentary Credits* (UCP) and the Incoterms enjoy universal application. The ICC also has its Arbitration Rules and a Court of Arbitration, which allow the enterprises from various countries to settle their trade disputes efficiently by arbitration.

4 The Cultural Environment of International Business

The cultural environment is also one of the critical components of the international business. It seems more difficult to understand the cultural environment, because it is essentially unseen. The "culture" has been described as a shared, commonly held body of general beliefs and values that determine what is right for one group. National culture is described as the body of general beliefs and values that are shared by a nation. Beliefs and values are generally seen as formed by factors such as history, language, religion, geographic location, government, and education.

Entities and natural persons need to understand what beliefs and values they may find in countries where they do business. In fact, a number of models of cultural values have been proposed by scholars. The most well-known is that developed by Hofstede in 1980. This model proposes four dimensions of cultural values including individualism versus collectivism, uncertainty avoidance, power distance and masculine versus feminality. Individualism is the degree to which a nation values and encourages individual action and decision making. Uncertainty avoidance is the degree to which a nation is willing to accept and deal with uncertainty. Power distance is the degree to which a national accepts and sanctions differences in power. And masculinity is the degree to which a nation accepts traditional male values or traditional female values. This model of cultural values has been extensively used because it provides data for a wide array of countries. Many academics and managers found this model helpful in exploring management approaches that would be appropriate in different cultures. For example, in a nation that is high on individualism (such as the U.S.), individual goals, individual tasks, and individual reward systems to be effective, whereas the reverse would be the case in a nation that is low on individualism.

Keep in mind that cultural factors will also influence a party's attitude toward how disputes are settled. For example, Americans are notorious litigators, tending to quickly turn to the courts to get remedies. Their combative stance can result in a "win or lose" mentality. However, Asians are generally notable for going to great lengths to seek an amicable settlement. After all, in Asian culture, it is a virtue to seek harmony and a vice to seek discord. These differences are evident in the way business people from different countries concluding contract or conducting business negotiations. For example, it is quite common for Americans to include their attorney or corporate counsel as a member of the negotiating team. But to some Asians, this may seem a little confrontational or a little unnecessary. Of course, in actual circustances, these attitudes may differ from country to country or from person to person, and no generalizations should be made. But one thing is certain, i.e. cultural factors have actual impact on the way of conducting business transactions.

Chapter Summary

This Chapter provides a framework for understanding both international business and the legal environment in which it operates. From the historical perspective, trade is almost as old as the civilization. In the twentieth century, the emerging globalization has greatly increased the economic interdependence among countries. The economics had exerted a strong influence on the shape and development of international business. The theories of absolute advantage, comparative advantage, and competitive advantage have justified that international business would be beneficial to both exporting and importing countries, although they are not wholly satisfying in explaining all phenomenon of trade. Different types of government and government controls over trade in a country will have a great impact on the international business transactions. Last but not the least, the cultural environment is also one of the critical components of the international business.

Laws differ from country to country, and there are differences in the role of legislatures, the role of judges and the courts in applying and interpreting the law, and in legal procedures between the civil law system and the common law system. No entity or individual can neglect the differences when conducting international transactions in different countries. The international law in modern sense derives from different sources including international treaties and conventions and international customs, which lay a fundation for the rules governing international business. In the sphere of international trade, a number of intergovernmental organizations and nongovernmental organizations are active and important to the development of international business and international business law. Some of them, for example, the ICC and the UNCITRAL, have achieved considerable progress in the harmonization and unification of national laws in trade.

Exercises

I. True or False Statements

1. Economic interdependence among countries around the world has great impact on the law in the field of international business.

2. Trade on the Silk Road was also a significant factor in the development of the civilizations of China, ancient Egypt, Mesopotamia, Persia, India and Rome, and helped to lay the foundations for the modern world.

3. Nations should concentrate their efforts on producing those goods that they can make most efficiently, with a minimum of effort and waste. The above statement is based on the theory of comparative advantage.

4. Management of interntional business is the management of risk. Such risks may include transactions risks, risks of exposure to foreign laws and courts, as well as political risks.

5. The ICC, UNCITRAL and UNIDROIT are nongovernmental organizations with a task to unifying national laws on trade.

6. Case law is the major characteristic of common law legal system, and no written law is passed in either the U.S. or the U.K.

7. Nowadays common law consists of case law and statutes, and in case of discrepancy between case law and statutes, the former will prevail.

8. The origin of modern international law dates to 1645 and is the Treaty of Westphalia.

9. The international law simply governs the state-state relationships.

10. This civil law legal system is characterized by the use of codes that establishes both basic principles and detailed rules for regulating the conduct of individuals.

II. Case Problems

Frigaliment (Plaintiff), a Swiss corporation, entered into contracts to purchase chicken from BNS International Sales Corporation (Defendant), a New York corporation. The English language contracts between them stated: "US Fresh Frozen Chicken, Grade A, Government Inspected, Eviscerated 2½-3 lbs. and 1½-2 lbs., each chicken individually wrapped in cryovac, packed in secured fiber cartons or wooden boxes, suitable for export: 75,000 lbs. 2½-3 lbs at $33.00; 25,000 lbs. 1½-2 lbs at $36.50." When the chickens were shipped to Switzerland, Plaintiff found 2-lb sizes were mature stewing chicken or fowls, but not young broiling chicken as they had expected. Plaintiff protested and claimed that in German the term "chicken" referred to young broiling chicken. Defendant pointed out the reference to "US fresh frozen chicken, grade A". The USDA defined the term "chicken" as subsuming different grades of chicken, including broilers and fowls, as well as other types such as capons, stags, and roosters.

Questions:

1. What is the focus issue in this case?

2. If you were the judge, what kind of chicken did Plaintiff order? Was it "broiling chicken" as the plaintiff argued, or any chickens weighing 2 lbs as the defendant insisted on?

3. What can you infer from this case? What would the parties have done to avoid this ambiguity?

III. Reading Materials

1. COVID-19 and International Business①

COVID-19 pandemic is considered one of the major challenges the world has faced. The pandemic effects were felt on all levels: individuals, businesses, countries, and supranational institutions. All have to deal with this new reality and the devastating impacts of COVID-19.

COVID-19 is significantly impacting businesses. Tourism, food service, and retail are some of the sectors most affected by the pandemic. MNCs are facing supply chain breakdown, demand and supply shocks, loss of revenue and profits, and other operational

---

① The excerpt is edited based on the article written by Ilan Alona and Vanessa Bretasb, selected from *Globalization, Business and Society in Pandemic Times* edited by Tony Fang and John Hassler and published by Emerald Publishing in 2021.

problems derived from travel restrictions. According to the World Bank's report about the impact of COVID-19 on foreign investors, the pandemic has affected 80% of MNCs. The top 5000 MNCs made downward revisions of their 2020 earnings by 30% (UNCTAD, 2020). Countries have established largely uncoordinated national policy responses and inter-country distancing measures, as travel limitations and border closures. The crisis gave rise to conflicts between nations over pharmaceutical and medical developments. Some countries have limited the export of medical supplies. The U.S. was accused of "modern piracy" due to the diversion of masks from Germany (BBC, 2020). France also complained about the difficulty of buying medical supplies because American buyers outbid them. At the same time, some attempts of international collaboration to develop and test vaccines and medicines were happening (Zimmermann et al., 2020). The world is seeing the rise of techno-nationalism, which includes biotechnology, in addition to usual suspects (e.g., dual-use technologies). Aid to Italy and Spain was shown to come from Russia and China and less from neighboring countries, as countries in the Schengen agreement have closed borders and limited the movement of people, even within the European Union.

COVID-19 is also impacting globalization flows. Globalization comprises four main types of flows—the movement of people, information, money, and products. And increases in the mobility of these flows have allowed for international business to prosper. However, cross-country differences impact these flows, facilitating or inhibiting the circulation of tangible and intangible assets between nations, markets, and companies. Due to the complexity of globalization movements, not only the physical geographic distance between countries is relevant. The CAGE distance framework disaggregates the concept of distance into four dimensions: cultural, administrative, geographic, and economical. The framework offers a broader view of distance and helps explain the patterns in the globalization flows. Cultural distance refers to values and social norms that shape the behavior of individuals (Ghemawat, 2011; Hofstede, 1980). For instance, countries might differ in social attitudes towards globalization. Administrative distance encompasses historical, political, and institutional relationships between countries, such as colonial relationships, trade agreements, and currency. The geographic distance considers how far countries are from each other and aspects such as borders sharing, size, and time zone. Finally, economic distance involves differences in wealth and income, availability of resources, infrastructure, organizational capabilities, among others (Ghemawat, 2011). Differences in these dimensions can encourage or discourage cross-border interactions.

The pandemic affected the CAGE-related barriers that limit cross-border integration.

It also accelerated some trends towards virtual integration, which might reduce some of these distances.

The COVID-19 crisis has an enormous impact on people's mobility. According to the International Organization for Migration, travel restrictions substantially increased in response to the pandemic. On March 10, 2020, there were 5,430 restrictions imposed by 105 countries. By March 23, the figures rose to 33,712 restrictions imposed by 164 countries (CCSA, 2020). The World Tourism Organization, a United Nations agency that promotes tourism, predicts that international arrivals in 2020 will decrease by 60% to 80% with respect to 2019 (UNWTO, 2020). The International Civil Aviation Organization verified that, in April 2020, the air traffic fell drastically to nearly zero. The number of passengers dropped by 56% in the first half of 2020, compared with 2019. The longer the restrictions on the movement of people persist, the bigger the impact it will have on persistent behaviors, both at the personal and at the firm levels. Even after some regions or countries will be open for business, adverse effects will continue to be observed on migration, tourism, and business travel flows.

People are seeking new ways to connect to obtain and exchange information due to mobility restrictions. The average daily traffic of entertainment, work, and study-related websites and apps have shown growth since the beginning of the pandemic. China has shown an increase of 58% in their local social media apps, as Wechat. As a consequence of the increase in internet usage, digital security risks such as corona virus-related scams and phishing campaigns also grew.

Even before COVID-19, money has become increasingly paperless. COVID-19 will accelerate the use of virtual money. This trend will benefit MNCs such as Alibaba, Tencent, Apple, Visa and Master Card. Mobile wallets as Alipay and WeChat Pay, which connect bank cards to smartphone apps, have already reached a considerable mass of consumers, including rural areas (Aveni & Roest, 2017). Innovations in digital money, such as Bitcoin and Facebook Libra, will also increase the fluidity of money across borders. Other specialized companies, such as TransferWise, dramatically reduce international transaction costs by matching buyers and sellers of currencies and sidestepping the international banking settling mechanisms. Countries will find it harder to control the value of their currencies through capital controls. Soft currencies are particularly vulnerable to sharp fluctuations. COVID-19 economic hardships will necessitate quantitative easing and fiscal loosening that many countries cannot afford. Sovereign debt crises might follow as a result. The post-COVID-19 world will see increasing value fluctuation, virtualization and internationalization of capital.

Portfolio investments have reacted earlier and had an even more intense shock from COVID-19 than FDI, due to their liquidity. Countries in weaker economic situations, such as developing and emerging markets, had massive outflows of portfolio investments. According to the International Monetary Fund, an amount of US$ 83 billion of capital outflowed from emerging markets. This is the largest outflow registered by the institution, including the 2008 global financial crisis. The Institute of International Finance estimates an outflow of US$ 103 billion from emerging economies between mid-January and mid-May 2020.

Products and services will follow similar patterns as investments. In the second quarter of 2020, global trade of goods decreased by 18.5%, compared to the same period in 2019. The global trade of services had a reduction of 10.4%. The most affected countries and regions in terms of exports decrease were the United States, Japan, the European Union, and Latin America. The Chinese economic downturn was smaller than the global average because of their relatively fast reopening (ECLAC, 2020).

2. How the International Court of Justice Works

There is no international regulatory agency or system of courts universally accepted for controlling international business behaviors or resolving international conflicts among businesses or countries. International law can be enforced to some degree through (1) international arbitration, (2) the courts of an individual country, or (3) the International Court of Justice.

Certain disputes between states may be taken to the International Court of Justice (ICJ) for resolution. The ICJ is headquartered at the Hague, Netherlands, and is a part of the United Nations. Of the six principal organs of the United Nations, it is the only one not located in New York (United States of America). The Court's role is to settle, in accordance with international law, legal disputes submitted to it by states and to give advisory opinions on legal questions referred to it by authorized United Nations organs and specialized agencies. The Court is composed of 15 judges, who are elected for terms of office of nine years by the United Nations General Assembly and the Security Council. It is assisted by a Registry, its administrative organ. Its official languages are English and French.

The Court may entertain two types of cases: legal disputes between states submitted to it by them (contentious cases) and requests for advisory opinions on legal questions referred to it by United Nations organs and specialized agencies (advisory proceedings).

Contentious Cases

Only states (state members of the United Nations and other states which have become parties to the Statute of the Court or which have accepted its jurisdiction under certain conditions) may be parties to contentious cases.

The Court is competent to entertain a dispute only if the states concerned have accepted its jurisdiction in one or more of the following ways:

By entering into a special agreement to submit the dispute to the Court;

By virtue of a jurisdictional clause, i.e., typically, when they are parties to a treaty containing a provision whereby, in the event of a dispute of a given type or disagreement over the interpretation or application of the treaty, one of them may refer the dispute to the Court;

Through the reciprocal effect of declarations made by them under the Statute, whereby each has accepted the jurisdiction of the Court as compulsory in the event of a dispute with another state having made a similar declaration. A number of these declarations, which must be deposited with the United Nations Secretary-General, contain reservations excluding certain categories of dispute.

Advisory Proceedings

Proceedings may be instituted in one of two ways:

Through the notification of a special agreement: this document, which is bilateral in character, can be lodged with the Court by either or both of the states parties to the proceedings. A special agreement must indicate the subject of the dispute and the parties thereto. Since there is neither an “applicant” state nor a “respondent” state, in the Court’s publications their names are separated by an oblique stroke at the end of the official title of the case, e.g., Benin/Niger.

By means of an application: the application, which is unilateral in character, is submitted by an applicant state against a respondent state. It is intended for communication to the latter state and the Rules of Court contain stricter requirements with regard to its content. In addition to the name of the party against which the claim is brought and the subject of the dispute, the applicant state must, as far as possible, indicate briefly on what basis—a treaty or a declaration of acceptance of compulsory jurisdiction—it claims that the Court has jurisdiction, and must succinctly state the facts and grounds on which its claim is based. At the end of the official title of the case the names of the two parties are separated by the abbreviation v. (for the Latin versus), e.g., Nicaragua v. Colombia.

Only countries have standing to go before the Court; individuals and businesses have no standing to initiate a suit. The countries decide whether to pursue claims on behalf of their citizens. ICJ decisions providing monetary judgments or injunctive relief may be referred to the United Nations Security Council for enforcement. However, the decisions of the above tribunals in resolving international business disputes can be enforced only if the countries involved agree to be bound by them.

Part II Fundamentals of International Business Law

Learning Objectives
(1) Understanding the definition of international business law (2) Getting to know the history of international business law (3) Having a command of international treaties, international trade customs and usages, national law as well as international model law governing international business transactions (4) Understanding the legal framework of international business law

1 Definition of International Business Law

As a discipline of law, the international business law in its modern perception has been largely developed by Clive Schmitthoff[①] through defining international trade law. Clive Schmitthoff provided a delimitation of international trade law in his book, *Export Trade: The Law and Practice of International Trade*: "[t]he law of international trade covers an unusually wide spectrum of business activity. It includes The International Sale of Goods; Marketing Organization Abroad; Finance of Export; Insurance of Exports; Transportation of Exports; International Commercial Dispute Settlement; Construction and Long Term Contracts; and Customs Law." In a more conceptual manner, he added: "International business transactions relate to the exportation of goods and services from one country to another... These transactions are referred to as export transactions. The

① Clive M. Schmitthoff (1903–1990) is regarded to be the most important founder of modern international business law. His books included but not limited to *The Sale of Goods*, *The English Conflict of Laws*, *Legal Aspects of Export Sales* and, most notably, *Schmitthoff's Export Trade*. The latter made its first appearance in 1948 and continued through ten editions. The tenth edition of *Schmitthoff's Export Trade* was edited by Leo D'Arcy, Carole Murray and Barbara Cleave and published by Sweet & Maxwell in 2000. Some of his essays have been translated into Chinese by Professor Zhao Xiuwen and published in 1992 in China.

conduct of export transactions can be divided into two categories: transactions founded on the contract for the international sale of goods and those having as their object the supply of services abroad, such as the construction of works and installation in another country." Even the above statements were made in 1960's, today's definition and coverage of international business law are still substantially based on them. Schmitthoff saw the international business law as a separate body of legal rules and one of the outstanding features of the legal development. He argued it is a remarkable fact that the law of international business shows a striking similarity in all national systems, thus some efforts should be made to achieve the uniformity of rules governing international business in nations. It was directly motivated by his enduring efforts, the United Nations Commission on International Trade Law (UNCITRAL), an organization aiming to facilitate the harmonization of the law for international business, was established in 1966.

It is generally agreed that **international business law is the body of rules and norms that regulates the cross-border transactions in goods and services between parties**. A transaction will qualify to be international or cross-border, if elements of more than one country are involved, not only limited to the nationality of the parties. Here "parties" include natural persons, legal persons, and international organizations. Under some circumstances, states may also be a party to international transactions in the capacity of commercial not sovereign entity. Of course, states more often play a unique role in regulating and supervising the international business between private parties in its capacity of a sovereign. Thus, international business law, in particular, regulates the business transactions of private persons internationally.

Some scholars define the international business law in a broader way. International business law is a body of law, regulation, or practice affecting business interests.① While lacking clearly defined limits, international business law can be taken to include treaties and agreements between nations, either bilaterally or multilaterally; international organizations together with their charters, rules and procedures; domestic law affecting the rights of any actors, be international or alien, within its territorial limits; domestic law of any nation intended to have an effect beyond its territorial limits; business practice that has become sufficiently universal as having the force of law; private business arrangements (i.e. contracts) involving international elements (parties, subject matter, or performance).

---

① See John H. Willes & John A. Willes, *International Business Law: Environments and Transactions*, The McGraw-Hill Companies, Inc., 2005, p.65–66.

2 History of International Business Law

International business is an area of law in constant change. The development of international business law can be roughly divided into three stages: medieval law merchant stage (twelfth century through seventeenth century); nationalized stage (eighteenth century through nineteenth century); modern international business law stage (after World War II).

At the beginning, the rules and norms governing international business are basically the creation of merchants. In the twelfth century, medieval Europe experienced a renaissance of trade and commerce. Merchants traveling by caravan or camel met at trade fairs to exchange goods such as wine, fruit, and porcelain. To meet the demand of trading over long distance, primary banking systems and new legal instruments (forerunners of today's bank checks) were created to facilitate the payment. Over time, the merchants developed a set of customs for exchanging goods and it is an unwritten code on how to bargain, barter, and sell goods at trade fairs or city markets. For example, it is a widely accepted consensus that if one bought the goods at a trade fair and later discovered the goods had been stolen, the innocent buyer will incur the loss anyway. By relying on these customs, merchants would know what was expected of both parties to a transaction and how to avoid and resolve a dispute. Formally these customs became known as **lex mercatoria or law merchant**. They were "enforced" by the merchants themselves rather than by the courts. That is, considering their reputation and the importance of maintaining permanent good business relationships, merchants would follow these customs in transactions voluntarily.

As trade spanned greater distances and involved more complicated skills, merchants took on greater risks, and transactions required more complex legal rules. By the eighteenth century, as the state power of European countries turned to be strong enough to regulate various business relations, the domestic courts recognized the law merchant and made it a part of the common law in England. In the continent of Europe, the law merchant was incorporated into stricter legal codes, for example, the French Civil Code of 1804 and the German Civil Code of 1896.

As the business world became more complex, and with the dawn of air travel and worldwide communication, a clearer and uniform set of modern rules governing international business are needed in the twentieth century. However, most countries used their own laws to regulate cross-border trade, which was proved to be ineffective in practice. So in this time period, unified rules characterized by efficiency, convenience and popularization are needed. So the international business law has grown and shaped up significantly in the twentieth century, especially after World War II. The leaders of the nations fighting against Germany, Italy and Japan realized a push to arrange a comprehensive network of multilateral agreements to settle the world's political and economic problems. In July 1944, they met in Bretton Woods determining to create a system of rules and obligations that would promote trade liberalization and multilateral economic cooperation. Under the Bretton Woods System, the International Monetary Fund (IMF) and the International Bank for Reconstruction and Development (IBRD or World Bank) were established. However, the International Business Organization, an institution planned to establish, only resulted in the *General Agreement on Tariffs and Trade*, which came into effect in 1947 (GATT 1947). Its articles established rules governing customs procedures, quantitative restrictions, subsidies, anti-dumping and countervailing duties, and state trading. Its contracting parties agreed to honor the most-favored-nation principle and the principle of national treatment. Unlike proposals discussed immediately after World War II, the GATT had no provisions dealing with employment, international investment, restrictive business practices, or international commodity agreements. A small secretariat (the GATT Organization) was set up in Geneva, Switzerland to oversee the operation of the GATT Agreement.

The contracting parties of the GATT 1947, among which most of the states allied with the United States and Europe during the Cold War, regularly participated in multilateral trade negotiations (or "Rounds") to negotiate trade concessions. And finally The Final Act Embodying the Results of the Uruguay Round of Multilateral Trade Negotiations provided for the establishment of a World Trade Organization (WTO), which came into existence on January 1, 1995. Other international organizations such as the United Nations Commission on International Trade Law and the International Chamber of Commerce greatly promoted the unification and standardization of global trade laws and customs. The international business law is developing rapidly in this time period.

3 Sources of International Business Law

The modern international business law is derived from a number of sources. Before determining the sources of this law, it is necessary to know the meanings of "sources of law". Strictly speaking, the concept of sources of law has two meanings: substantive sources and formal sources. The former refers to the substance of the principles and rules of law—what the law is, what the regulation is; the latter denotes constitution, treaty, statute, or customs that provide authority for legislation and for judicial decisions. The latter meaning is more often used in legal literature. In this sense, sources of international business law include international treaties and conventions, international trade usages and customs, national law, and other sources such as model law.

3.1 International Treaties and Conventions

Treaties are legally binding agreements between two (bilateral treaties) or more states (multilateral treaties). Conventions are legally binding multilateral treaties on matters of common concern, usually negotiated via conferences and open to adoption by many countries. In the field of international business, the purpose of some treaties (such as the GATT) is to liberalize trade between the contracting states. Another group of treaties or conventions aims at unification of trade laws in countries. They introduce common substantive rules for regulating the transactions between individuals and entities. Most of the unifying treaties or conventions provide rules for specific situations with an international dimension, for example, international transportation or international sale of goods. The provisions of the treaties or conventions have become part of the national law of the contracting states. Of course, for a specific treaty or convention, only the contracting states are bound by it. A number of treaties are, for instance, not yet in force or at present only apply in a limited number of countries. For that reason, many unifying law treaties or conventions, in fact, achieve only a limited or a regional unification.

There are some important international treaties or conventions as the sources of international business law. They include but not limited to: the *United Nations Convention on Contracts for the International Sale of Goods* (CISG 1980) in the field of international sale of goods, the *Convention on the Unification of Certain Rules of Law Relating to Bills of Lading* (Hague Rules 1924), the Warsaw Convention and the *Convention for the Unification of Certain Rules for International Carriage by Air* (Montreal Convention 1999) in the area of international transportation, the *International Convention on the Protection of Industrial Property* in 1883 and revised in 1979 (Paris Convention 1979) in the field of trade in intellectual property, and the *Convention on the Recognition and Enforcement of Foreign Arbitral Awards* (New York Convention 1958) in the sphere of international commercial arbitration.

3.2 International Trade Customs and Usages

International trade customs and usages stem from the tradition of law merchant or the lex mercatoria in the history of international business. They refer to the general rules and practices in international business activities that have become generally adopted through unvarying habit and common use. In fact, each sector of industry has developed its own practices and usages, which are adapted to the needs of the sector. Thus there are specific usages in the bank sector, grain trade, the oil industry, etc. International business customs and usages, in their nature, are not law, but they are undeniably important in international business. Since trade customs and usages are usually widely recognized in the specific industry, they are often incorporated into international sales contracts or standard clauses to specify the rights and obligations of the parties.

International trade customs and usages used to be oral rather than in writing. In recent decades some nongovernmental organizations, with the view to facilitating the use of trade customs and usages, have collected and compiled them into sets of rules in a written form. The *International Rules for the Interpretation of Trade Terms* (Incoterms) published by the International Chamber of Commerce serve as a good example. The term Incoterms is an acronym for "International Commercial Terms" and was first published in 1936. They had been updated periodically since that time. Incoterms underwent major revisions in 1953 and 1990, and were republished with new terms in 1967, 1976, and 1980. The current version of Incoterms was published in 2020, and is known as Incoterms 2020. Incoterms provide rules for determining the obligations of both seller and buyer when goods are to be carried from one location to another as part of the sale transaction. They state what acts seller must do to deliver, what acts buyer must do to accommodate delivery, what costs each party must bear, and at what point in the delivery process the risk of loss passes from seller to buyer. Each of these obligations may be varied for different commercial terms (e.g. F.O.B. and C.I.F.). The International Chamber of Commerce has also published the *Uniform Customs and Practice for Documentary Credits* (UCP), the widely accepted rules and guidelines for handling letter of credits in international sale of goods. This document was newly revised in 2006 (known as " UCP 600") and took effect as of 2007.

3.3 National Laws

Although there are increasing number of international treaties or conventions, and trade usages, national law is and will still be an important source of international business law in the foreseeable future. Every state has established its own legal system governing domestic transactions. For instance, on sale of goods there are *Civil Code of the People's Republic of China* (PRC) in China, the *Uniform Commercial Code* in the United States① and the *Sale of Goods Act* in Britain.② The international cross-border transaction linking with different states, leads to the possibility that different legal systems will govern the transaction. In absence of a uniform governing law, conflict of law rules will be used to determine which law will apply to the transaction in question. For example, the conflict of law rules on contracts run parallel, to a great extent, in different legal systems. All systems recognize the possibility of choice of law. If there is no express choice of law clause in the contract, under most legal systems, the rule of most significant connection will apply to determine the applicable law.

3.4 Other Sources

Some nongovernmental organizations draft rules and norms on the international business for the free choice of nations. These rules and norms are often embodied in model laws. A model law is a proposed series of rules pertaining to a specific subject, which the states may choose to adopt or reject, in whole or in part. If a state adopts the model law, it becomes the statutory law of that state. The purpose of a model law is to attempt to homogenize all states' laws on a particular subject.

In the field of international business, typical examples of model law are the *UNCITRAL Model Law on International Commercial Arbitration* and *Principles of International Commercial Contract*. The former was drafted by the UNCITRAL in 1985. It is designed to assist states in reforming and modernizing their laws on arbitral procedure so as to take into account the particular features and needs of international commercial arbitration. It covers all stages of the arbitral process from the arbitration agreement, the composition and jurisdiction of the arbitral tribunal and the extent of court intervention to the recognition and enforcement of the arbitral award. It reflects worldwide consensus

---

① The *Uniform Commercial Code* (UCC) is the primary body of law for commercial transactions in the United States. The UCC covers many areas of commercial law including the sale of goods, bank deposits and negotiable instruments. The UCC has been adopted in all 50 states of the United States, however, Louisiana has not adopted the Article 2 on the sale of goods, preferring to follow its French-influenced Civil Code.

② The *Sale of Goods Act 1979* is an act which regulates contract law and commercial law in respect of goods that are sold and bought in the United Kingdom. The act consolidated the original *Sale of Goods Act 1893* and subsequent legislation. Since 1979, there have been numerous minor statutory amendments and additions to the 1979 Act.

on key aspects of international arbitration practice having been accepted by states of all regions and the different legal or economic systems of the world. Amendments to Articles 1(2), 7, and 35(2), a new chapter "IVA" to replace Article 17 and a new article "2A" were adopted by UNCITRAL on July 7, 2006. The revised version of Article 7 is intended to modernize the form required in an arbitration agreement to better conform to international contract practices. The newly introduced Chapter IVA establishes a more comprehensive legal regime dealing with interim measures in support of arbitration. And Article 1(1) of the *UNCITRAL Model Law on International Commercial Arbitration* provides: "This law applies to international commercial arbitration, subject to any agreement in force between this State or any other States or State." The *Principles of International Commercial Contract* were drafted by the International Institute for the Unification of Private Law (UNIDROIT) in 1994. The Preamble of the *Principles of International Commercial Contract* states: "These Principles set forth general rules for international commercial contracts. They shall be applied when the parties have agreed that their contract be governed by them. They may be applied when the parties have agreed that their contract be governed by general principles of law, the lex mercatoria or the like. They may be applied when the parties have not chosen any law to govern their contract. They may be used to interpret or supplement international uniform law instruments. They may be used to interpret or supplement domestic law. They may serve as a model for national and international legislators."

In addition, resolutions of international organizations are sometimes binding. For example, all members of the United Nations are bound by the resolutions of the Security Council by virtue of the UN Charter. Resolutions and recommendations of the International Labor Organization are binding on the member states if the member states are obliged by a treaty to give effect to these resolutions and recommendations in their national legislations.

Chapter Summary

The development of international business requires a set of rules and norms to regulate and facilitate cross-border transactions in goods and services. At the beginning, the customs governing international business are basically the creation of merchants. These customs were embodied in lex mercatoria or law merchant. Later, as the state power turned to be strong enough to regulate various business relations, lex mercatoria or law merchant is partly recognized and incorporated into domestic law. After World War II, international organizations such as the United Nations Commission on International Trade Law and the International Chamber of Commerce greatly promoted the unification and standardization of global trade laws and customs. The international business law in modern sense derives from different sources, including international treaties and conventions, international trade customs and usages, national law and other sources such as model law.

Exercises

I. True or False Statements

1. International business law only deals with the business relationship between people from different countries.

2. International business law regulates the cross-border business transactions between private persons.

3. There is no difference between international business law and international economic law.

4. Lex mercatoria or law merchant, formed in medieval Europe, was a written law and enforced by states.

5. The sources of international business law only include international treaties and conventions, international trade customs, and national business laws.

6. International trade customs and usages are not binding on parties unless the parties have incorporated them in the contract.

7. National law such as the Civil Code of PRC is not a kind of source of international business law.

8. The parties involved in transnational commercial activities may choose the domestic law of a country as the governing law.

9. The UCP 600 are binding on the parties when the text of the letter of credit expressly indicates that it is subject to the UCP rules.

10. Incoterms are internationally accepted trade terms which determine the passing of risk and the rights and obligations of the parties to an international contract of sale.

II. Chapter Questions

1. How will you define the international business law and the coverage of it?

2. What is your understanding of the statement that the international trade customs

are not law but important to the international business?

3. What are the sources of international business law? Give an example for each form of source.

4. How do you understand the model law? Is the *UNCITRAL Model Law on International Commercial Arbitration* binding on member states of the UNCITRAL?

5. Name two international trade customs and usages.

III. Case Problem

Company A is an entity set up by an American businessman, having its place of business in Xiamen, China. In March 2020, Company A signed a sales contract for 1,000 computers with Company B having its place of business in Fuzhou. The sales contract required that the goods will be delivered before June of the same year at the place of business of Company B. It is also stipulated in the sales contract that any dispute arising from this contract shall be settled by both parties through friendly negotiation. If no agreement can be reached through negotiations, the case shall be submitted to Xiamen Intermediate People's Court for settlement in accordance with the *United Nations Convention on Contracts for the International Sale of Goods*. Later, due to the failure of Company A to deliver the goods on time, both parties had a dispute over the amount of damages and filed a lawsuit to Xiamen Intermediate People's Court.

Question:

What should be the applicable law in the contract? Please explain.

IV. Reading Material

The following is an excerpt from Article 2 Sales of the *Uniform Commercial Code.* Read and make a comparison with those corresponding articles of the Civil Code of PRC.

§ 2-106. Definitions: "Contract"; "Agreement"; "Contract for sale"; "Sale"; "Present sale"; "Conforming" to Contract; "Termination"; "Cancellation".

(1) In this Article unless the context otherwise requires "contract" and "agreement" are limited to those relating to the present or future sale of goods. "Contract for sale" includes both a present sale of goods and a contract to sell goods at a future time. A "sale" consists in the passing of title from the seller to the buyer for a price (Section 2-401). A "present sale" means a sale which is accomplished by the making of the contract.

(2) Goods or conduct including any part of a performance are "conforming" or

conform to the contract when they are in accordance with the obligations under the contract.

(3) "Termination" occurs when either party pursuant to a power created by agreement or law puts an end to the contract otherwise than for its breach. On "termination" all obligations which are still executory on both sides are discharged but any right based on prior breach or performance survives.

(4) "Cancellation" occurs when either party puts an end to the contract for breach by the other and its effect is the same as that of "termination" except that the cancelling party also retains any remedy for breach of the whole contract or any unperformed balance.

[...]

§ 2-201. Formal Requirements; Statute of Frauds.

(1) Except as otherwise provided in this section a contract for the sale of goods for the price of $500 or more is not enforceable by way of action or defense unless there is some writing sufficient to indicate that a contract for sale has been made between the parties and signed by the party against whom enforcement is sought or by his authorized agent or broker. A writing is not insufficient because it omits or incorrectly states a term agreed upon but the contract is not enforceable under this paragraph beyond the quantity of goods shown in such writing.

(2) Between merchants if within a reasonable time a writing in confirmation of the contract and sufficient against the sender is received and the party receiving it has reason to know its contents, it satisfies the requirements of subsection (1) against such party unless written notice of objection to its contents is given within 10 days after it is received.

(3) A contract which does not satisfy the requirements of subsection (1) but which is valid in other respects is enforceable

(a) if the goods are to be specially manufactured for the buyer and are not suitable for sale to others in the ordinary course of the seller's business and the seller, before notice of repudiation is received and under circumstances which reasonably indicate that the goods are for the buyer, has made either a substantial beginning of their manufacture or commitments for their procurement; or

(b) if the party against whom enforcement is sought admits in his pleading, testimony or otherwise in court that a contract for sale was made, but the contract is not enforceable under this provision beyond the quantity of goods admitted; or

(c) with respect to goods for which payment has been made and accepted or which have been received and accepted (Sec. 2-606).

§ 2-202. Final Written Expression: Parol or Extrinsic Evidence.

Terms with respect to which the confirmatory memoranda of the parties agree or which are otherwise set forth in a writing intended by the parties as a final expression of their agreement with respect to such terms as are included therein may not be contradicted by evidence of any prior agreement or of a contemporaneous oral agreement but may be explained or supplemented

(a) by course of dealing or usage of trade (Section 1-205) or by course of performance (Section 2-208); and

(b) by evidence of consistent additional terms unless the court finds the writing to have been intended also as a complete and exclusive statement of the terms of the agreement.

§ 2-203. Seals Inoperative.

The affixing of a seal to a writing evidencing a contract for sale or an offer to buy or sell goods does not constitute the writing a sealed instrument and the law with respect to sealed instruments does not apply to such a contract or offer.

§ 2-204. Formation in General.

(1) A contract for sale of goods may be made in any manner sufficient to show agreement, including conduct by both parties which recognizes the existence of such a contract.

(2) An agreement sufficient to constitute a contract for sale may be found even though the moment of its making is undetermined.

(3) Even though one or more terms are left open a contract for sale does not fail for indefiniteness if the parties have intended to make a contract and there is a reasonably certain basis for giving an appropriate remedy.

Part III Law of International Sale of Goods

Chapter 1

Law of the Contract for International Sale of Goods

Learning Objectives
(1) Getting to know the fundamentals of contracts and international sales contracts
(2) Having a command of different sets of rules that may govern the contact for international sale of goods
(3) Having a deep understanding of the application scope of the CISG
(4) Grasping the rules that govern the formation of the contact for international sale of goods
(5) Having a deep understanding of remedies for breach of the contract for international sale of goods

Nowadays making contract is universally recognized as the basic legal way of conducting either domestic or international business transactions. In fact, greatly owing to the spread of rule of law, contracts also play an increasingly important role in everyday life. A person, from the cradle to the grave, may never commit a crime. However, it is hard to imagine the person has not ever entered into a contract. In international business context, the parties usually rely on the sales contract to provide the rights and obligations of the parties including the transfer of title to the goods, the arrangement of transportation, payment and insurance, the way to settle any potential dispute and many other matters agreed by them. The sales contract is essential because it sets out rights and obligations that may extend well into the future. The sales contract allows buyer and seller to agree on all essential terms of the contract in advance, and to begin performance, knowing their rights and obligations are understood.

1 Fundamentals of Contracts and International Sales Contracts

A contract has been defined by scholars and legislators from various perspectives. The most concise definition may be the one found in *Black's Law Dictionary.* It states a contract is "An agreement between two or more parties creating obligations that are enforceable or otherwise recognizable at law".[①]

Under common law, contracts tend to be regarded as a promise or promises. Contract is "A promise or a set of promises that the law will enforce or at least recognize in some way".[②] Such definition is adopted by the *Restatement (Second) of Contracts of the United States* as "a promise or a set of promises for the breach of which the law gives a remedy, or the performance of which the law in some way recognizes as a duty".

Under civil law, the nature of contract is a "meeting of minds" or "mutual assent". For instance, Article 1101 of French Civil Code provides: "A Contract is a mutual assent with which one person or more is obligated to give a thing, to do or not to do a thing to one person or more persons." Civil Code of PRC provides a concise definition for contracts. Article 464 of the Code states: "A contract is an agreement establishing, altering, or terminating a civil juristic relationship between civil subjects."

Due to different purposes contracts may serve, a variety of contracts are widely used in reality. There are sales contracts, employment contracts, lease contracts, construction contracts, agency contracts, warehousing contracts, brokerage agreements, license agreements for transfer of technology, contracts for transport and transportation of people and cargo, etc. In fact, the list may be endless.

As for the form of contracts, there are written contracts and oral contracts. The term of "contract" is often used to refer to a written document, which embodies an agreement. But for legal purposes, an agreement, even though it is oral, may be a binding and enforceable contract in most circumstances. For example, you take a taxi and agree to pay a fee. Then the taxi driver drops you at your destination. An oral contract has been made and performed without signing a written document. The written contract may take the form of agreement, letter or electronic message including telegram, telex, facsimile, electronic

---

① Bryan A. Garner, *Black's Law Dictionary*, 9th ed., West Publishing Co., 2009, p.365.

② E. Allan Farnsworth, *Contracts*, Little, Brown and Company, 1990, p.3.

data exchange and electronic mail, etc. which is capable of expressing its contents in a tangible form. However, a written document is necessary according to some laws. Article 469 of Civil Code of PRC provides that a contract may be made in written, in oral, as well as in any other form. But a contract shall be in written if a relevant law or administrative regulation so requires or so agreed by the parties. And in accordance with the *Uniform Commercial Code*, contracts such as for the sale of land or sale of goods of $500 or more must be written.

Considering the different validity of contracts, there are valid, void and voidable contracts. Valid contracts are the usual contracts, which may be enforced by either party. Void contracts, although there is contradiction in terms, are those agreements that have no legal effect. Voidable contracts are those contracts which one party may at his option either enforce or not enforce. Articles 143–157 of Civil Code of PRC specifically provide the circumstances for a void contract and a voidable contract. A contract is void under the following circumstances: (1) A civil juristic act performed by a person who has no capacity for performing civil juristic acts. (2) The parties perform a civil juristic act based on a false expression of intent. (3) A civil juristic act which is in violation of any mandatory provision of any law or administrative regulations. (4) A civil juristic act which is contrary to the public policy. (5) A civil juristic act performed through malicious collusion between the parties harms the lawful rights and interests of another person. A contract is voidable under the following circumstances: (1) A civil juristic act performed is based on material misunderstanding. (2) A party induces the other party to perform a civil juristic act by fraudulent means. (3) A civil juristic act performed by the other party is based on a third person's fraudulent act. (4) A civil juristic act performed is based on duress. (5) The civil juristic act performed is obviously unfair. Under these circumstances, either of the parties may petition the people's court or an arbitration institution for revocation of the contract. However, to achieve the purpose of efficiency, the law requires a party must exercise the right of petition for revocation within one year, commencing on the date when the party knew or should have known the cause for the revocation.

In view of the rights and obligations allocated between parties to a contract, there are bilateral contracts and unilateral contracts. Bilateral contract is a contract which consists of an exchange of promises, that is, both parties promise to do something. Unilateral contract refers to a contract in which only one party promises to do something, and the other party is free to act. In reality most of the contracts are bilateral ones, and gift contract is an example of unilateral contracts.

Under common law, there are contracts sometimes called "quasi-contracts". They must be distinguished from contracts. A quasi-contract, in fact, is not contract at all. It is rather the term used by some courts to denote a recovery imposed by law where justice so requires, even though the parties have not made any agreement in advance. For example, a physician who rendered emergency services to an injured pedestrian he found on the sideway unconsciously might be allowed to recover the costs in the name of quasi-contract, even though his services were not requested by the victim. The quasi-contract is designed by the law to avoid unjust enrichment in some cases. But there is a limitation on requesting for a quasi-contract recovery. The quasi-contract cannot be invoked by the party who has conferred a benefit on someone else unnecessarily or as a result of misconduct or negligence. For example, you take your car to the local car wash and ask to have it run through the washer and to have the gas tank filled. While it is being washed, you go to a nearby shopping center for two hours. In the meantime, one of the workers at the car wash mistakenly believed that your car is the one needed hand wax. When you come back, you are presented with a bill for a full tank of gas, a wash job, and a hand wax. Are you under the obligation to pay the bill for a hand wax? The answer is no.

An international sales contract is an agreement between a buyer and a seller that identifies the elements for a cross-border sale such as parties in the transaction, the goods or services being sold, the terms and conditions of the sale, the price to be paid and the governing law. In a contract for the international sale of goods, at least one party is likely to have its rights decided under the law of a foreign country. In the absence of a "choice of law" provision in a contract, a court would have to determine which law will govern—and that could be the law of the country where the contract was made, where it was to be performed, where the goods were to be delivered, where the subject matter is located, where either party resides or has its principal place of business, or in some other country with a closest connection to the contract. This could lead to some different results. Because different countries, even with modern codes, often have different rules for interpreting contracts, for remedies and awarding damages, or even for determining if a contract exists at all. This is especially true when buyer and seller come from countries with different legal systems—common law, civil law, or Islamic law.

2 Rules Governing the Contract for International Sale of Goods

2.1 United Nations Convention on Contracts for the International Sale of Goods

As the trade brought the world closer together, there were calls for more organized efforts at unifying the sales laws of diverse countries around the world. The process of making national laws more uniform is known as the unification of law. The unification of modern sales law has been ongoing since the early part of the twentieth century. Early efforts were made by the League of Nations, and by private organizations and law societies, although those largely turned out to be unsuccessful. In 1966, the United Nations created a new organization responsible for unifying trade law, the United Nations Commission on International Trade Law (UNCITRAL). The UNCITRAL plays an important role in furthering the progressive unification of the law of international sales of goods. The UNCITRAL's work led to a very successful effort—the adoption of the *United Nations Convention on Contracts for the International Sale of Goods* (CISG) in 1980. The CISG came into force on January 1, 1988 with the original 11 states. By the year of 2021, the number of contracting states has reached 94 including Australia, Canada, China, France, Germany, Italy, Russia, Singapore, Swiss, Switzerland, United States, Japan, Vietnam and other major countries in world trade covering countries from every geographical region, every stage of economic development and every major legal system.① Thus the CISG is regarded to be one of the most successful instruments of international sales law harmonization.

The CISG is divided into four parts. Part I deals with the scope of application of the Convention and the general provisions. Part II contains the rules governing the formation of contracts for the international sale of goods. Part III deals with the substantive rights and obligations of buyer and seller arising from the contract. Part IV contains the final clauses of the Convention concerning such matters as how and when it comes into force, the reservations and declarations that are permitted and the application of the Convention to international sales where both states concerned have the same or similar law on the subject. The CISG is the primary subject of this Chapter. Details concerning the CISG for

① A significant absentee for the CISG is the United Kingdom. For the whole list of contracting states to the CISG, you may refer to the website of the UNCITRAL.

international sale of goods will be discussed in this Chapter.

2.2 National Sales Law

Despite the great influence of the CISG on the international sale of goods, national sales law is still an important source for rules governing the sale of goods, which is partly due to the incomplete coverage of contractual issues by the CISG, and partly attributed to the legal and cultural tradition of different countries.

In common law countries, traditionally the principles and rules governing the sale of goods are embodied in case law. However, in recent decades in order to relieve the complexity of case law and facilitate the uniformity of sales law, statutes have been adopted. In 1951, a new commercial law was proposed by the American Law Institute and the National Conference of Commissioners on Uniform State Laws in the United States. It is the *Uniform Commercial Code* (UCC), the primary commercial law for domestic transactions in the United States. The purposes of the UCC are as follows: (1) to simplify, clarify, and modernize the law governing commercial transactions; (2) to permit the continued expansion of commercial practices through custom, usage, and agreement of the parties; and (3) to uniform the law among the various jurisdictions (states) (See UCC 1-102). The UCC was drafted as a model law to be enacted by a particular state. Now it has been adopted by all U.S. states, only partially in Louisiana. It covers many areas of commercial laws, covering sales of goods, leases, commercial paper, bank deposits and collections, L/C, bulk transfer, warehouse receipts, B/L, investment securities and secured transactions. It does not, however, cover the sale of real estate or services, insurance, intellectual property, etc. Article 2 of the UCC applies to "sales and contracts of sales". Many early principles of the law merchant are still found in Article 2 in a modern, codified form such as trade terms. Contracts not covered by the UCC or other statutes are governed by the common law. That is where the UCC is silent, the case law of contracts applies to the transaction. Since the United States has been a contracting state to the CISG since 1988, for many international sales involving U.S. companies, the UCC has been supplanted by the CISG.

In England, the *Sale of Goods Act 1893* had codified many rules from law merchant. And this Law was revised in 1979. In recent years, new statutes related to the regulation of contracts such as *Supply of Service Act* and *Consumer Rights Act* have been passed to adapt to new social and technology changes. Article 1 of the *Sale of Goods Act 1979* states the Act applies to:

"(1) Contracts of sale of goods made on or after (but not to those made before) 1

January 1894.

(2) In relation to contracts made on certain dates, this Act applies subject to the modification of certain of its sections as mentioned in Schedule 1 below.

(3) Any such modification is indicated in the section concerned by a reference to Schedule 1 below.

(4) Accordingly, where a section does not contain such a reference, this Act applies in relation to the contract concerned without such modification of the section.

(5) Certain sections or subsections of this Act do not apply to a contract to which Chapter 2 of Part 1 of the Consumer Rights Act 2015 applies.

(6) Where that is the case it is indicated in the section concerned."

In civil law countries, the principles and rules governing contracts for sale of goods are usually found in codes, supplemented with some newly passed statutes. For example, in France, there are French Civil Code of 1804 and French Code of Commerce of 1807 and in Germany there is German Civil Code of 1896.

In China, the laws governing sale of goods have undertaken great changes since 1978. These laws witnessed China's transition from a planned economy to market one. On October 1, 1999, Contract Law of PRC came into effect, which repealed the previous three laws of contracts—Economic Contract Law, Foreign Economic Contract Law, and Technology Contract Law. Contract Law of PRC has drawn on accepted legal concepts and principles from both civil law and common law legal systems, as well as international conventions such as the CISG, and then adapted them to the economic, political and cultural situations of China. It applies not only to the sale of goods, but also contract for supply of electricity, water, gas or heat, gift contract, loan agreement, lease contract, finance lease contract, contract for hired work, contract for construction project, contract for transport and transportation of people and cargo, contract for transfer of intellectual property, deposit contract, warehousing contract, agency contract and brokerage contract. On January 1, 2021, Civil Code of PRC came into effect, which repealed, *inter alia*, General Principles of the Civil Law of 1986, General Rules of Civil Law of 2017, and Contract Law of 1999. Civil Code of PRC is the dominant law governing sale of goods in China, Book Three of which titled "Contracts".

2.3 Principles of International Commercial Contracts

As we have discussed in Part II of this textbook, model law also plays an undeniable role in international trade law. In the area of international sale of goods, the *Principles of*

International Commercial Contracts serve as such a good example.

In 1968 at the celebration ceremony of the 40th anniversary of UNIDROIT, a NGO aiming at the unification of national private laws, President of UNIDROIT at that time proposed to initiate a "restatement of law" at international level. This initiative was included in the Work Program of UNIDOIT in 1971. After the Work Program was approved by the member states of UNIDROIT, a small Steering Committee was set up, consisting of Professors Clive Schmitthoff, Rene David and Tudor Popesu to make preliminary inquiries. In 1980 a special Working Group was established to prepare the draft of the *Principles of International Commercial Contracts.* Members of the Group were legal scholars, leading experts in contract law and international trade law, as well as some prestigious judges and officials. The Working Group finished the last reading of different chapters in the draft in February 1994, after which the draft was submitted to a Special Editorial Committee for review. Finally the *Principles of International Commercial Contracts* were published in 1994 (amended in 2004) by the UNIDOIT. To facilitate its worldwide use, the text of the *Principles of International Commercial Contracts* has been translated into over two dozen of languages besides English.

The *Principles of International Commercial Contracts* are applicable to all contracts, not just sales of goods, and the provisions are set forth in more general terms. It consists of a Preamble and 185 articles organized into ten chapters including "General Provisions", "Formation", "Validity", "Interpretation", "Content", "Performance", "Non-performance" and others. And among them, "Performance" has two sections dealing with "Performance in General" and "Hardship". "Non-performance" covers four sections: "non-performance in General", "Right to Performance", "Termination" and "Damages".

In the Preamble to the *Principles of International Commercial Contracts*, it states that these rules only apply to international commercial contracts, and that the concept of international commercial contracts should be understood in the broadest possible way to include not only international transactions in goods, but also transactions in services and investment. The *Principles of International Commercial Contracts* have established a number of principles including freedom to contract, good faith and fair dealing, and *favor contractus*, which, like threads, run through the *Principles of International Commercial Contract*. For example, freedom to contract is expressly stated in Article 1.1. It reads: "The parties are free to enter a contract and to determine its content." The comment of this article explains that "the right of business people to decide freely to whom they will offer their goods or services and by whom they wish to be supplied, as well as the possibility for them freely to agree on terms of individual transactions, are the cornerstones of an open, market-oriented and competitive international economic order" . That is, under the principle of freedom to contract, the parties are free to conclude contracts with any other person, irrespective of their nationalities, and the parties are also free to agree on any terms and choose any law as the governing law in their contracts unless otherwise provided in the *Principles of International Commercial Contracts*. And the principle of *favor contractus* means endeavoring to facilitate the formation and existence of contract. Such principle has been embodied in Article 2.1 of the *Principles of International Commercial Contracts*, and it states that a contract may be concluded either by the acceptance of an offer or by conduct of the parties that is sufficient to show agreement. And Para. 2 of Article 2.1 states that a reply to an offer which purports to be an acceptance but contains additions or modifications may nonetheless lead to the conclusion of a contract, if the additional or different terms do not materially alter the terms of the offer and the offeror does not object to the discrepancy without undue delay. Moreover, if the offeror does not object, the terms of the contract are the terms of the offer with the modifications contained in the acceptance.

Unlike the CISG, which is a binding convention on member states, the *Principles of International Commercial Contracts* are drafted as a model law, not a binding legal document. However, the considerable functions of it cannot be denied. First, it can be used as a model for national and international legislators. Second, it is not only the subject of a substantial body of legal writings, but is more frequently being used in international contract practice and dispute resolution. That is, it can be chosen to be the governing law by the parties to an international commercial contract as an alternative of national law and the CISG. And it can be used by international commercial arbitrators, and even by judges where local law is ambiguous. Third, compared with the CISG, the *Principles of International Commercial Contracts* cover more categories of sales rather than sale of goods. It covers almost all the contractual issues from the formation to performance of sales contract, however, the CISG keeps silent on some issues, for example, the requirements for validity of contract. Moreover, the substantive rules of the *Principles of International Commercial Contracts* are often different from those of the CISG, because it was not drafted by official delegations of governments, and the individual drafters could adopt what they considered to be "best practices" in commerce.

2.4 International Customs and Usages: Incoterms

Frequently, parties to a contract are unaware of the different trading practices in their respective countries. This can give rise to misunderstandings, disputes and litigation, with all the waste of time and money that this entails. In order to remedy these problems, the International Chamber of Commerce (ICC) first published in 1936 a set of international rules for the interpretation of trade terms. These rules were known as "Incoterms 1936". Amendments and additions were later made in 1953, 1967, 1976, 1980, 1990, 2000, 2010 and presently in 2020 in order to bring the rules in line with current international trade practices.

The purpose of Incoterms is to provide a set of international rules for the interpretation of the most commonly used trade terms in foreign trade. Thus, the uncertainties of different interpretations of such terms in different countries can be avoided or at least reduced to a considerable degree.

It appears that two particular misconceptions about Incoterms are very common. First, Incoterms are frequently misunderstood as applying to the contract of transport rather than to the contract of sale. Second, they are sometimes wrongly assumed to provide for all the duties, which parties may wish to include in a contract of sale. It should be stressed that **the scope of Incoterms** is limited to **matters relating to the rights and obligations of the parties to the contract of sale with respect to the delivery of goods sold**.

Incoterms deal only with the relation between sellers and buyers under the contract of sale. Incoterms deal with a number of identified obligations imposed on the parties—such as the seller's obligation to place the goods at the disposal of the buyer or hand them over for transport or deliver them at place—and with the distribution of risk between the parties in these cases. Further, they deal with the obligations to clear the goods for export and import, the packing of the goods, the buyer's obligation to take delivery as well as the obligation to provide proof that the respective obligations have been duly fulfilled. Although Incoterms are extremely important for the implementation of the contract of sale, a great number of problems which may occur in such a contract are not dealt with at all, like transfer of ownership and other property rights, breaches of contract and the remedies for such breaches as well as exemptions from liability in certain situations. These questions must be resolved by other stipulations in the contract of sale and the applicable law.

In view of the changes made to Incoterms from time to time, it is important to ensure that **where the parties intend to incorporate Incoterms into their contract of sale, an express reference of the version shall always be made**. A failure to refer may then result in disputes as to whether the parties intended to incorporate the current version or an earlier version as a part of their contract. Parties wishing to use Incoterms 2020 should therefore clearly specify that their contract is governed by Incoterms 2020.

◆ **The Division of Incoterms**

Incoterms give the parties a menu of different terms to be used in their sales contract with respect to the delivery of goods sold. There are different types of division among these terms. Under Incoterms 2000, two types of divisions are used. One division is between those six terms, which require the involvement of water-borne transportation and those seven other terms, which are applicable to any mode of transportation, including multi-model transportation. A second division, based on duties imposed on the seller, classifies the terms into four groups: Group E, Group F, Group C and Group D. However, Incoterms 2010 (See **Exhibit III-1**) and Incoterms 2020 (See **Exhibit III-2**) only adopt one type of division (Mode of Transport).

Exhibit III-1

Division of Incoterms 2010 (Mode of Transport)

Group 1. Incoterms that apply to any mode of transport are:

EXW	Ex Works
FCA	Free Carrier
CPT	Carriage Paid To
CIP	Carriage and Insurance Paid To
DAT	Delivered At Terminal
DAP	Delivered At Place
DDP	Delivered Duty Paid

Group 2. Incoterms that apply to sea and inland waterway transport only:

FAS	Free Alongside Ship
FOB	Free On Board
CFR	Cost and Freight
CIF	Cost, Insurance, and Freight

Exhibit III-2

Division of Incoterms 2020 (Mode of Transport)

Group 1. Incoterms that apply to any mode of transport are:

EXW	Ex Works
FCA	Free Carrier
CPT	Carriage Paid To

CIP	Carriage and Insurance Paid To
DAT	Delivered At Terminal
DPU	Delivered At Place Unloaded
DDP	Delivered Duty Paid

Group 2. Incoterms that apply to sea and inland waterway transport only:

FAS	Free Alongside Ship
FOB	Free On Board
CFR	Cost and Freight
CIF	Cost, Insurance, and Freight

Incoterms 2020 have kept the spirit of Incoterms 2010 at a high rate. The differences between the version 2010 and version 2020 are: (1) One term of the 2010 version (DAT—"Delivered at Terminal") was removed, and is replaced by a new term (DPU—"Delivered at Place Unloaded") in the Incoterms 2020. (2) The insurance to be provided under terms CIF and CIP has changed, increasing from Institute Cargo Clauses (C) to Institute Cargo Clauses (A). Under the trade term of CIF, the Institute Cargo Clauses (C) remains the default level of coverage, giving parties the option to agree to a higher level of insurance cover. Taking into account feedback from global users, the trade term of CIP now requires a higher level of cover, compliant with the Institute Cargo Clauses (A) or similar clauses. (3) The transportation is allowed to be done with both the seller's and buyer's transportation vehicles under the trade terms of FCA, DAP, DPU and DDP. Apart from these, there are no major modifications between the two versions.

EXW is the term in which the seller's obligation is at its minimum: the seller has to do no more than place the goods at the disposal of the buyer at the agreed place—usually at the seller's own premises. Moreover, as a matter of practical reality, the seller would frequently assist the buyer in loading the goods on the latter's collecting vehicle.

FCA means that the seller delivers the goods to the carrier or another person nominated by the buyer at the seller's premises or another named place. The parties are well advised to specify as clearly as possible the point within the named place of delivery, as the risk passes to the buyer at that point. FCA requires the seller to clear the goods for export, where applicable. However, the seller has no obligation to clear the goods for import, pay any import duty or carry out any import customs formalities.

CPT means that the seller delivers the goods to the carrier or another person nominated by the seller at an agreed place. The seller must contract for and pay the costs of transport necessary to bring the goods to the named place of destination. When CPT, CIP, CFR or CIF is used, the seller performs its obligation to deliver when it hands the goods over to the carrier and not when the goods reach the place of destination. This rule has two critical points, because risk passes and costs are transferred at different places. The parties are well advised to identify as precisely as possible in the contract both the place of delivery, where the risk passes to the buyer, and the named place of destination to which the seller must contract for the transport. If several carriers are used for the transport to the agreed destination and the parties do not agree on a specific point of delivery, the risk passes when the goods have been delivered to the first carrier. CPT requires the seller to clear the goods for export, where applicable. However, the seller has no obligation to clear the goods for import, pay any import duty or carry out any import customs formalities.

CIP means that the seller delivers the goods to the carrier or another person nominated by the seller at an agreed place. The seller must contract for and pay the costs of transport necessary to bring the goods to the named place of destination. The seller also contracts for insurance coverage against the buyer's risk of loss of or damage to the goods during the transport. The buyer should note that under CIP the Institute Cargo Clauses (C) is the default level of coverage, while it gives parties the option to agree to a higher level of insurance coverage.

DAT means that the seller delivers when the goods, once unloaded from the arriving means of transport, are placed at the disposal of the buyer, at a named terminal, at the named port or place of destination. "Terminal" includes any place, whether covered or not, such as a quay, warehouse, container yard or road, rail or air cargo terminal. The seller bears all risks involved in bringing the goods to and unloading them at the terminal at the named port or place of destination. The parties are well advised to specify as clearly as possible the terminal and, if possible, a specific point within the terminal at the agreed port or place of destination, as the risks to that point are for the account of the seller. The seller is advised to procure a contract of transport that matches this choice precisely. DAT requires the seller to clear the goods for export, where applicable. However, the seller has no obligation to clear the goods for import, pay any import duty or carry out any import customs formalities. Moreover, if the parties intend the seller to bear the risks and costs involved in transporting and handling the goods from the terminal to another place, the DAP or DDP rules should be used.

DPU means that the seller delivers when the goods are placed at the named place of destination and unloads the goods. There are no restrictions on the named place—for example, it can be a transport hub, a warehouse or the buyer's depot. The seller is responsible for arranging transport and for delivering the goods, unloaded from the arriving means of transport, at the named place. Risk transfers from seller to buyer when the goods have been unloaded. This is the only trade term that requires the seller to unload the goods in order to complete delivery. The buyer is responsible for import clearance and any applicable local taxes or import duties. DPU is well suited for container operations where the seller bears responsibility for the main transport.

DDP means that the seller delivers the goods when the goods are placed at the disposal of the buyer, cleared for import on the arriving means of transport ready for unloading at the named place of destination. The seller bears all the costs and risks involved in bringing the goods to the place of destination and has an obligation to clear the goods not only for export but also for import, to pay any duty for both export and import, and to carry out all customs formalities. DDP represents the maximum obligation for the seller. The parties are well advised to specify as clearly as possible the point within the agreed place of destination, as the costs and risks to that point are for the account of the seller. The seller is advised to procure contracts of transport that match this choice precisely. The parties are well advised not to use DDP if the seller is unable directly or indirectly to obtain import clearance.

FAS means that the seller delivers when the goods are placed alongside the vessel (e.g., on a quay or a barge) nominated by the buyer at the named port of shipment. The risk of loss of or damage to the goods passes when the goods are alongside the ship, and the buyer bears all costs from that moment onwards. The parties are well advised to specify as clearly as possible the loading point at the named port of shipment. The seller is required either to deliver the goods alongside the ship or to procure goods already so delivered for shipment. Where the goods are in containers, it is typical for the seller to hand the goods over to the carrier at a terminal and not alongside the vessel. In such situations, the FAS rule would be inappropriate, and the FCA rule should be used.

FOB means that the seller delivers the goods on board the vessel nominated by the buyer at the named port of shipment or procures the goods already so delivered. The risk of loss of or damage to the goods passes when the goods are on board the vessel, and the buyer bears all costs from that moment onwards. The seller is required either to deliver the goods on board the vessel or to procure goods already so delivered for shipment. FOB may not be appropriate where goods are handed over to the carrier before they are on board the vessel, for example goods in containers, which are typically delivered at a terminal. In such situations, the FCA rule should be used.

CFR means that the seller delivers the goods on board the vessel or procures the goods already so delivered. The risk of loss of or damage to the goods passes when the goods are on board the vessel. The seller must contract for and pay the costs and freight necessary to bring the goods to the named port of destination. CFR requires the seller to clear the goods for export, where applicable. However, the seller has no obligation to clear the goods for import, pay any import duty or carry out any import customs formalities.

CIF means that the seller delivers the goods on board the vessel or procures the goods already so delivered. The risk of loss of or damage to the goods passes when the goods are on board the vessel. The seller must contract for and pay the costs and freight necessary to bring the goods to the named port of destination. The seller also contracts for insurance coverage against the buyer's risk of loss of or damage to the goods during the transport. CIF now requires a higher level of insurance coverage, compliant with the Institute Cargo Clauses (A) or similar clauses. The seller should not obtain insurance only on minimum cover under CIF.

In practice, it frequently happens when the parties themselves add words to an Incoterm to seek further precision than the term could offer such as "EXW loaded". It should be underlined that Incoterms give no guidance whatsoever for such additions. Thus, the parties may encounter serious problems when no consistent understanding of the additions could be proven. For these reasons, the parties are strongly advised to clarify the intentions or meanings of such additions in the contract. Consequently, if the contract fails to expressly describe the parties' intentions, the parties may bear much unnecessary troubles and costs.

One thing is worth noting that all contracts made under Incoterms 2010 remain valid even after the publication of Incoterms 2020. Moreover, although Incoterms 2020 are recommended to be used after their publication, parties to a contract for the sale of goods can agree to choose any version of the Incoterms rules. It is important however to clearly specify the chosen version—Incoterms 2020, Incoterms 2010 or any earlier version.

3 The Applicability of the CISG

◆ Three Conditions

The first six articles of the CISG define its scope of application. According to Article

1 of the CISG, the CISG applies if the following three conditions are met: (1) The contract is for the commercial sale of goods. (2) The contract is between parties whose places of business are in different countries. (3) The places of business are located in countries that have ratified the CISG. The CISG itself does not expressly define "sale", "goods" or "commercial". However, according to the cases decided under the CISG, generally it is understood that a "sale" is the passing of title from the seller to the buyer for a price. "**Goods**" are assumed to be things that are movable and tangible. "Commercial" means the goods are traded for business purposes, that is, for industrial production or resale, rather than for personal use or household use. As for "international", Article 1 thereof requires that a sale of goods contract be deemed to be "**international**" if the places of business of the parties are located in different contracting states to the CISG. In other words, it does not require that the goods be shipped between different states, nor the negotiations of the contract occur in different nations. Neither the location of the goods themselves, nor the citizenship or nationality of the parties, is necessarily decisive. Instead, the "**place of business**" of each party must be located in a different contracting state to the CISG. Therefore, in a contract involving two Austrian citizens, one of whom had his place of business in Italy, the court held that the CISG applied, and not Austrian law.

What is "a place of business"? Although the term in the English language version may be ambiguous, the term in the French (établissement) and Spanish (establecimiento) language versions of the CISG refers to a permanent place of business. And the drafting history of the CISG suggests that a permanent establishment is required and that neither a warehouse nor the office of a seller's agent qualifies as a "place of business". This interpretation has been adopted by the courts. A seller's "liaison office" in buyer's nation was held by the Paris Court of Appeal not to be a "place of business", because it was not an autonomous legal entity, so that orders through that office were not subject to the CISG.

This "**place of business**" standard will cause difficulty whenever one or both parties have more than one place of business. That is, if a party has multiple places of business, one of which is in the same state as the other party's place of business, the issue of "international" becomes more complicated. However, the CISG does provide the resolution in such situations by specifying which "place of business" is to be considered. Which place of business shall be used to determine the applicability of the Convention? The Article 10(a) of CISG directs that use of the place of business having "the closest relation to the contract and its performance". Thus, the determinative "place of business" depends upon the relationship of the transaction to a particular office. Where one office is more closely associated with the formation of the contract and a second office is more closely associated with a party's performance of its contractual obligations, there is an unresolved issue concerning which one of those offices is the relevant "place of business". The assistance furnished by Article 10(a) in such situations is to limit the usable facts in making a choice. These facts are limited to those circumstances known to the parties before or at the conclusion of the contract. Of course, well-advised parties may resolve these possible ambiguities by directly stating in the contract which office of each party they believe to be the "place of business".

This "place of business" method provides certainty to the parties in designing the transaction and to courts in analyzing and deciding issues from such transactions. In addition, the CISG also offers a second method to determine the "international" nature of the international sales contract. Places of business of the parties are in different states when the rules of private international law lead to the application of the law of a contracting state [See Article 1(1)(b)] .Thus, a contract between a seller in France (a contracting state) and a buyer in the United Kingdom (not a contracting state) would be governed by the CISG if the applicable rules of private international law make the law of the seller's place of business the governing law. Because the second method depends on a various conflict-of-laws rules and some states, including China and the United States, have precluded this method by making reservation to the CISG. Therefore, a contract of sale between a party whose place of business is located in China (or a United States party) and another party in a non-contracting state to the CISG, will not be governed by the CISG.

◆ **Choice of Law Clause**

When the above-discussed three requirements are met, the CISG does apply. However, the parties to a contract may exclude (i.e., they may "opt out") or modify the application of the CISG by a "**choice of law clause**". Opting out of the CISG is allowed in all legal regimes of contracting states, but it requires the clarity of the choice of law clause. A simple statement that a contract "shall be governed by the law of China" is somewhat ambiguous, because in a strict sense the CISG has become an integral part of the laws of China after China adopted the CISG. "Opting out" of the CISG would require at least: "This contract shall be governed by the laws of China applicable to domestic contracts of sale, and shall not be governed by the United Nations Convention on Contracts for the International Sale of Goods, 1980." Or in this way: "This contract shall be governed by the Civil Code of PRC and other laws of China governing domestic sale of goods." There are many attorneys who will seek to "opt out" of the CISG for all contracts under all conditions, simply because they do not understand it as well as they do about their domestic law. Such a practice seems particularly popular among the U.S. attorneys. However, such action may not be in the clients' interests. There may be many circumstances when a seller of goods in an international transaction will be placed in a much more awkward position by the domestic law. At least one author has stated that automatically opting out of the CISG in negotiating an international sales contract, without understanding how it affects the client's interests, constitutes malpractice.①

The following case helps to further your understanding of "opt out" of the CISG.

Case III-1

American Biophysics Corp. v. Dubois Marine Specialties

411 F.Supp.2d D.R.I., 2006

ABC is a Delaware corporation with its principal place of business in North Kingstown, Rhode Island. Dubois is a Canadian corporation with its principal place of business in Selkirk in the Province of Manitoba, Canada.

On February 19, 2002, the parties entered into a "Non-Exclusive Distributorship Agreement" (the Agreement), pursuant to which Dubois was to purchase and resell "Mosquito Magnets" manufactured by ABC, which are designed to attract and kill mosquitoes. The Agreement required Dubois to make payment within thirty (30) days after receiving ABC's invoice and it provided for interest on overdue amounts "at the greater of (a) eighteen percent (18%) per annum or (b) the highest rate of interest allowed by the laws of the State of Rhode Island". Subsection 11(h) of the Agreement provided: "This Agreement shall be construed and enforced in accordance with the laws of Rhode Island. The parties agree that the courts of the State of Rhode Island, and the Federal Courts located therein, shall have exclusive jurisdiction over all matters arising from this Agreement."

The complainant alleges that Dubois owes $513,985.94 for goods sold and delivered, plus $96,512.75 in interest accrued through July 22, 2005, the date on which suit was commenced.

In support of its motion to dismiss, Dubois has filed an affidavit stating, in

① See Ronald A. Brand, *Professional Responsibility in a Transnational Transactions Practice*, 17 Journal of Law and Commerce 301, 301 (1998).

effect, that it has no contacts with Rhode Island; an excerpt from the *United Nations Convention on Contracts for the International Sale of Goods*, 1980 ("the CISG"); and copies of Manitoba statutes that deal with excluding the CISG from contracts to which it might otherwise apply.

Analysis

1. Effect of Forum Selection Clause

It is well established that a party may waive its right to challenge personal jurisdiction by entering into a contract that contains a forum selection clause. Therefore, in this case, the threshold question is whether the forum selection clause contained in subsection 11(h) of the Agreement between ABC and Dubois is valid and binding.

2. Validity of Subsection 11(h)

Forum selection clauses are considered "prima facie valid and should be enforced unless enforcement is shown by the resisting party to be 'unreasonable' under the circumstances". Thus, a party challenging a forum selection clause must present "evidence of fraud, undue influence, overweening bargaining power or such serious inconvenience in litigating in the selected forum that it is effectively deprived of its day in court". Here, Dubois has made no such showing. Dubois has presented no evidence of fraud or undue influence and has made no showing that litigating this dispute in Rhode Island, as agreed, would, effectively, deprive Dubois of its day in court. Dubois hints at suggesting that Subsection 11(h) should be viewed as a contract of adhesion by describing ABC as a "large manufacturer" with "customers throughout the world" and by characterizing its own operation as a "small, Manitoba based, family run" dealership. However, Dubois states that it has organized a network of over 100 Canadian dealers to distribute the Mosquito Magnets and that its annual gross revenue exceeds $1,000,000, and there is no indication that it was under any compulsion to enter into the Agreement with ABC.

3. Effect of the CISG

Dubois seeks to avoid the forum selection clause by asserting that the Agreement with ABC is governed by the *United Nations Convention on Contracts for the International Sale of Goods* (CISG), codified at 15 U.S.C. App. (West 1998), to which the United States and Canada are both signatories, but it fails to explain how the CISG would preclude this action from being brought here.

In any event, it appears that the CISG is inapplicable. The CISG governs "contracts for the sale of goods where the parties have places of business in different nations, the nations are the CISG signatories, and the contract "does not contain a choice of law provision". More specifically, Article 6 of the CISG provides that: "The parties may exclude the application of this Convention or, subject to Article 12, derogate from or vary the effect of any of its provisions." Here, as already noted, Subsection 11(h) of the Agreement provides that the Agreement "shall be construed and enforced in accordance with the laws of the state of Rhode Island". That provision is sufficient to exclude application of the CISG. It has been affirmed in many cases such as *Delchi Carrier SpA v. Rotorex Corp.*, 71 F.3d 1024, 1028 n.1 (2d Cir. 1995) ("The Convention makes clear that the parties may by contract choose to be bound by a source of law other than the CISG..."); *Viva Vino Import Corp. v. Farnese Vini S.r.l.*, 2000 WL 1224903, (E.D.Pa. Aug. 29, 2000) (The CISG governs contracts for sale of goods between parties of signatory nations "unless the contract contains a choice of law provision to the contrary".); and *Claudia v. Olivieri Footwear Ltd.*, 1998 WL 164824. (S.D.N.Y., April 7, 1998) ("When two foreign nations are signatories to this Convention ... the Convention governs contracts for the sale of goods ... absent a choice-of-law provision to the contrary.")

Conclusion

For all of the foregoing reasons, Dubois's motion to dismiss is denied.

If the parties can "opt out" of the CISG, can they also "opt in"? In fact, whether the parties can "opt in" depends on the rules of the state where this question comes up. Usually parties to an international sales contract are allowed to "opt in" the CISG by choice of law clause. For example, they agree that this contract shall be governed by the laws of Italy, including the *United Nations Convention on Contracts for the International Sale of Goods*, 1980.

◆ Sales Excluded from the CISG

Articles 2 and 3 of the CISG exclude a series of types of transactions from application. Except the exclusion of "opting out" by the parties, there are eight circumstances not governed by the CISG. They are:

(1) Consumer goods sold for personal, family, or household use;

(2) Goods bought at auction;

(3) Stocks, securities, negotiable instruments, or money;

(4) Ships, vessels, or aircraft;

(5) Electricity;

(6) Assembly contracts for the supply of goods to be manufactured or produced wherein the buyer provides a "substantial part of the materials necessary for such manufacture or production" ;

(7) Contracts that are in "preponderant part" for the supply of labor or other services; and

(8) Liability of the seller for death or personal injury caused by the goods.

For your better understanding, we may classify these exclusions into two categories: goods and types of sales. In the following the exclusions of goods and types of sales will be discussed respectively.

For the exclusions of goods, firstly, the **goods sold for personal, family or household use** are excluded. Such exclusion is designed to protect consumers by avoiding conflict with special national legislation. However, some ambiguities may arise from it. One ambiguity is whether the goods must be so used by the immediate buyer in the transaction. Or, can it be eventually used by that buyer's sub-buyer or other remote buyers? The U.S. interpretation has uniformly held the former, that is, the buyer must intend to use the goods in such a manner. Other issues relate to whether buyer's intended use must be known to seller at the time of the conclusion of the contract, and whether seller has a duty to inquire about intended use. An Austrian court, in a contract for the sale of Lamborghini automobile, stated that application of the exclusion language① depended upon the proposed use of the car as understood by the parties, and not on the actual use, and ruled that the CISG did not govern the sale.

The exclusion of consumer goods contains an exception which allows the CISG to apply if seller "neither knew nor ought to have known" of buyer's use for personal purposes [Article 2(a)]. Thus, if buyer's purchase is in fact for "personal, family, or household use", seller would seem to have the burden of proving that it neither knew of that use, nor should have realized such intended use from the transaction facts. This may explain the results in some cases. In the Lamborghini sale, the Austrian court observed that seller had not presented evidence that it neither knew nor ought to have known of buyer's personal use.

Secondly, **sales of ships, vessels, hovercraft and aircraft** are also expressly

① See CLOUT Case 190.

excluded. This exclusion is made in the CISG because ships, vessels, hovercraft and aircraft were often treated as "immovable" (real property) under the domestic laws of civil law countries, and such goods were strictly subject to registration. However, sales of parts of aircraft are covered by the CISG, even though those parts themselves may be precisely identifiable by serial number and may be subject to registration. This has been established by case law.[①]

Thirdly, sales of some intangible rights or claims of **stocks, securities, negotiable instruments, or money** as well as **electricity** are expressly excluded from the CISG, even though they may have a tangible "token". A Swiss court has held that a contract for the purchase of corporate shares is not covered by the CISG, and an arbitral tribunal determined that a contract for the transfer of a quota relating to goods was not governed by the CISG. Contracts for the transfer of information (an intangible) which is contained in a tangible (e.g., a computer disc) create special difficulties in interpreting the term "goods". Under the CISG it is presumed that contracts concerning intellectual property rights (patent, copyright and trademark) are not for the sale of goods, but a disc, a computer or a camera, containing intellectual property right is a "good". In a transaction, a German court held that a contract for market research was not a contract for the sale of "goods", even though the market research was to be contained in a written report to be furnished to the buyer. The court emphasized that the concept of goods required that the tangible thing delivered be the principal object of the contract.[②] Contracts for the sale of computer hardware, such as computer components, have been held to be governed by the CISG. A contract calling for the submission of a manuscript for a book is not a contract for the sale of goods, even though the manuscript will be on paper or a disc. It is basically a contract for the author's services. However, a contract for the commercial sale of a lot of printed books (or only one book) is for the sale of tangible items—the books, not the printer's services. There is no such clear bright line in software sales, since many software sales involve some adaptation to the user's precise situation. Nevertheless, a standard which is based on the difference between "off the shelf" software and individually designed software may be helpful.

For the types of sales excluded from the CISG, there are many "transactions in goods" which may or may not be "sales". **Auction sales** are excluded from the CISG. This

---

① See United Technologies International Pratt & Whitney Commercial Engine Bus *v.* Malev Hungarian Airlines, UNILEX Case D. 1992-40.

② See UNILEX Case D. 1994-21.

is another type of contract, which is often subject to specialized national law. Therefore such sales are precluded from the CISG. For similar reasons, issues of liabilities of the seller for death or personal injury caused by the goods are excluded from the provision of the CISG. **Services contracts** (mixed sales) are also expressly excluded from the CISG. However, there are many contracts which involve both obligations to provide goods and also obligations to provide related services. In such circumstances, will the CISG be the governing law? The stated standard is that the CISG does not apply when the "preponderant part of the obligations of the party who furnishes the goods consists of labor or other services". The courts seem to be in agreement that a "preponderant part" requires that more than 50% of the purchase price be attributed to labor or other services. Thus, the sale of a water tank did not become a "services contract" just because the contract required both provision and installation of the goods. Further, for a mixed service and sale contract, if less than 50% of the purchase price be attributed to labor or other services, the CISG is applicable and will govern both sales and services aspect of that contract, unless the contract is divisible under national law.

Article 3(b) of the CISG excludes contracts where the preponderant part of one party's obligations is labor or other services. However, there is a second CISG provision, which is expressly applicable when the party who "orders the goods" also supplies some of the materials for producing those goods. The CISG then makes an exception, however, for those transactions in which the purported buyer ("the party who orders the goods") will provide "a substantial part of the materials necessary" for the completed goods. Note that the deliberate use of "a substantial part" in Article 3(1) is in contrast with the use of "the preponderant part" in Article 3(2), and indicates that the purported buyer needs not provide as much as 50% of the necessary materials in order for this exclusion to become applicable. An Austrian court has ruled that a transaction was excluded from the CISG in which an Austrian firm provided the raw materials to a Yugoslav company to process into brushes and brooms. There was no discussion of any materials being furnished by the Yugoslav company.[①]

◆ **Contractual Issues Excluded from the CISG**

The CISG does not cover all the issues related to the contract for international sale of goods. The Convention expressly includes two sets of issues arising under a sale contract, and expressly excludes two sets of contractual issues from its coverage. The issues covered

① See UNILEX Case D. 1994-27.

by the CISG are **the formation of the contract** and **the rights and obligations of the parties to the contract**. The excluded issues are the validity of the contract, and property right (or title) to the goods (See Article 4). These issues excluded from the coverage of the CISG will be left to the governing of the law indicated by private international law rules or by choice of law clause. For the contractual issues to which both the CISG and domestic law apply, the CISG will preempt to domestic law.

◆ **Interpretation of the CISG**

Articles 7–13 cover "General Provisions". These provisions deal with interpretation of the CISG and interpretation of international sales contracts, which are used to fill gaps in its provisions. Article 7 is designed to assist in interpretation of the CISG itself. It establishes the rules that the underlying goal of the CISG is the creation of a uniform body of international commercial sales law, and in deciding questions governed by the CISG, **a court is to look to the following sources, in the following order**: (1) the CISG itself, (2) the general principles on which the CISG is based, and (3) the rules of private international law. In interpreting the words of the CISG itself, a court is to consider: the international character of the Convention, the need to promote uniformity in the Convention's application, and the observance of good faith.

Articles 8 and 9 are designed to provide guidance in interpretation of terms in international sales contracts. Article 8 is intended to establish **rules for interpreting the sales contract and its terms**. It sets up a three-tier hierarchy: (1) Where the parties have a common understanding on the meaning of a provision, that common understanding is to be used in any interpretation. (2) Where the understanding of the parties diverges, and one party "knew or could not have been unaware" of the other's intent, the latter party's interpretation prevails. (3) Where the parties were unaware of the divergence, their statements and conduct are each to be subject to a "reasonable person" standard. In other words, in determining the meaning of a provision in contract, the CISG directs courts to turn to the "subjective" intent of a speaker, but only if "the other party knew or could not have been unaware" of the speaker's intent. When a speaker's intent is not clear, the CISG directs the court to look at "objective intent". Subjective intent is what the party was actually thinking at the time. Objective intent is determined from the party's statements and other conduct "according to the understanding that a reasonable person of the same kind as the other party would have had in the same circumstances". In evaluating party conduct and statements, a court can look to the negotiation history of the contract and to the actual administration of contractual terms by the parties.

Article 9 allows **the parties to include "any usage" to which they have agreed**. This Article states that parties are bound by "any practices which they have established between themselves", and usages which they have agreed to, and any usages "of which the parties knew or ought to have known and which in international trade is widely known to, and regularly observed by parties of contracts of the type involved in the particular trade".

Article 10 concerning multiple places of business has been already discussed in the above part. Article 11 provides the requirement for the form of international sales contract. It states that a contract for international sale of goods is enforceable, even though it is not written. And Article 13 then defines "writing" as used in the CISG, to include a telex or telegram. That is, according to the CISG, a contract for international sale of goods may be proven in any means. However, Article 12 and Article 96 allow a contracting state to make a reservation on Article 11, allowing the domestic law of that contracting state to govern the form requirements of the sales contract. China has formerly declared a reservation on Article 11 when it ratified the CISG in 1988. Because at that time one of the contract laws of China—Foreign Economic Contract Law required that international sales contract shall be made in writing. However, the Contract law of PRC 1999 repealed the former contract laws including Foreign Economic Contract Law, requiring the form of contract be in written or oral form unless relevant law or administrative regulation requires contract to be in writing or the parties have so agreed.① Then China withdrew the reservation on Article 11 of the CISG in 2013. For the requirement for the form of contracts, Article 469 under Civil Code of PRC states:

"The parties may conclude a contract in writing, orally, or in other forms.

"A writing refers to any form that renders the content contained therein capable of being represented in a tangible form, such as a written agreement, letter, telegram, telex, facsimile, or the like.

"A data message in any form, such as electronic data interchange and e-mails, that renders the content contained therein capable of being represented in a tangible form and accessible for reference and use at any time is deemed as a writing. "

We may infer that the contract for international sale of goods is no longer required to be in writing in China.

---

① See Article 10 of Contract Law of PRC 1999.

4 Formation of the Contract for International Sale of Goods

Part II (Articles 14–24) of the CISG contains the contract formation provisions. Part II of the CISG focuses on "offer" and "acceptance". Under the CISG, a contract is concluded (becomes binding) when an acceptance of an offer becomes effective. There is no need for consideration (like under the UCC), and no formal requirements.

4.1 The Offer

Under the CISG, an "offer" has four requirements. First, it must be "a proposal for concluding a contract". Second, it must indicate "an intention to be bound in case of acceptance". Third, the proposals must be addressed to a specific person or persons. The proposals addressed to the general public will be presumptively not offers "unless the contrary is clearly indicated." Fourth, an offer must be "sufficiently definite". This provision requires **the proposal should contain at least three contract terms: the description of the goods, their quantity and their price**. Other terms can be left open, but not those three. The offer is definite enough if the goods are "indicated", which does not seem to require that they be described with any particularity. Similarly, an offer is definite if it "expressly or impliedly fixes or makes provision for determining the quantity and the price". The above requirements for an offer are based on the reason that the proposal has to describe the goods with sufficient clarity so that the parties know what is being offered, and other elements of the proposal can be implied from the conduct of the parties or from similar contracts used in the trade.

Attention shall be paid to distinguish an **offer** and an **invitation to offer**. The laws of some countries hold that a public advertisement cannot create the power of offer. In Germany, for example, advertisements addressed to the public in general are mere invitation to offer. In the United States, while treating most advertisements as mere invitation to offer, they do recognize that specific advertisements that describe the goods, their quantity and price may be considered an offer. In China, under its Civil Code of PRC, auction announcements, bidding announcements, stock prospectuses, bond prospectuses, fund prospectuses, commercial advertisements and promotions, and mailed price catalogs, and the like, are invitations to offer. However, a commercial advertisement and promotion is deemed an offer if its contents meet the requirements of an offer (Article 473, Civil Code of PRC). However, a commercial advertisement is deemed an offer if its contents meet the requirements of an offer (Article 15, CISG). It seems the CISG takes a middle way by providing that an advertisement or circular is not an offer unless the contrary is clearly indicated by the person making the proposal. Thus in international commercial practice a seller may want to include a notice in all of its price catalogs and literature that the material does not constitute an offer.

Article 14 of the CISG provides the requirements for an offer, and the three following articles concern the **withdrawal**, **revocation** and **termination of an offer**. "Withdrawal" of an offer is permissible only before or at the same time as the offer is received by the offeree. After such receipt, the only recourse of the offeror is to attempt to "revoke" the offer. Under the CISG, **any attempt to revoke an offer must be received by the offeree before the offeree has dispatched an acceptance**. However, not all offers are revocable. There are two ways in which an offer can become irrevocable under Article 16 of the CISG: (1) Through the offeror's statements. An offeror can indicate that an offer is irrevocable "by stating a fixed time for acceptance or otherwise". (2) Through reasonable reliance by the offeree. The first of these approaches incorporates civil law norms, while the second applies common law norms. The criteria for irrevocability of an offer after reasonable reliance by an offeree under Article 16(2)(b) of the CISG seem to follow United States case law and the *Restatement (Second) of Contracts of the United States*. Article 17 states that an offer, even it is irrevocable, is terminated when a rejection reaches the offeror.

4.2 The Acceptance

A contract comes into being at the time an offer is accepted. The CISG requires no particular form for acceptance; it only requires that the offeree communicate his assent (by statement or other conduct) to the offeror within the time period specified in the offer. If no time period is given, then the offeree is given a "reasonable" time in which to accept. It is very common for a would-be buyer to place an order to purchase goods (an offer) but seller responds simply by shipping the goods required, not by verbal or written confirmation. However, the general rule in most countries is that the offeree's silence should not be interpreted as an acceptance. That is, if you unexpectedly receive goods that you did not order, you should not have the duty to pay them. It would be unfair if a seller could force you to take goods simply by stating: "If I don't hear from you, I will assume you would take these goods and pay for them." However, an exception will come up when the previous dealings between the parties entitle one party to interpret the other's silence as acceptance. For instance, during the past six years, Company A regularly purchased raw materials from Company B. At first Company B confirmed all the orders. Soon for the cost-saving purpose, Company B stopped sending any confirmation and just shipped within one month. This time Company A placed the order but Company B never shipped. Thus Company A suffered damages when unexpectedly running out the raw materials. Company A can sue against Company B for breach of contract on the basis the established practice of the acceptance.

Under the CISG, **an acceptance is not effective until it reaches the offeror** (**"Receipt Rule"**). Thus, **the offeree may withdraw the acceptance any time before or at the same time as the acceptance reaches the offeror**. Here "**reach**" means the acceptance is made orally to the addressee or delivered by any other means to him personally, to his place of business or mailing address. In case that he does not have a place of business or mailing address, to his habitual residence (Article 24, CISG). Partly due to the undeveloped status of information technology in 1980's, the CISG does not define the meaning of "reach" where the electronic means such as e-mail is used to make an acceptance. For this point, Article 16 of Contract Law of PRC (repealed) may provide some reference. It states: "When a contract is concluded by the exchange of electronic messages, if the recipient of an electronic message has designated a specific system to receive it, the time when the electronic message enters into such specific system is deemed its time of arrival; if no specific system has been designated, the time when the electronic message first enters into any of the recipient's systems is deemed its time of arrival."

The Receipt Rule under the CISG allows the offeree to speculate for a day or two while the offeror is bound when an acceptance is sent by a slow transmission method. However, on the other hand, the offeror's power to revoke the offer under the CISG is terminated upon dispatch of the acceptance [Article 16(1), GISG].

Under the CISG the effective rules for acceptance follow the basic rules in China and other civil law countries. They are different from those rules established by the common law. Under the common law, the acceptance becomes effective upon the acceptance is dispatched by the offeree ("Mailbox Rule"). In case of an acceptance made by letter, the time of dispatch is the time the letter is put into the hands of the postal authority. This rule makes some sense. A seller of fresh flowers may expect the contract is formed upon the dispatch of the acceptance rather than wait until the arrival of acceptance. However, it also means the offeree may not have any opportunity to regret by withdrawing the acceptance once the acceptance is dispatched.

For the late acceptance, it is effective if without delay the offeror orally so informs the offeree or dispatches a notice to that effect. In simple words, when the offeror receives a late acceptance, it is at his option to make the late acceptance effective or not. If the offeror does not, without delay, orally or dispatches a notice to the offeree stating he would like to accept the late acceptance, the late acceptance will be ineffective. Under the circumstances in which an acceptance would have reached the offeror in due time if its transmission had been normal, the late acceptance will be presumed to be effective unless without delay the offeror informs the offeree that he considers his offer as having lapsed or dispatches a notice to that effect.

4.3 Battle of the Forms

A battle of the forms arises when two parties are negotiating the terms of a contract for the international sales of goods, one party offers to buy goods from the other party on its standard terms but the other party purports to accept the offer on the basis of its own standard terms. In the commercial reality, a contract for the international sales of goods is often formed after several rounds of negotiation. The chains of correspondence or exchange of documents between seller and buyer often make it difficult to tell which one is offer and which one is acceptance. Most countries follow **the mirror image rule**. The rule requires that the terms in an acceptance match the terms of the offer exactly, unequivocally, and must not change. Under this rule, a purported acceptance that contains different or additional terms is considered a counteroffer and thus a new offer. The requirements under mirror image rule present special problems when both parties negotiate back and forth via standard business forms such as purchase order or order confirmation. According to the mirror image rule, if buyer's purchase order form and seller's order confirmation form differ in any term, there will be no acceptance. Instead, there is counteroffer, followed by a rejection of that original offer. Thus, theoretically the parties cannot "conclude" a contract by exchanging conflicting forms; and if one party reneges on its obligations, before performance, it probably is not bound to perform. However, a vast majority of transactions involving exchanges of such conflicting forms are performed by the parties. Once the goods have been shipped, accepted and paid for, there has been a transaction, and a contract underlying that transaction has been formed by the parties. Then what are its terms? To put the same question in a different way, is it the seller's shipment of the goods "conduct" which accepts the terms in the buyer's purchase order? Or, is it the buyer's acceptance and payment for the goods "conduct" which accepts the terms in the seller's confirmation form? When such a problem occurs, the lawyers in common law countries often call it in a vivid way "battle of forms".

The common law analysis would make the terms of the form last sent to another party controlling, since that last form (usually seller's) would be a counteroffer and a rejection and termination of all prior unaccepted offers. It may be worth noting that both the United States and civil law regimes have developed more sophisticated methods of dealing with the "battle of the forms" than the "mirror-image" rule followed by the "last shot" doctrine, but they each use different mechanisms. The CISG drafters showed great resistance against going back to nineteenth century contract principles. They seemed to agree that the mirror-image and last-shot doctrines should not be resurrected, and thus there are more sophisticated tools to resolve the battle of forms under the CISG.

Article 19(1) of the CISG establishes the mirror image rule as a general doctrine. However, as an express exception to the mirror image rule, Article 19(2) provides that a non-mirror image response can be an acceptance if it contains additional or different terms, which do not materially alter the terms of the offer. Here "**materially alter**" is defined in the last paragraph of Article 19, and would include **any term, which relates to "the price, quality and quantity of the goods, place and time of delivery, settlement of disputes or the extent of one party's liability to the other"**. This list is so broad that almost any term could conceivably be interpreted as "material". A purported acceptance that contains additional or different terms that do materially alter the terms of the offer would constitute a rejection of the offer and a counteroffer. However, under the CISG an acceptance containing new terms that do not materially alter the terms of the offer becomes a part of the contract, unless the offeror promptly objects to the change. Suppose that a German Company, Pillow International Inc. sends a purchase order to Fort, a U.S. supplier of feathers. Fort replies with a confirmation adding a clause that a charge of 1% per month will be applied to the outstanding balances if the account is not paid within thirty days. Pillow International Inc. said nothing more. If the seller (Fort) ships, it might not have recourse against Pillow for refusing the goods. Because under the CISG, the new term has materially altered the terms in the offer, and the confirmation made by Fort constitutes a counteroffer to Pillow's purchase order, thus no contract is formed to protect the seller.

5 Performance of the Contract for International Sale of Goods

5.1 Seller's Obligations

A seller is required to deliver the goods, hand over any documents relating to them, and insure that the goods conform to the contract. In fact the CISG just provides basic rules for these obligations and leaves most of the things to be determined by the contractual terms.

5.1.1 Obligations of Delivery

"Delivery" under the CISG relates to transfer of possession or control of the goods. The CISG draftsmen did not attempt to consolidate all the aspects of sale—physical delivery, passing of risk of loss, passing of title, etc. into a single concept or make them turn on a single event, as has been done in many sales statutes. Instead, they provide separate provisions for each of these concepts.

As to **the place of delivery**, the CISG recognizes four distinct types of delivery: (1) destination contracts or delivery contracts in which the seller must deliver to the place specified in the contract; (2) shipment contracts, in which the contract "involves transport of the goods," but does not require delivery to any particular place; (3) sales of goods at a known location which are not expected to be transported; and (4) sales of goods whose location is not known or specified, and which are not expected to be transported.[①]

In "destination" or delivery contracts, the seller may be obligated to deliver the goods to the buyer's place, or to any location specified in the contract. However, it should be noted that the CISG has no provisions directly describing seller's duties in such contracts, and all interpretation is left to contract terms only. The goods must be conforming when delivered not merely when shipped, unless performance is excused by *force majeure*.[②]

In a shipment contract, the seller has no obligation to accomplish delivery of goods to their destination, or to any particular place, but it is clear that transportation of the goods by an independent third party carrier is involved. The usual reference of such a contract is through trade terms like "FOB" or "CIF". Since the goods are to be "handed over" to

---

① See Article 31 of the CISG.

② See Article 36 and Article 69 of the CISG.

the carrier and not to the buyer, transactions involving transport by the buyer seem to be excluded. The shipment contract may require seller to take more than one action to accomplish its obligation of "delivery". First, the seller must transfer ("hand over") the goods to a carrier—the first carrier. There is no duty under the CISG for seller to arrange for the transport of the goods. It is trade terms that may impose such a duty. Second, depending upon the sale contract terms, seller must either "effect insurance" coverage of the goods during transit or, at buyer's request, provide the buyer all available information necessary to effect insurance. Third, if the goods are not "clearly identified to the contract" by the shipping documents or by their own markings, seller must notify buyer of the consignment specifying the goods. Fourth, the contract may require seller to arrange for the transportation of the goods, in which case seller must contract for "appropriate" transport under "usual terms".[①]

Where **transport of the goods is not "involved"**, the buyer may or may not be told where the goods are or will be. Absent from a contrary provision in the contract, in such a transaction, if buyer is told the location of the goods he is expected to pick them up at that location; otherwise at the seller's place of business. The seller's obligation under the CISG is to put the goods "at buyer's disposal" at the appropriate place.

Where **the delivery of the goods is to be accomplished by tender or delivery of documents**, the CISG merely requires that the seller conform to the terms of the contract. The second and third sentences of Article 34 establish the principle that a seller who delivers defective documents early may cure the defects until the date due under the contract, if possible, buyer must take the cured documents, even though the original tender and cure has caused damage to buyer.

The **time requirements for seller's performance**, as stated in the CISG, all relate to the contract terms: the goods or documents must be delivered on or before a stated or determinable date set in the contract, within a stated or determinable span of time specified in the contract, or, if no date or span of time is set, within a "reasonable time". "Reasonable time" is not defined, and will depend on trade usage, but at least it precludes demands for immediate delivery.

The CISG has no provisions concerning seller's duties in regard of export and import licenses and taxes, but leaves the determination of these incidents of delivery to the contract terms, or usage. Where these issues are not covered by the contract terms or

① See Article 32(2) of the CISG.

usage, the concepts are to be interpreted according to the general principles of the CISG.

5.1.2 Obligations of Conforming Goods

One of the primary responsibilities of the seller is to deliver conforming goods. Article 35 of the CISG states: "The seller must deliver goods which are of the quantity, quality and description required by the contract and which are contained or packaged in the manner required by the contract." Goods that do conform to the requirements of the contract are said to be conforming. Conforming goods are: (1) that the goods be fit for ordinary use, (2) that the goods be fit for any particular use made known to the seller, (3) that the goods are properly packaged, and (4) that they conform to any goods which seller has held out as a sample or model. However the parties may "agree otherwise" and limit seller's obligations concerning quality. ①

There are no specific legal rules on the imposition on seller of the obligation of fitness for ordinary use. For example, foodstuffs must be sold in a condition "fit for human consumption". In a contract for wine purchase, the wine delivered by the seller became chaptalized (i.e. it turned to vinegar). Because the chaptalized wine is obviously not fit for the ordinary use of it—be sold as drinking wine. Thus the seller has breached the contract.

The obligation of fitness for a particular purpose arises only if (1) the buyer makes the particular purpose known to the seller (expressly or impliedly) at or before the "conclusion of the contract", (2) the buyer also relies on seller's skill and judgment, and (3) such reliance is reasonable. There is no express requirement that the buyer inform the seller of the buyer's reliance, but only that the buyer informs the seller of the particular purpose. More importantly, there is no requirement that the buyer inform the seller of any of the difficulties which the buyer may know are involved in designating or designing goods to accomplish this particular use. However, it is likely that courts can avoid any abuse of these gaps in the statute by the "reasonable reliance" criterion.

Seller is relieved of any of the obligations under Article 35(2) of the CISG against defects in quality whenever buyer is aware or "could not have been unaware" of a defect at the time the contract is "concluded". However, knowledge gained at the time of delivery or inspection of the goods will not affect seller's obligation, as the "could not have been unaware" language is the subject of much dispute among common law and civil law authorities. Most common law authorities consider it to be "subjective" and relate to

① See Article 35(2) (a)–(d) of the CISG.

buyer's actual state of mind, rather than to impose "constructive knowledge" on the buyer for items he should have learned. In practice, the usual dispute seems to arise out of the sale of used goods, where the courts refuse to allow claims for defects which are not notified to the buyer, but which seem to be predictable for such goods.

Under Article 35 of the CISG, a seller is generally not obligated to supply goods that conform to the public laws and regulations in the buyer's state. However, there are at least three exceptions to this general rule. First, if those laws and regulations are identical to those in the seller's state, the goods must conform to them. Second, if the buyer informs the seller of the laws and regulations in its state, the goods must conform to them. And, third, if the seller knew or should have known of the laws and regulations in the buyer's state due to special circumstances, such as having a branch office in buyer's state, then the goods must conform to them.

How long do these obligations of delivering conforming goods continue? Under the CISG, even after the risk of loss has passed to the buyer, the seller is still liable for the nonconformity of goods, even if such nonconformity is discovered later.① Thus, the buyer is still able to recover for any non-conformity, which becomes apparent long after delivery, but the buyer may have to prove that the defect was present at delivery and was not caused by buyer's use, maintenance or protection of the goods.

If the goods are defective, seller may have **a disclosure obligation**. Under Article 40 of the CISG there is an obligation to notify buyer of any non-conformity not only if known to seller, but also if "he could not have been unaware". If seller does know of a defect and does not notify, then seller may not be able to rely on buyer's failure to inspect the goods quickly or to notify seller of any discovered defects. Thus, even though the buyer may lose its right to rely on a nonconformity because the buyer did not inspect the goods "within as short a time as is practicable or did not notify the seller of any defects, specifying the nature of the defects, within a reasonable time after it discovered" or "ought to have discovered" them, the buyer's right to rely on the nonconformity revives if the seller, in turn, knew of the nonconformity and did not notify the buyer of it. However, in any event the buyer loses the right to rely on a lack of conformity of the goods if he does not give the seller notice within a period of two years from the date on which the goods were actually handed over to the buyer.

Can seller exclude these obligations concerning the quality of the goods by terms

① See Article 36 of the CISG.

in the contract? Article 6 of the CISG states that the parties may, by agreement, derogate from any provision of the Convention, and Article 35(2) of the CISG supports that ability to limit obligations concerning the quality of the goods.

5.1.3 Obligations of Property Issues

Even though Article 4(b) of the CISG states that the CISG is not concerned with property or title to the goods sold, the CISG does impose obligations on sellers that **the goods be sold free of any claims concerning title to the goods or claims on infringement of intellectual property rights** (Article 42, CISG). Seller's obligation concerning title to the goods under the CISG is to deliver the goods not only free from any encumbrances on their title, but also free from any claim of a third party. The legal issue is whether the CISG language should be interpreted to require that seller convey title that is free from all claims, or only title that is free from valid claims. The language in the English version is not clear and, the debates and legislative history suggest conflicting interpretations, but the language in French and Spanish versions suggest that the goods are to be free from all claims. There are no CISG cases yet which analyze the issue. The parties may derogate from the terms of these provisions of the CISG by agreement, but buyer's knowledge that the goods are subject to a bailee's lien does not necessarily imply such an agreement. Instead, buyer may expect seller to discharge the lien before tender of delivery.

In addition to good title, **seller is obligated to deliver the goods free from patent, trademark and copyright claims under the law of the buyer's "place of business" or the place where both parties expect the goods to be used or resold**. This obligation is, however, subject to multiple qualifications. First, seller's obligations arise only with respect to claims of which "seller knew or could not have been unaware". Second, seller has no obligation with respect to intellectual property rights or claims of which buyer had knowledge when the contract was formed. Third, seller is not liable for claims which arise out of its use of technical drawings, designs or other specifications furnished by buyer, if seller's action is in "compliance with" buyer's specifications. Fourth, seller is excused from these obligations if buyer does not give notice to seller specifying the claim of the third party within a reasonable time unless seller knew of the claim, which knowledge may be required in order to create liability initially.

With all these qualifications on the seller's obligation, does the mere assertion of an intellectual property infringement claim create a violation of seller's title obligations? In order to have a violation, the buyer must show that "seller knew or could not have been unaware" the third party claims. One survey of the legislative history concludes that it does not require the seller to research the trademark and copyright registries of the buyer's country, but only requires seller to use due care.

5.2 Buyer's Obligations

Buyer has two primary obligations in a sale contract under the CISG: (1) to pay the price and (2) to take delivery of the goods.① The former duty is more important than the latter.

5.2.1 Obligations of Payment

Unless the sale contract expressly grants credit to buyer, the sale is a cash sale, and payment and delivery are concurrent conditions. Further, payment is due when seller places the goods, or their documents of title, "at buyer's disposal according to the contract". If the sales contract involves transport of the goods, seller may ship the goods under negotiable documents of title and demand payment against those documents, even though no particular method of payment was actually agreed upon by the parties. In such circumstances, buyer still has a right of inspection before payment. If, however, buyer has expressly agreed to "pay against documents" (such as through the use of CFR or CIF term), the buyer has agreed to pay upon tender of the documents, regardless of whether the goods have yet arrived, and without inspection of the goods.

If the buyer is to pay against "handing over" of the documents, or handing over the goods, the place of "handing over" is the place of payment. Otherwise, **the place of seller's business is the place of payment unless the contract provides otherwise**. Such a provision requires the buyer to "export" the funds to seller, which is a critical issue when buyer is from a country with a "soft" currency, or with other restrictions on the international transfer of funds. In addition the buyer has an obligation to cooperate and take all necessary steps to enable payment, including whatever formalities may be imposed by the buyer's country to obtain administrative authorization to make a payment abroad. Failure to take such steps may create a breach by the buyer even before payment is due.

Where the parties agreed to a sale without stating a price, but essentially "agreed to agree" later on the price for each shipment, the purported offer neither contained a price

---

① See Article 53 of the CISG.

term nor made a provision for determining the price. However, where the seller and buyer agreed to a sale with no price term, then the goods were shipped and accepted by buyer, the courts found that a binding contract existed.

The buyer's second obligation, to take delivery, also imposes duties of cooperation. The buyer must not only take over the goods, but also do everything that could reasonably be expected in order to enable the seller to make delivery. This includes a duty to make the expected preparations to permit seller to make delivery and may include such acts as providing for containers, transportation, unloading and import licenses.

5.2.2 Obligations of Inspection and Notice of Defects

The buyer has a right to inspect the goods before taking delivery and duty to notify the seller of any nonconformity of the goods. Where the contract involves the transport of goods, the buyer may defer the inspection until the goods have arrived at their destination. Timeliness of inspection is important, and several decisions hold that the buyer is not permitted to pass the goods on to sub-purchasers and await their complaints, but has an affirmative duty to inspect the goods immediately when they arrive.

The buyer may also have a natural incentive to inspect at the place of delivery because the goods must be conforming at the time the risk passes, which will be at the place or port of shipment in the usual FCA, FOB or CIF contract. There are numerous specialized inspection companies that will, for a fee, inspect goods for a distant buyer.

The buyer must notify the seller within a reasonable time after the buyer discovers any non-conformity. The notice must specify the nature of the lack of conformity. If it fails to duly notify the seller without a reasonable excuse, the buyer may not rely on the lack of conformity in any remedy proceeding. If there is a reasonable excuse, the buyer may still reduce the price of the goods in accordance with Article 50 of the CISG.

The contract may include such terms as a provision on how many days the buyer will have to inspect, where the inspection will take place, how many days the buyer will have to notify the seller of the defects, how and where the notice is to be sent, and a statement as to when specification of a defect is sufficient.

If the seller delivers nonconforming goods, it will often wish to cure any defect in the goods delivered. It is for that reason that the CISG requires early notice by the buyer to the seller of any defects in the goods or their tender of delivery. The CISG has different rules for cure, which depend upon whether the defects are discovered before or after the contract date for delivery.

Where a non-conforming goods is delivered before the contract date for delivery, the seller has the right to remedy any lack of conformity, "provided that the exercise of this right does not cause the buyer unreasonable inconvenience or unreasonable expense". The cure may be repair, replacement or making up a shortage in quantity. If seller cures the non-conformity, it is still liable to the buyer for any damages caused by the defects (Article 37, CISG). If the buyer prohibits the seller from attempting cure, that is a breach of buyer's obligations, so the buyer will be responsible for any damages, which arise from not permitting the cure.

Even **the date for delivery has passed,** the seller may remedy the non-conformity but its right to do so is subject to more conditions. In addition to not causing the buyer unreasonable inconvenience or unreasonable expense, the seller must cure without unreasonable delay. Unlike the specific references in Article 37 of the CISG to various ways a non-conformity tender might be remedied, Article 48 of the CISG says only that the seller may remedy any failure. If asked whether it will accept cure, the buyer apparently has the option to say "No". If the buyer does so and the seller proceeds nevertheless to make a conforming tender, the buyer would not be obligated to accept the tender. One arbitral award has stated that the seller's right to cure after the delivery date is dependent on the consent of the buyer. If the buyer does agree to the seller's offer of cure, it may not seek a remedy which as inconsistent with seller's offered performance, such as avoidance of the contract. If the buyer wishes to avoid the contract after seller has made an offer to cure the nonconformities, which is still possible under the opening clause of Article 48(1) of the CISG. However, to be authorized to avoid the contract, the buyer must comply with one of the requirements of Article 49 of the CISG.

5.3 Excused Performance

Under the CISG, performance of an obligation of a party is excused when the following conditions are met: (1) that party's failure to perform the obligation was due to an "impediment" which was **beyond that party's control**, and which the party "**could not reasonably foresee**" when the contract was made. (2) The party seeking excuse must prove that it could **neither avoid nor overcome** the "impediment". (3) The excuse is available only so long as the impediment continues, and the party seeking excuse must **notify** the other party to the contract both of the "impediment" and of its effect on performance.①

① See Article 79 of the CISG.

Even if the party seeking excuse proves all these elements, it is protected only from damages claims. It is not protected from other remedial actions by the other party, such as avoidance of the contract or restitution of benefits received from the other party or derived from goods received.

A summary of the provisions of Article 79 of the CISG demonstrates that great weight is placed on the concept of "impediment". The drafters of the CISG provisions deliberately rejected a proposal to use the word "circumstances", rather than "impediment". In part, that word of "impediment" was chosen because it was believed to be not an operative word used to define excused performance in any current legal regime. "Impediment" was thought to reflect a requirement of an outside force, which arose to prevent performances, rather than a change in the general economic climate. Thus, economic recessions or increases in inflation rates were not expected to qualify as impediments, and relief has been denied where the price of goods increased by 30%.① A buyer is not excused from payment because the funds were stolen from a foreign bank through allegedly criminal conduct. Transferring the funds to seller is a part of buyer's obligation and should be at buyer's risk.② Most of the cases involve defaults by seller's suppliers. The CISG provisions establish a high standard for obtaining excuse because a third party such as seller's supplier has defaulted. The party to the sales contract (seller) is excused by a default of a third party (supplier) only if both the seller and the supplier can prove they failed due to an impediment which was beyond their control, unforeseeable, unavoidable and cannot overcome.

The language in Article 79 of the CISG does not, however, resolve the issue of whether it can excuse only a complete failure to perform (deliver or pay for goods), or whether it can also be used to excuse defective performance (late delivery or delivery of non-conforming goods). The debates in the working group indicate that it was intended to excuse only the obligation to deliver or pay, and not to include obligation to deliver conforming goods.

Parties that prefer to establish their excuses for performance may incorporate a ***force majeure* clause** into a contract. The term ***force majeure*** means "superior force". A *force majeure* clause in a contract is an exculpatory clause. It excuses a party from failing to perform on the occurrence of an event specified in the clause. The events included in the

① See CLOUT Case No. 54 (1994).

② See UNILEX Case D. 1998-52.

force majeure clause are determined by negotiation of the parties. The list of events usually includes fire, acts of government, acts of God, quarantine restrictions (e.g. COVID-19), strikes and others. It is advised that *force majeure* clauses should be tailored to the special nature of the contract and the type of business involved. *Force majeure* clauses for the steel industry would not be the same as those for the textiles industry. The events included in the clause are determined by negotiation of the parties.

6 Remedies for Breach of the Contract for International Sale of Goods

Remedies for breach of the contract for international sale of goods are provided by the sales laws in almost every country, which are intended to give the parties the benefit they expected to obtain from the contract and to put the parties into the economic position they would have been in had the breach not occurred. The remedies available to a buyer or seller under the CISG are drawn from both common law and civil law systems. These remedies include (1) suspension of performance, (2) avoidance of the contract, (3) damages, (4) specific performance, (5) seller's right to cure, (6) seller's additional time to perform, and (7) price reduction. The remedies of (1), (2), (5), (6) and (7) may be undertaken without judicial intervention, the rest remedies involve proceedings in court or before an arbitration tribunal. The remedies which do not require judicial intervention are usually preferred by businessmen because of their low cost. And businessmen who have traded with each other in the past, and hope to do so in the future, are much more likely to use these remedies than to go to court. We discuss these remedies by following the order in the above list. However, it by no means indicates the varying importance of them in international sales practice.

6.1 Suspension of Performance

Suspension of performance is a kind of remedy for **anticipatory breach**. Anticipatory breach occurs when one party expressly states or indicates by its conduct that it will not perform its obligations or a substantial part of its obligations before the date for performance of the contract comes.

Either party may stop performing (suspend performance) under a contract once **it becomes clear that the other party will fail to perform a "substantial part" of his obligations because of a lack of ability, a lack of creditworthiness, or inadequate**

preparation such as a failure to open a letter of credit or to provide specifications for the goods.[①] If a seller has shipped goods with a carrier and it learns that the buyer is insolvent or that there is a serious deficiency in his creditworthiness, the seller may order the carrier not to hand over the goods to the buyer. The provision is neutral between buyers and sellers. Thus, a buyer who has agreed to pay, or to prepay, for the goods may suspend that performance if it learns that there is a "serious deficiency" in seller's ability to perform, or that necessary preparations for performance, including making shipping insurance arrangements or obtaining the proper documents, have not been made.

A party who suspends performance must give reasonable notice to the other party of that suspension in order to permit him to provide adequate assurance. If sufficient adequate assurance has been provided by the other party, the party who suspends performance must continue to perform, otherwise a breach will be deemed to be committed by the party. Failure to notify triggers the other party's rights to a remedy in accordance with the remedies provisions of the CISG. None of these remedies authorizes the other party to treat the suspension as ineffective before no notice has been given. However, the non-notified party may have an immediate cause of action for damages.

The CISG permits a seller to suspend performance, if possible, after shipment of the goods but before delivery of them—stoppage in transit. The CISG provision, however, only deals with rights and duties between the parties to the contract. There is a second question concerning whether a carrier will comply with the seller's direction to stop delivery. The CISG does not require the carrier to do so, and the carrier's obligations are left to other law. After the carrier has delivered the goods to the buyer, then it is no longer possible to stop delivery under the CISG. What the seller would have to do is to seek other remedies for breach of contract such as damages.

Instead, if, **prior to the date for performance of the contract, it is clear that one party will not perform his obligations, the other party may avoid the contract.**[②] In contrast to the right to suspension just discussed, avoiding the contract is allowed where one party will be unable to perform the contract. For example, the seller or the buyer has declared that he will not perform his obligation, the seller's plant has been burnt down or an embargo in the seller's country makes it legally impossible to ship the contracted goods. However, the party avoiding the contract also must give reasonable notice to the other

---

① See Article 71 of the CISG.

② See Article 72 of the CISG.

party, unless the other party has declared that he will not perform his obligation.

Similar remedies for anticipatory breach are also provided by Civil Code of PRC. Article 578 of the Code states: "Where a party explicitly expresses or indicates by act that it will not perform the contractual obligations, the other party may, prior to expiration of the period of performance, request the former party to bear default liability."

6.2 Avoidance of the Contract

"Avoidance of contract", a terminology used in the CISG, is the equivalent of "cancellation of contract". Either buyer or seller can avoid a contract under conditions that there has been a fundamental breach committed by the other party, and the party avoiding the contract has given notice to the other party within a reasonable time.

What constitutes a "fundamental breach"? Article 25 of the CISG defines a **fundamental breach** as one that will "**substantially deprive him of what he is entitled to expect under the contract**". The focus is on the contract and what the aggrieved party is entitled to reasonably expect. According to the cases decided under the CISG, **the seller's shipment of seriously defective goods that cannot be repaired, or that have no value to the buyer under the contract is probably a fundamental breach. So too would be the seller's failure and refusal to ship at all or the buyer's failure and refusal to pay. A partial shipment may also constitute a fundamental breach if it presents a serious problem for the buyer and one that cannot quickly be solved.** Of course the further interpretation of fundamental breach will have to be left up to the courts.

The two U.S. court decisions have created an overwhelmingly high standard to meet the "fundamental breach" test. In one case, compressors for air conditioning units were delivered which did not have either the cooling capacity or the power consumption contained in the contract specifications. The court held that cooling capacity was an important factor in determining the value of air conditioner compressors, so the buyer did not in fact receive the goods, it was entitled to expect.[①] In the other case, mammography units were seized for non-compliance with U.S. administrative regulations. When the court decided that the seller in this case was obligated to furnish goods that conformed to the buyer's laws, it also held that a breach of that obligation was a fundamental breach.[②]

① See Delchi Carrier *v*. Rotorex Corp., 71 F.3d 1024 (2d Cir. 1995).

② See Medical Marketing Int'l Inc. *v*. International Medico Scientifica, S.r.l., 1999 WL 311945 (E.D. La 1999).

German courts have adopted the same approach. In a case the buyer stated that "it was unable to work with" the substandard steel wire delivered by the seller, the court held that since buyer was unable to use the goods, the defect was a fundamental breach.① However, where the buyer alleged only that the material used in the goods was different from the contract specifications, but did not allege that the goods could not be used or resold, the breach was not considered fundamental.② When a seller contracted to "deliver in July, August, and September" and the buyer expected monthly installment deliveries, it was not a fundamental breach to deliver the goods on September 30. Such delivery was within the agreed delivery period, so any delay was not a fundamental defect.

Whereas **installment contract** is involved, there are separate criteria for the avoidance with respect to an individual installment and with respect to the whole contract. For example, although the sale of the first installment is a fundamental breach with respect to the first installment, it might not be a fundamental breach for the whole contract. To permit avoidance with respect to the whole contract, the buyer would have to give "good grounds to conclude" that a fundamental breach will reoccur with respect to future installments.

Given the uncertainties of the "fundamental breach" test, sometimes it will be difficult for buyer, or buyer's attorney, to know whether "avoidance of contract" is permissible or not. Articles 47 and 49(1)(b) of the CISG attempt to cure these uncertainties. If the seller fails to deliver the goods on the agreed delivery date, the buyer may notify the seller that performance is due by a stated new date (after the contract date for performance), and the seller's failure to perform by the new date permits the buyer to declare the contract avoided. The following case concerns disputes over performance of an international sales contract, and the focus is on determination of "fundamental breach".

Case III-2

Sinochem International (Overseas) Pte. Ltd. v. ThyssenKrupp Metallurgical Products GmbH

The Supreme People's Court Min-Si-Zhong-Zi [2013] No. 35

Facts

On April 11, 2008, the Sinochem International (Overseas) made the Contract

① See CLOUT Case 235 (Ger. 1997).

② See UNILEX Case 1994-2.

with the ThyssenKrupp Company, agreeing that:

(i) The Sinochem International (Overseas) will purchase 25,000 tons of fuel-grade petroleum cokes from the ThyssenKrupp Company, the quantity of which can be fluctuated by 10% and the range of HGI (Hardgrove Grindability Index) value of the cokes shall be between 36 and 46;

(ii) The loading port for the petroleum cokes is Pittsburg in the State of California, and the destination port is a Chinese port, which shall be specifically determined by the Sinochem International (Overseas);

(iii) The independent inspector confirmed by the parties shall test and inspect samples on the ships at the loading port and issue an inspection certificate, and the inspection result shall be final and binding on the parties. The Sinochem International (Overseas) shall have the right to inspect the quantity and quality of the petroleum cokes at the unloading port, while the ThyssenKrupp Company shall have the right to entrust an independent inspector to witness the abovementioned inspection process. Where the Sinochem International (Overseas) finds that the quality or quantity of petroleum cokes is not in conformity with the quality or quantity determined at the loading port, it shall send a notice of claim to the ThyssenKrupp Company and have the right to claim damages against the ThyssenKrupp Company under Section 7.2.3 of the Contract within 60 days from the date of arrival of the petroleum cokes at the destination port; and

(iv) The Contract shall be concluded, governed and interpreted in accordance with the laws of the State of New York in force at the time.

On August 8, 2008, the A.J.EDMOND Company, an independent inspector confirmed by the parties, issued an inspection certificate at the loading port stating that the HGI of the petroleum cokes was at 32. On July 31, 2008, the Sinochem International (Overseas) had opened a Letter of Credit ("L/C") at the Bank of Communications (China) Singapore Branch (hereinafter referred to as "the Bank"). The L/C 45A stated that the HGI of the petroleum cokes involved in this case would be CA.36–46. On August 27, 2008, the ThyssenKrupp Company submitted negotiation documents to the Bank which included the inspection certificate issued by the A.J. EDMOND Company at the loading port. The Bank paid the goods. In total, the Sinochem International (Overseas) paid $7,756,828.55 to the ThyssenKrupp Company.

The petroleum cokes arrived at the Nanjing Port on September 8, 2008, and on November 10, 2008, a verification certificate issued by China Certification & Inspection Group Jiangsu Co., Ltd. stated that the HGI of the petroleum cokes was at 32.

From October to December 2008, the price of petroleum cokes in the Chinese market continued to fall. The EXW price of the medium-sulfur cokes fell to RMB 2,048/ton in October, RMB 1,357/ton in November and RMB 1,305/ton in December, respectively. The Sinochem International (Overseas) sued the ThyssenKrupp Company for avoidance of the Contract and damages.

Analysis

The Sinochem International (Overseas) argued that the HGI value of the petroleum cokes delivered by the ThyssenKrupp Company of 32 was not in conformity with the Contract, making difficulty to resell these goods in the Chinese market, and thus the acts of the ThyssenKrupp Company constituted a fundamental breach of contract. In order to support its claim, the Sinochem International (Overseas) provided the Explanation on the Characteristics of Petroleum Cokes issued by the School of Materials Science & Engineering of Shanghai University. The Explanation states that the hardness of fuel-grade petroleum cokes (HGI value) is the core index. Generally speaking, large-scale enterprise buyers usually demand the hardness index of the fuel-grade petroleum cokes with a HGI not below 45. When certain mill grinding procedures allow, some petroleum cokes with a HGI above 35 may also be partially accepted, however, the use for fuel-grade petroleum cokes with a HGI below 35 is very limited. Therefore, demand for petroleum cokes with a HGI below 35 is very limited in the Chinese domestic fuel-grade petroleum coke market.

But the ThyssenKrupp Company believed that, although the HGI of the petroleum cokes delivered was at 32, its delivery did not constitute a breach of contract because the HGI agreed upon in the Contract was a range of typical values, and the delivered petroleum cokes with an HGI at 32 could still be sold in the Chinese market. In order to support its claim, the ThyssenKrupp Company applied for admitting the in-court testimony of multiple witnesses, including Mr. F, who had been working in the petroleum coke industry for more than 30 years, Mr. Wang from the Chinalco Zhengzhou Light Metal Research Institute, and Professor Li from the North China Electric Power University. The three expert witnesses unanimously recognized that the HGI refers to the grinding index of petroleum cokes, which means the lower the index is, the greater the hardness of the petroleum cokes and the greater the grinding difficulty are. In addition, Mr. Wang stated that, when using the petroleum cokes with a high hardness, it would be necessary to adjust the grinding parameters such as the feeding speed, wind pressure, flow rate, and speed of the grinding mill before putting them into use. Mr. Li said that the HGI was the basis for selecting the fuel milling system and could not be used as a basis for judging whether it was acceptable fuel or not. This meant that the petroleum cokes involved in this case with a HGI at 32 still was of value by changing the grinding equipment before using petroleum cokes.

The ThyssenKrupp Company also argued that the Sinochem International (Overseas) sold the petroleum cokes involved in this case to its parent company (the Sinochem Group) at the same price as agreed in the Contract, without any loss. The Sinochem International (Overseas) recognized its sales contract with the Sinochem Group on the petroleum cokes, and that the sales price was basically the same as the price agreed in the Contract, but insisted that there was no real sales relationship between them but rather an entrusted sales relationship. The intended purpose of the sales contract between it and the Sinochem Group is to have the Sinochem Group resell the petroleum cokes involved in this case in China. In order to support its above claim, the Sinochem International (Overseas) submitted its letter of entrustment to the Sinochem Group regarding selling the petroleum cokes involved in the case.

1. The Applicable Law

This case involves a dispute over a contract for international sale of goods. In this case, the parties' places of business are located in Singapore and Germany respectively. These two countries are both contracting states to the CISG. The parties agreed that the contract shall be concluded, governed and interpreted in accordance with the laws of the State of New York in force at the time of concluding the contract. Such a choice-of-law clause is valid. However, the United States is also a contracting state to the CISG, and the choice-of-law clause did not exclude the application of the CISG. During the trial of first instance, the parties unanimously chose to apply the CISG as the basis for determining their rights and obligations. Therefore, it is correct to adjudicate the case by applying the provisions of the CISG. Where the CISG is silent for the issues involved in this case, the laws of the State of New York chosen by the parties shall apply. The *UNCITRAL Digest of Case Law* on the *United Nations Convention on Contracts for the International Sale of Goods* is not an integral part of the CISG and thus cannot be (directly) used as the legal basis for this case.

2. Has the Act of the Thyssenkrupp Company Constituted a Fundamental Breach of Contract

The typical range of HGI values for petroleum cokes agreed upon by the parties in the Contract was 36–46, while the HGI actually delivered by the Thyssenkrupp Company was at 32, which was lower than the minimum value of the typical HGI agreed, and thus was not in conformity with the Contract.

The focus of the dispute in this case is whether the abovementioned performance (breach of contract) by the Thyssenkrupp Company has constituted a fundamental breach of contract. First, in terms of the chemical and physical property specifications of petroleum cokes, the parties agreed upon seven indicators—the moisture rate, sulfur content, ash content, volatile (matter) content, size, calorific value, and hardness of the petroleum cokes (HGI value)—in the Contract. According to the established facts, the Sinochem International (Overseas) only expressed that one of the seven aspects—the HGI value—of the petroleum cokes delivered by the Thyssenkrupp Company was not in conformity with the agreement, and did not raise any objections to the other six indicators. Based on the testimonies of the expert witnesses submitted by the parties and the statements of the witnesses in court, the HGI indicates the grinding index of petroleum cokes. The lower the index means the greater the hardness of the petroleum coke and the more difficult the grinding. However, just as the Jiangsu Higher People's Court in the judgment of first instance pointed out, even the explanatory document issued by the School of Materials Science and Engineering of Shanghai University and submitted by the Sinochem International (Overseas) does not deny that petroleum cokes with an HGI at 32 would only have limited value of use. Accordingly, it can be concluded that the HGI of the petroleum cokes was not in conformity with the Contract but such cokes still had some value of use. Second, during the first instance of the trial of this case, the Sinochem International (Overseas) actively resold the petroleum cokes for the purpose of reducing losses, and clearly stated in a letter to the Thyssenkrupp Company that the resale price of petroleum cokes involved was "not below the reasonable market price". This fact indicates that the petroleum cokes involved in the case could be sold at a reasonable price. Third, considering the decisions made by other jurisdictions on the interpretation of fundamental breach of contract under the CISG, even if the goods delivered by the seller are defective, however, the nonconformity in the quality of the goods delivered shall not be deemed to be a fundamental breach of contract under the CISG, provided that the buyer can use or resell the goods even at discount without causing the buyer unreasonable burden. Therefore, the Court held that the Thyssenkrupp Company's act of delivering the petroleum cokes with the HGI at 32 had not constituted a fundamental breach of contract. Consequently, a sufficient basis for the Thyssenkrupp Company's appeal regarding the fact that their act did not constitute a fundamental breach of contract can be established, which is supported by the Court.

In view of the fact that the Thyssenkrupp Company's act did not constitute a fundamental breach of contract, the Sinochem International (Overseas) would not have the right to declare the contract avoided. Since the issue raised in the Thyssenkrupp Company's appeal regarding whether the avoidance of the contract declared by the Sinochem International (Overseas) was made within a reasonable time was based on the alleging ground of a fundamental breach of contract, there is no need for further review, and the Court will no longer comment and offer judgement on this issue.[①]

Conclusion

In accordance with Article 145 of the *General Principles of the Civil Law of the People's Republic of China*, Articles 1, 4, 25, 39, 40, 49, 74 and 78 of the *United Nations Convention on Contracts for the International Sale of Goods*, Item 2, Paragraph 1 of Article 170 of the *Civil Procedure Law of the People's Republic of China*, and Article 2 of the *Interpretation of the Supreme People's Court on Several Issues Concerning the Application of the Law of the People's Republic of China on the Application of Law for Foreign-Related Civil Relations (I)*, the Court made the following judgment:

(i) Revoking the first item of the Civil Judgment of the Jiangsu Higher People's Court (Su-Min-San-Chu-Zi [2009] No. 0004);

(ii) Altering the second item of the Civil Judgment of the Jiangsu Higher People's Court (Su-Min-San-Chu-Zi [2009] No. 0004) so that the ThyssenKrupp Company shall compensate the Sinochem International (Overseas) for the economic losses of goods in the amount of $1,610,581.74 within 30 days from the date that this judgment becomes effective, and pay the interest accrued from September 25, 2008, the date of

---

① In addition to the two claims, this judgment involves analysis on other claims between the parties such as the relationship between the Sinochem International (Overseas) and its parent company (the Sinochem Group). Such analysis is omitted.

the payment, to the date of payment determined in this judgment (calculated on the basis of the dollar loan interest rate at the Bank of China for the same period);

(iii) Altering the third item of the Civil Judgment of the Jiangsu Higher People's Court (Su-Min-San-Chu-Zi [2009] No. 0004) so that the ThyssenKrupp Company shall compensate the Sinochem International (Overseas) for the loss of stowage expenses in the amount of $98,442.79 within 30 days from the date that this judgment becomes effective; and

(iv) Dismissing other claims of the Sinochem International (Overseas).

If the abovementioned payment obligations are not fulfilled by the party held liable within the period specified in this judgment, the debt interest during the period of delayed performance of payment shall be doubled in accordance with the provisions of Article 253 of the *Civil Procedure Law of the People's Republic of China.*

The case acceptance fee of first instance is RMB 306,432, and the ThyssenKrupp Company and the Sinochem International (Overseas) shall bear the case acceptance fee of RMB 183,859.20 and RMB 122,572.80 respectively. The case acceptance fee of second instance is RMB 306,432, and the ThyssenKrupp Company and the Sinochem International (Overseas) shall bear the case acceptance fee of RMB 183,859.20 and RMB 122,572.80 respectively.

Commentary

This case is a typical dispute over a contract for the international sale of goods which involves two main legal issues: first, the issue of identifying the applicable law, and second, the issue of identifying whether the Defendant's act has constituted a fundamental breach of contract. The Court first confirmed the application of the CISG in this case, and in doing so clarified that the issues not covered by the CISG would otherwise be governed by the third country's law chosen by the parties. Further, referring to the provisions of the CISG and the specific facts of this case, the Court fully analyzed whether the Defendant's act constituted a fundamental breach of contract. Therefore, the judgment of this case has significance in deciding a case of contracts for the international sale of goods.

1. Identification of the Applicable Law

Both parties agreed that the Contract should be concluded, governed and interpreted in accordance with the laws of the State of New York in force at the time of contract formation. Such agreement is a valid one, as it does not violate any provisions of Chinese laws. Meanwhile, the places of business of the parties to the Contract are located in two contracting states to the CISG. Article 1 of the CISG states: "(1) This Convention applies to contracts for sale of goods between parties whose places of business are in different countries: (a) when the states are contracting states..." And the parties did not explicitly exclude the application of the CISG in this case. During the trials of first and second instances, it was clearly stated by the parties that the CISG should be used as the legal basis for determining the rights and obligations of the parties. Therefore, the applicable law in this case should be the CISG at first. However, Article 4 of the CISG states: "This Convention governs only the formation of the contract of sale and the rights and obligations of the seller and the buyer arising from such a contract. In particular, except otherwise expressly provided in this Convention, it is not concerned with: (a) the validity of the contract, or of any of its provisions, or of any usage; (b) the effect which the contract may have on the property the goods sold." According to the above provision, the CISG does not govern the validity of the contract, the issue on the validity of the Contract under the case should be subject to the laws of the State of New York, as chosen by the parties hereto.

2. Analysis of Whether the Defendant's Act Constituted a Fundamental Breach of Contract

The question of whether the Thyssenkrupp Company's act constituted a fundamental breach of contract is also a focal dispute in this case. Article 25 of the CISG stipulates: "A breach of contract committed by one of the parties is fundamental if it results in such detriment to the other party as fundamentally to deprive him of what he is entitled to expect under the contract, unless the party in breach did not foresee and a reasonable person of the same circumstances would not have foreseen such a result." Specifically, the court of second instance made a final determination on the issue of whether the Defendant's act constituted a fundamental breach of contract based on certain factors. It considered whether the goods still had the value of use even if certain indicators measuring the goods involved in the case did not conform to the contractual requirements; whether the goods involved in the dispute could be sold at a price not lower than the market price; and took the relevant judgments of other jurisdictions into consideration to understand the provision of fundamental breach under the CISG. Overall, the judgment of this case has guiding significance of solving similar disputes in China.

6.3 Damages

Articles 74–78 of the CISG provide the aggrieved party (seller or buyer) is entitled for damages for any breach of a party's obligations, and damages can be available when the contract has been "avoided" and also even when the defects in its performance have been successfully cured. There is no requirement that the aggrieved party should prove that the party in breach was "at fault" as a prerequisite to damage recovery. As long as the aggrieved party can prove the other party has committed a breach of contract and he suffers economic loss from such a breach, courts will grant damages under the CISG.

The CISG provides that the party in breach shall be liable for damages in an amount sufficient to make the aggrieved party whole in the event of a breach. Article 74 of the CISG states that **damages to an aggrieved party shall consist of a sum equal to the loss**. Damages under the CISG may also include an amount for lost profits. **The damages for lost profits**① **are limited under Article 74 to those losses that "the party in breach foresaw or ought to have foreseen at the time of the conclusion of the contract" ("foreseeability rule")**.

There are some reasons underlying the so-called "**foreseeability rule**". In the ordinary breach of contract circumstances, the court will attempt to protect the plaintiff's (the aggrieved party) expectation interests, that is, the court will try to put the plaintiff in the position he would have been in had the contract been performed. In some circumstances, however, sometimes the plaintiff may sustain unusual and great losses as a result of a breach of contract. For example, the sender of a telegram may lose a million-dollar deal if the postal office mistransmits his bid. For a long time the courts have realized that awarding the plaintiff full compensation for all of his losses due to the breach (no matter how strange or unforeseeable these losses are) would be unfair for the defendant, and possibly affect the commerce as well. Therefore the courts have developed certain limits on damages the plaintiff may recover.

The so-called "**foreseeability rule**" originates from the principles established by the famous English case of *Hadley v. Baxendale* (See **Case III-3**).

---

① Under common law and the UCC, the damages for lost profits arising from breach of contract are often called "consequential damages".

Case III-3

Hadley v. Baxendale (1854)

9 Exch. 341, 156 Eng. Rep. 145

Facts

A shaft in Hadley's (Plaintiff) mill broke rendering the mill inoperable. Hadley hired Baxendale (Defendant) to transport the broken mill shaft to an engineer in Greenwich so that he could make a duplicate. Hadley told Baxendale that the shaft must be sent immediately and Baxendale promised to deliver it the next day. Baxendale did not know that the mill would be inoperable until the new shaft arrived.

Baxendale was negligent and did not transport the shaft as promised, causing the mill to remain shut down for an additional five days. Hadley had paid 2 pounds 4 shillings to ship the shaft and sued for 300 pounds in damages due to lost profits and wages. The jury awarded Hadley 25 pounds beyond the amount already paid to the court and Baxendale appealed.

Issue

What is the amount of damages to which an injured party is entitled for breach of contract?

Decision

An injured party may recover those damages reasonably considered to arise naturally from a breach of contract, or those damages within the reasonable contemplation of the parties at the time of contracting.

The court held that the usual rule was that the claimant is entitled to the amount he or she would have received if the party in breach had performed; i.e. the plaintiff is placed in the same position she would have been in had the party in breach performed. Under this rule, Hadley would have been entitled to recover lost profits from the five extra days the mill was inoperable.

The court held that in this case however the rule should be that the damages were those fairly and reasonably considered to have arisen naturally from the breach itself, or such as may be reasonably supposed to have been in the contemplation of both parties at the time the contract was made.

The court held that if there were special circumstances under which the contract had been made, and these circumstances were known to both parties at the time they made the contract, then any breach of the contract would result in damages that would naturally flow from those special circumstances.

Damages for special circumstances are assessed against a party only when they were reasonably within the contemplation of both parties as a probable consequence of a breach. The court held that in this case Baxendale did not know that the mill was shut down and would remain closed until the new shaft arrived. Loss of profits could not fairly or reasonably have been contemplated by both parties in case of a breach of this contract without Hadley having communicated the special circumstances to Baxendale. The court ruled that the jury should not have taken the loss of profits into consideration.

In the above case, the situation in which an enterprise of a mill might be shut down for lack of a shaft would not normally be foreseen by one in the position of the Defendant. Therefore the damages did not fall in the first class of "natural" damages. Nor did the Plaintiff give the Defendant notice of the possibility of the shutdown of the mill. Therefore the damages did not fall in the second class of "special" damages. The above rules of *Hadley v. Baxendale* are followed and refined in other similar cases such as *Victoria Laundry Ltd. v. Newman Industries Ltd.* (1949), *Koufus v. Czarnikow Ltd.* (*The heron II*) (1969), *Parsons v. Uttley Ingham* (1978), etc. And similar foreseeability rule is also developed in civil law countries and incorporated into their civil codes.

Case III-4

Victoria Laundry Ltd. v. Newman Industries Ltd.

[1949] 2 KB 528

Facts

Newman Industries Ltd. was meant to deliver a boiler for Victoria Laundry (Windsor) Ltd. The delivery was five months late. As a result of not having enough laundry capacity, Victoria Laundry lost a lucrative cleaning contract from the Ministry of Supply. Victoria Laundry sued for the ordinary profit that it had forgone through not having the boiler on time. The question was whether it could also claim the extraordinary profit it would have made, had it been able to take advantage of the lucrative Ministry of Supply contract.

Issue

What part of the plaintiff's profits can they recover?

Rule

When there is a breach of contract, the breaching party should be liable for damages that naturally arise from the breach, or damages that both of the parties contemplated at the time they made the contract.

Analysis

The court says it is reasonable to think that since the defendant knew that the plaintiff was in the laundry business, it was foreseeable that the lack of a boiler would keep them from receiving the profits laundry people usually get. The engineering company cannot plead ignorance as to what the boiler was for because any reasonable person would understand that it is essential to their business.

The court issued six "propositions" :

1. The rule that damages try to put the aggrieved party in the same position as if his contractual rights had been observed, can be too harsh at times, because some damages are too unpredictable or improbable.

2. Only damages which are "reasonably foreseeable" from the breach are recoverable.

3. What was "reasonable" depends on the knowledge of the party that commits the breach.

4. Knowledge can be imputed ("ordinary course of things") or of "special circumstances outside the ordinary course of things of such a kind that a breach ... would be liable for more loss".

5. It is not necessary to prove that the wrongdoer contemplated the loss. "Parties at the time of contracting contemplate not the breach of the contract, but its performance. It suffices that, if he had considered the question, he would as a reasonable man have concluded that the loss in question was liable to result".

6. It is not necessary to foresee "that a breach must necessarily result in that loss. It is enough if he could foresee it was likely so to result. It is indeed enough ... if the loss ... is a serious possibility" ... "real danger" or "in the cards".

Conclusion

Asquith LJ in the Court of Appeal held that Newman Industries only had to compensate for the ordinary, not the extraordinary loss of profits that the defendant did not know about.

Under Civil Code of PRC, the foreseeability rule is embodied in Article 584. This Article states: "Where a party fails to perform the contractual obligation or the performance does not conform to the agreement so that the other party suffers losses, the amount of damages shall be equivalent to the losses caused by the breach of contract, including the benefits expected to be obtained should the contract had been performed, except that the damages may not exceed such losses that the party in breach foresaw or should have foreseen at the time of conclusion of the contract. "

Besides, Civil Code of PRC also entitles the parties to agree on liquidated damages or deposits for the performance of their contract. Article 585 states that the parties may prescribe that if one party breaches the contract, it will pay a certain sum of liquidated damages to the other party in light of the degree of breach, or prescribe a method for calculation of damages for the loss resulting from a party's breach. Where the amount of liquidated damages prescribed is below the loss resulting from the breach, a party may petition the people's court or an arbitration institution to increase the amount; where the amount of liquidated damages prescribed exceeds the loss resulting from the breach, a party may petition the people's court or an arbitration institution to decrease the amount as appropriate. The scheme of earnest money is found in Article 586. It provides: "The parties may agree that one party provides earnest money with the other party to secure the claim. An earnest money contract is formed upon actual delivery of the earnest money. The amount of the earnest money shall be agreed by the parties, except that it may not exceed 20% of the value of the object of the principal contract, and any excessive amount does not have the effect of earnest money. Where the amount of the earnest money actually delivered is more or less than the agreed amount, the agreed amount of the earnest money is deemed to have been changed."

To have a proper understanding of the foreseeability rule, due attention should be paid to several aspects of it. **First**, the time for measuring "foreseeability" is the time when the contract is concluded. Where the defendant acquires knowledge of possible consequences after the contract is concluded, this knowledge is irrelevant to the application of foreseeability rule. **Second**, in determining whether the party in breach foresaw or should have foreseen particular damages for lost profits, the facts and matters the party in breach knew or ought to have known as a possible consequence of the breach of contract shall be taken into account. These facts and matters may include customs in the trade parties involved in, the trade relationships between parties, and the sophistication of the party in breach, etc. In determining the "foreseeability", there are subjective test and objective test.

The subjective test is usually used to determine the "foresaw" state of breaching party, i.e. whether the party in breach has actually foreseen the possible consequence of his breach of contract at the time of conclusion of the contract. While the objective test is usually used to determine the "should have foreseen" state of breaching party, i.e. whether a reasonable party would have foreseen the possible consequence of his breach of contract at the time of conclusion of the contract under such circumstances. **Third**, it is important to distinguish between the question whether particular damages were foreseeable and the question whether particular damages can be proved with adequate certainty. "Foreseeability" relates to whether the possibility of the damages was likely at the time of concluding the contract, while "certainty", on the other hand, requires that the aggrieved party must not only show that he has suffered lost profits, but must show the amount of these lost profits.

Of course, the parties to contracts for international sale of goods are free to allocate the risks by express agreement in a way different from foreseeability rule. One way they can do this is for the non-breaching party to give notice to the party in breach of special circumstances at the time of concluding the contract. Alternatively, the parties may agree that the party in breach will not be liable for certain reasonably foreseeable consequences, which would otherwise deemed to be foreseeable under the foreseeability rule.

A party who relies on a breach of contract (the aggrieved party) must take "reasonable measures" to **mitigate its damages**, including loss of profits (Article 77, CISG). For example, when the seller's breach of contract occurs, if similar goods may be purchased in the market, the most usual reasonable measures of the buyer is to buy substitute goods as a way to mitigate or reduce the losses arising from a breach of contract. To some degree, mitigation of damages is a duty imposed on the non-breaching party by law. This rule is justified by the purpose to encourage the efficient use of economic resources and to avoid the avoidable losses. Since mitigation of damages is a kind of legal duty, liability will incur if such a duty is not fulfilled. Article 77 of the CISG requires that if the aggrieved party fails to take such reasonable measures, the breach party claims a reduction in the damages in the amount by which the loss should have mitigated.

6.4 Specific Performance

Specific performance is used when a court requires a breaching party to perform a contract. This remedy is available to both seller and buyer. In case of nonperformance, the seller may petition the courts to enforce the buyer to pay the price, and the buyer may also enforce the seller to deliver the goods as required in the contract rather than damages by the order from the courts.

In establishing the scheme of specific performance, the difficulty the drafters of the CISG face is illustrated by the facts: specific performance is the preferred remedy at civil law, while the action for damages is preferred at common law. Under common law, specific performance is considered a harsh remedy to be used only damages cannot be calculated or are inadequate, which may occur when the subject matter of the contract is unique. For instance, in a dispute over the sale of a prized race horse, a common law court may require a seller to deliver it to the buyer because of the unique nature of goods. However, the civil law courts will prefer the use of specific performance under much more circumstances, without regard to whether money damages are inadequate. This reflects the basic civil law theory that legal compulsion of performance is the best relief to an aggrieved buyer, and that seller's actual performance is preferable to substitution relief (such as a monetary award).

Finally the CISG draws strongly on the civil law's acceptance of specific performance as a remedy for breach of contract. Under Article 46 of this Convention, a court may grant specific performance only if all of the following conditions are met: (1) the buyer had not resorted to any "inconsistent" remedy such as avoidance of contract. Since avoidance would terminate the contract, there would be no contract to enforce after avoidance; (2) the seller had failed to deliver or in the case of non-conforming goods, the non-conformity was so serious that it constituted a fundamental breach; (3) the buyer had given timely notice to the seller that the goods were non-conforming; (4) the buyer had made a timely request that the seller provide substitute goods. However, the above provision of the CISG may not have much effect on the use of specific performance in common law countries, because the CISG has provided a limitation on the buyer's right to seek specific performance. Article 28 of the CISG provides that a court need not grant specific performance unless it would do so under its own law. However, it has a negligible effect on civil law courts because they are authorized to order seller's performance in many more cases. Thus, if specific performance is sought in a civil law court, it will usually apply Article 46 of the CISG and order the seller to perform its obligations.

The CISG provision gives buyer the right to seek specific performance, rather than damages, but does not require it to do so. Thus, any preference for this remedy must arise from buyer's perspective, not from the court's. Even in civil law jurisdictions, buyers will often prefer to recover damages and purchase substitute goods.

Under Civil Code of PRC, Article 577, Article 580 and Article 581 provide the remedy of specific performance for breach of contract. It states that if a party fails to pay the price or remuneration, the other party may require payment thereof. And where a party fails to perform, or renders non-conforming goods, the other party may require performance, except where: (1) Performance is impossible in law or in fact. For example, the subject matter of the contract is unique and was ruined by fire. (2) The subject matter of the obligation does not lead itself to enforcement by specific performance or the cost of performance is excessive; for example, the obligation of providing personal service under a service contract. (3) The other party does not require performance within a reasonable time. Where a party fails to perform the contractual obligation, if the obligation may not be enforced by virtue of its nature, the other party may request such party to bear the expenses of a substitute performance by a third person.

6.5 Other Remedies Available under the CISG

In addition to refusing to accept goods, which do not conform to the contract through avoidance of the contract, the aggrieved buyer has another informal remedy which appears to give it the power of self-help. Under the CISG, the buyer who receives non-conforming goods "may reduce the price" it pays to the seller. This remedy of **price reduction** is available whether the buyer has already paid or not. If the buyer has paid, the remedy is likely to require an action in court, rather than self-help.

The CISG provision spells out a mathematical formula for calculating the permissible amount of the price reduction. The reduction requires a comparison of the value that the goods actually delivered at the time of that delivery to the value that conforming goods would have had at the time of that actual delivery. That ratio is to be applied to the contract price to determine the price to be paid under Article 50 of the CISG. There is little guidance in the provision on how to determine the value of the actual goods delivered at the time of delivery, or as to what evidence of value should be sent to the seller. The provision for **price reduction, therefore, seems better suited to deliveries which are defective as to quantity, rather than as to quality**. One United States court decision has indicated that, if the buyer resells the defective goods, the resale price is evidence of their value at the time of delivery; the seller is entitled to discover the resale prices. Several foreign courts have dispensed with the formula stated in the provision and, where the buyer had the defective goods repaired, have given the buyer the costs of repair under Article 50 of the CISG.

Article 577 of Civil Code of PRC provides in circumstances of a party failing to perform the contractual obligations or the performance does not conform to the contract, it shall bear the liability such as continuing to perform the obligations, taking remedial measures, or compensating for losses.

As we have discussed in the part of buyer's obligations, **a seller who has delivered some goods to the buyer prior to the delivery date, even if the goods are non-conforming or the shipment is incomplete had the right to cure or correct the problem by sending substitute or replacement goods if it can be done before the date for performance**. The seller maintains this right to cure, and the buyer may not avoid the contract, until the time for performance expires. However, Article 37 of the CISG states that the seller may exercise this right only if it does not cause unreasonable inconvenience or expense to the buyer.

In the event that the seller has failed to deliver the goods, and the time for delivery under the contract has passed, the buyer may grant the seller extra time (**a grace period**) to do so. During this time, the buyer may not avoid the contract or resort to a remedy for breach of contract. If the seller does not perform within the grace period, the buyer may avoid the contract whether or not the breach was fundamental. Article 48 of the CISG contains a provision entitling the seller to invoke such a grace period, which allows a seller who fails to perform on time, or who delivers non-conforming goods, to cure performance if it does not cause the buyer "unreasonable delay" or "unreasonable inconvenience". If a seller asks for an extension of the grace period for delivery and the buyer fails to respond within a reasonable time, the seller may perform within the time requested by the grace period. These provisions of the CISG intend to encourage the parties to stay in their contract rather than to repudiate it in the event of a dispute.

Chapter Summary

This Chapter is intended to provide a thorough understanding on the legal framework governing international sale of goods. After introducing fundamentals of contracts, this Chapter discusses different sources which offer many alternatives for the rules governing international sale of goods, including the CISG, the *Principles of International Commercial Contracts*, the Incoterms and national law such as Civil Code of PRC and the U.S. *Uniform Commercial Code*. The CISG is regarded to be a success of uniform law worldwide, which is now binding on 94 contracting states in many respects of international sale of goods. The CISG governs sale of goods between the parties whose places of business are located in different contracting states. Neither the nationality of the parties nor the civil or commercial character of the parties or of the contract is to be taken into consideration in determining the application of the CISG. Where one or both parties have multiple places of business, the place of business is the one that has the closest relationship to the contract and its performance. However, the CISG does not cover all international sales or all aspects of issues of contract for international sale of goods. In fact, it governs only the formation of the contract of sale and the rights and obligations of seller and buyer arising from such a contract (including remedies for breach of contract). The contractual issues of the validity of the contract and passage of title to goods are left for applicable domestic laws. Under Article 2 of the CISG, six types of goods including goods bought for personal, family or household use, electricity, ships, etc. are excluded from the coverage of the CISG. And two kinds of mixed sales are also excluded from the coverage of the CISG under Article 3. Although not being a binding legal document in its nature, *Principles of International Commercial Contracts* can be chosen to be the governing law by the parties to an international commercial contract as an alternative of national law and the CISG. The Incoterms specify the rights and obligations of the parties to the contracts with respect to the delivery of goods sold, and provide a set of international rules for the interpretation of the trade terms most commonly used in international sales contracts. A thorough understanding upon the roles of these sources in governing international sale of goods will be of some help in reducing the occurrence of disputes to a considerable degree.

A contract for international sale of goods can be concluded through two steps: offer and acceptance. Offer is defined to be a proposal addressed to one or more specific persons, which is sufficiently definite indicating the goods, the quantity and the price. An offer should be carefully distinguished from an invitation to offer. An offer becomes effective when it reaches the offeree, and it may be withdrawn if the withdrawal reaches the offeree before or at the same time as the offer. An offer, if revocable, may be revoked if the revocation reaches the offeree before he has dispatched an acceptance. An acceptance, which indicates assent to an offer, can be made by statement or by other conduct. Under the CISG, an acceptance becomes effective when it reaches the offeror. And an acceptance can be withdrawn before or at the same time as the acceptance reaches the offeror. A purported acceptance, which is usually a standard form used by international merchants, contains additions, limitations or other modifications as a rejection of the offer and constitutes a counteroffer according to the mirror image rule. However, a purported acceptance that contains additions, limitations or other modifications, which do not materially alter the terms of the offer constitutes an acceptance, unless the offeror objects without delay. The terms of the contract will be the terms of the offer with such modifications contained in the acceptance. But if modifications do materially alter the terms in the offer, the purported acceptance shall be a counteroffer.

The CISG provides general obligations for the seller and the buyer, however, leaves a lot of opportunities for the parties to specify their respective obligations under the contract. The seller must deliver conforming goods, i.e. the goods which are of the quantity, quality and description required by the contract, hand over any documents relating to them and transfer the property in the goods. On the other hand, the buyer must pay the price for the goods and take delivery as required by the contract. As for the allocation of risk of loss, usually the trade terms incorporated into the contract will give the direction. Where no trade term is used, the risk of loss will pass from the seller to the buyer when the goods are handed over to the first carrier, if the seller is not required to deliver the goods to a particular place. If the seller is bound to hand the goods over to a particular destination, the risk will be on the seller until the goods are delivered to the particular destination. In respect of goods sold in transit, the risk passes to the buyer from the time of conclusion of the contract.

Remedies of suspending performance, avoidance of contract, specific performance, damages, price reduction, etc. are available for breach of contract under the CISG. The party seeking to resort to these remedies can reasonably choose one suitable remedy or remedies in accordance with relevant circumstances. In absence of *force majeure* clauses under the contract, the other party may invoke the occurrence of "an impediment", which is beyond the party's control, unavoidable, unforeseeable, and cannot be overcome as an excuse for his nonperformance.

The study of the CISG will help you to understand those rules established under Civil Code of PRC.

Exercises

I. True or False Statements

1. The UN Convention on Contracts for the International Sale of Goods (CISG) is the principal law governing international sale of goods. Here "international" means the nationalities of the parties are different.

2. The CISG defines a sale as the passing of title from the seller to the buyer for a price.

3. Under the CISG, a contract of sale need not to be concluded in writing. The contract may be proved by any means including witnesses.

4. Offers can be revoked if the notice to revoke reached the offeree before the acceptance becomes effective under CISG.

5. Dramatic increase of inflation can constitutes an impediment under the CISG, thus may be invoked by the party as an excuse for nonperformance.

6. To recover the damages for breach of contract, the aggrieved party must prove that the breaching party was at fault if CISG applies to the contract.

7. After duly avoiding the contract, the aggrieved party may still seek damages if he can prove damages have arisen from the fundamental breach committed by the other party.

8. Under the CISG, if a party seeking to claim damages fails to mitigate the losses suffered by the other party, the former will not be entitled to any damages at all.

9. A party may suspend performance under a contract once it becomes clear that the other party will fail to perform a substantial part of his obligations because of a lack of ability, or a lack of creditworthiness.

10. Under Civil Code of PRC, the court will grant specific performance only where the subject matter of the contract is unique goods.

II. Multiple Choices

1. For a sales transaction to be covered by the UN Convention on Contracts for the International Sale of Goods (CISG), the buyer and the seller must have their places of business in different states, and ________ .

A. both the buyer's state and the seller's state must be parties to the CISG

B. either the buyer's state or the seller's state must be a party to the CISG

C. the rules of private international law must lead to the application of the law of a state that has become a contracting party of the CISG

D. either A or C

E. either B or C

2. Which of the following is a legal issue regulated by the UN Convention on Contracts for the International Sale of Goods (CISG)?

A. the competency of the contracting parties

B. the formation of contracts

C. the legality of a contract

D. the liability of a party for death or personal injury

E. the rights of third parties

3. X agrees to ship 1,000 widgets from the United States for delivery to Y in Italy. X actually ships 1,500 widgets. According to the UN Convention on Contracts for the International Sale of Goods (CISG), Y may ________ .

A. accept the 1,500 widgets

B. accept only 1,000 widgets

C. reject all of the widgets

D. all of the above

E. either A or B

4. Which of the following international transactions is covered by the CISG?

A. sale of ships

B. sale of electricity

C. sale of parts of aircraft

D. sale of stocks

E. sale of cosmetics for personal use

5. CISG states the following are key terms of a contract that will materially alter the contract, except ________ .

A. price

B. time of delivery

C. quantity of goods

D. specifications of goods

E. settlement of disputes

6. A party is excused for a failure to perform a contract if he proves that the failure ________ .

A. was due to an event beyond his control

B. can not be reasonably foreseen by him when concluding the contract

C. can not be avoided

D. all of the above

E. only A and B

III. Chapter Questions

1. When considering the applicability of CISG to contracts for the international sale of goods, what questions will you take into account?

2. What are the sales excluded from the coverage of CISG? In your opinion what are

the reasons for these exclusions?

3. Under what circumstances will an offer be deemed to be irrevocable?

4. In China, if a real estate developer does not intend their advertisements to be treated as an offer in law, what suggestions will you put forward?

5. What are the rules for passing risk of loss under CISG? When the risk has passed from the seller to the buyer, will the seller be excused from damages for delivering non-conforming goods?

6. The seller must deliver conforming goods as required by the contract. How would you understand the concept of "conforming goods"?

7. If the seller knew the buyer was a middleman in international trade at the time of concluding the contract, can the damages for buyer's lost profits be recoverable if later the seller failed to perform the obligation of delivery? Please explain.

8. How do you understand the *force majeure* clauses in a contract?

9. Where no *force majeure* clauses have been incorporated into a contract, is there any other excuse for nonperformance the party may resort to?

10. Suppose the seller delivered 900 widgets to you rather than 1,000 widgets, which is the quantity required by the contract. There are similar widgets available in the local market, however, the price is somewhat higher than the contract price and you are in urgent need of the widgets. What remedies would you prefer to seek if CISG applies to the contract? Please explain.

IV. Case Problems

Analyze the following cases by applying the legal rules you have learned in this Chapter.

Filanto, the Plaintiff, is an Italian corporation engaged in the manufacture and sale of footwear. Chilewich, the Defendant, is an export and import firm incorporated in New York with its principal place of business in White Plains. On February 28, 1989, Chilewich's agent in the United Kingdom, Byerly Johnson, Ltd., signed a contract with Raznoexport, the Soviet Foreign Economic Association, which obligated Byerly Johnson to supply footwear to Raznoexport. Section 10 of the contract—the "Russian Contract" (This contract was signed by Byerly Johnson and Raznoexport)—is an arbitration clause, which reads in pertinent part as follows:

"All disputes or differences which may arise out of or in connection with the present

Contract are to be settled, jurisdiction of ordinary courts being excluded, by the Arbitration at the USSR Chamber of Commerce and Industry, Moscow, in accordance with the Regulations of the said [Chamber]."

Chilewich then entered into negotiation with Filanto to supply the shoes needed for the Russian contract. After a negotiation meeting, Chilewich sent Filanto a letter, dated July 27, 1989, that stated: "Attached please find our contract to cover the purchases from you. Same is governed by the conditions which are enumerated in the standard contract in effect with the Russian buyers, copy of which is also enclosed." Subsequently, Chilewich procured a letter of credit to the benefit of Filanto as required under the contract. Soon thereafter, Filanto began to perform on the contract.

On September 2, 1989, Chilewich received a letter from Filanto that included the following statement: Returning back the enclosed contracts signed for acceptance, "[I]f we do not misunderstand, regarding the Russian contract, we have to respect only the following points: packing and marking, way of shipment, delivery." After its Russian buyer rejected an earlier shipment of shoes, Chilewich never purchased a subsequent order of 90,000 pairs of boots. Chilewich commenced an arbitration action in Moscow. Filanto sought for an order directing that arbitration be held in New York rather than Moscow because of unsettled political conditions in Russia.

Questions:

1. What was the applicable law to the dispute?
2. Where should the arbitration be held? Please explain.

Chapter 2
Law of International Transport of Goods

Learning Objectives
(1) Getting to know the advantages and disadvantages of different modes of transportation of goods (2) Having a deep understanding of the functions of bills of lading (3) Having a command of carrier's liability and shipper's liability under international conventions on transportation of goods by sea (4) Getting to know the risks and coverage of marine cargo insurance (5) Having a deep understanding of the carrier's liability under international conventions on transportation of goods by air, rail and road

Beyond the terms regarding the goods to be exchanged as covered in the previous chapter, contracts for the international sale of goods must also address transportation of these goods. Once the buyer and the seller have negotiated the contract for the sale of goods, and how those goods will get from point A to point B, a carrier must actually transport those goods. Transportation or transport of those goods is governed by private contractual relations. But, for many instances, it is also enhanced by the international conventions concerning carrier's liability for loss, misdelivery, and monetary damages. In fact, an independent body of rules has been established for governing the international transport of goods.

There are five main modes of transportation: sea, air, road, rail, and pipeline. And with the wide use of containers, sometimes two or more modes are combined to accomplish international transport of goods, i.e. multimodal transport of goods. Each mode is characterized by a set of technical and commercial characteristics such as speed, capacity and cost. For example, pipeline routes are practically unlimited as they can be laid on land or underwater. Their purpose is to move liquids such as petroleum products over long distances in a cost-effective fashion. The longest gas pipeline links Alberta to Sarnia (Canada), which is 2,911 km in length. The longest oil pipeline is the Transiberian, extending over 9,344 km from the Russian arctic oilfields in eastern Siberia to Western Europe. A typical process of international transport of goods by sea is as follows: Goods are transported from a seller in Country A to an inland carrier and carried to a seaport for transport abroad. The inland carrier will deposit the goods in a warehouse or port depository for examination by customs officials and for consolidation with other goods if the load is not large enough to occupy a ship. A stevedore company or the ship's crew will load the goods and then stow the goods aboard ship, mark the goods and issue a bill of lading on behalf of the carrier to the shipper. At a seaport in Country B, the ship will be directed by port authorities to tie up at a pier or to anchor in the harbor. When the buyer presents the bill of lading, the ship's crew will unload the goods onto the dock. The crew or a stevedoring company will then deliver the goods to a customhouse or a bonded warehouse for inspection. Once the customs of Country B has inspected the goods and their related documents, and collected import duties, the goods will be released for entry into Country B. A local inland carrier may be employed to transport the goods to the buyer's place of business. When goods are transported by air, rail, or truck, much the same procedure is followed except that the carrier will issue an air waybill or similar non-negotiable receipt instead of a bill of lading. In this Chapter, we will focus on the legal issues in different modes of international transportation.

1 Transportation of Goods by Sea

Compared with most other options, transportation or transport of goods by sea is cheap, but slow, and transshipment (i.e. having to unload and reload goods between different modes of transport) may be necessary. Despite the decline in the number of passengers using sea transport, transportation of goods by sea has been growing for the past decades. Transportation of goods by sea is still the most effective mode to move large quantities of cargo over long distances. In fact, more than 75% of world trade is carried by sea. Therefore, transportation of goods by sea plays a vital role in transportation by far. Most transport of goods by sea is done by liners, i.e. a carrier holding itself to carry goods for more than one shipper, and an important document as a bill of lading is often used. However, sometimes a few shipments large enough to require the shipper to hire an entire vessel are generally carried by means of a charterparty, i.e. the contract to employ an entire vessel. We will come back to charterparties after discussing common transport.

1.1 Bills of Lading

1.1.1 Fundamentals of Bills of Lading

A bill of lading is a document that is issued by a carrier to a shipper upon receipt of goods from the shipper. A bill of lading serves three purposes: (1) It is a carrier's receipt for goods. (2) It is evidence of a contract of transport. (3) It is a document of title. First, a bill of lading signed by or on behalf of a carrier usually describes the goods put on board, states the quantity and conditions of the goods, and sets forth the terms on which those goods have been carried. The form of bill of lading is normally preprinted. Before issuing a bill of lading, the carrier's tally clerk will check to see that the goods loaded comply with the goods listed. However, the carrier is responsible only to check for the outward appearance of the goods—the labels comply and that the packages are not damaged. Second, the bill of lading is the evidence of the contract of transport between the shipper and the carrier. In the international sale when the bill of lading is negotiated to a third party (consignee), it may be deemed to be an evidence of the contract of transport between the carrier and the consignee. The terms in the bill of lading may be rebutted by other terms between the shipper and the carrier. However, the bill of lading becomes conclusive evidence of the terms of the contract of transport once it is negotiated to a good-faith third party. Because the third party's knowledge of the terms of the contract of transport is limited to what appears on the bill of lading. Third, bill of lading is described as the key that permits the holder to unlock the door to where the goods are held. The bill of lading evidences the ownership or title to the goods described therein. In other words, the holder of the bill of lading is the owner of the goods described therein. In an international sale of goods only when the buyer produces the bill of lading, will the ship's crew release the goods to him, where the goods are transported by sea.

Case III-5

Captain v. Far Eastern Steamship Co.

[1979] 1 Lloyd's Rep. 595

Facts

The plaintiff contacted the defendants' agents to make the shipping arrangements of the vans from Madras to Vancouver. The plaintiff was advised that the vans would be transhipped at some point in the voyage and carried on board a second vessel to Vancouver. The plaintiff and the defendants orally reached that goods were to be shipped below deck. The vans were loaded on the defendants' vessel, Pionerskaya Pravda on November 1, 1976, and the bill of lading issued on that date provided *inter alia*: "4. Period of Responsibility. The Carrier ... shall not be liable for loss of or damage to the goods during the period before loading and after discharge from the vessel howsoever such loss or damage arises. 6. ... The responsibility of the Carrier shall be limited to the part of the transport performed by him on vessels under his management and no claim will be acknowledged by the Carrier for damage or loss arising during any other part of the transport even though the freight for the whole transport has been collected by him". The plaintiff who had been in the shipping industry in India was aware that bill of lading. The defendants knew that the vans were water resistant but not waterproof. However, vans were not kept in covered storage when they were discharged in Singapore. The household effects were damaged by contact with fresh water as a result the plaintiff suffered damages. The only time they had been exposed to fresh water was on the docks in Singapore.

The plaintiff brought an action contending that the defendants were negligently in breach of their duty as a carrier forwarder, had delivered the goods severely damaged by water. The defendants argued that since, by clause 2 of the bill of lading, the contract between the parties incorporated the Hague Rules, the period that the vans were on the deck at Singapore was covered by the Hague Rules, and by Article IV Rule 5, their liability was limited to $500 per package or unit. If the Hague Rules did not apply, the defendants alleged that they were completely absolved from liability based on the bill of lading. The plaintiff denied that the clauses formed part of the contract since no effort had been made to bring them to his attention, they had never been discussed and he had not seen either the mate's receipt or the bill of lading until after the damage occurred.

Issues

1. Is the bill of lading a conclusive statement of the contract between the shipper and shipowner?

2. Do Hague Rules apply to the part of the contract under which the goods were on the deck at Singapore?

3. Can the defendants rely on exclusion of liability clauses which are the terms of the contract?

Reasoning

The plaintiff had been in the shipping industry in India and was aware of the use of bills of lading and of the existence of an Indian statute governing the carriage of goods by sea. Further he knew that a bill of lading would be issued to cover the shipment and that it would contain terms on the reverse side. No contractual document should be required when a contract is reached, though it is only an oral one. When the verbal arrangement was made, a contract came into existence, which as both parties well knew was to be covered by the usual bill of lading, including all its terms. Therefore the bill of lading including the Hague Rules were incorporated into the contract between the parties.

The operation of the Hague Rules is determined by the limits of the contract of carriage by sea and not by any limits of time. Under this reasoning, that part of the contract relating to holding the goods on the deck at Singapore awaiting loading upon the second vessel is not within the Hague Rules because it does not relate to "the carriage of goods by water".

If a party uses his superior power to impose an exemption or limitation clause on the weaker party, he will not be allowed to rely on it if he has himself been guilty of a breach going to the root of the contract. In other cases, the court will, whenever it can, construe the contract so that an exemption or limitation clause only avails the party when he is carrying out the contract in substance, and not when he is breaking it in a manner which goes to the very root of the contract. If he should happen to damage goods by some momentary piece of inadvertence, then he is able to rely on the exempting clause: because negligence by itself, without more, is not a breach which goes to the root of the contract. However, if a warehouseman were to handle the goods so roughly as to warrant the inference that he was reckless and indifferent to their safety, he would be guilty of a breach going to the root of the contract and could not rely on the exempting clause.

The oral term of the contract that the goods were to be shipped below deck equally obliged the defendant to protect them from the elements by keeping them under cover at the place of transshipment. Any reasonable person would know that the shipment exposed the goods to the risk of damage or total loss. The defendant performed the principal thing for which it contracted. Leaving the goods uncovered at Singapore constituted a fundamental breach.

Decision

Therefore Hague Rules did not apply to the part of the contract under which the goods were on the deck at Singapore. The defendant has broken the oral contract in a manner which went to its very root, and the plaintiff would have judgment for damages of $32,262.48 and costs.

Different types of bills of lading are used in international transport of goods to serve diverse purposes.

(1) Straight (non-negotiable) bills of lading and order (negotiable) bills of lading. These two types of bills of lading are also known in the trade as "white" and "yellow" for the different colors of paper on which they are often printed. Straight bills of lading are also called "air waybills", "sea waybills" and "freight receipts", depending upon the intended method of main transportation for the goods. Straight bills of lading are non-negotiable and are not documents of title. A non-negotiable or "straight" bill of lading is just a receipt for the goods, and serves as a contract with the carrier stating the terms and conditions of transport. Such a document is used by the ocean carrier only if the seller intends that the goods be delivered directly to a consignee, a specific person named in the document. The consignee may be the buyer or the buyer's bank or agent. Straight bills of lading are also used when the seller is shipping to its own agents such as its subsidiary company in the foreign country. The consignee is not required to produce the actual bill of lading in order to receive delivery.

An "order" or negotiable bill of lading serves all purposes of a bill of lading as a contract with the carrier, a receipt for the goods, and a document of title for the goods. A negotiable bill of lading is issued to a named person or "order". This allows the named person (the consignee) to endorse the bill of lading to "order" delivery of the goods to others. If possession of the bill of lading is transferred to a third party by endorsement, then the third party becomes a "holder" of the bill of lading. The original consignee may endorse the negotiable bill of lading either "in blank" by a bare signature of the endorser (e.g., "Richard Folsom") or by a "special endorsement", which specifies the name of the intended holder (e.g., "Deliver the goods to Michael George, or order, Richard Folsom"). Under a blank endorsement, any person in possession becomes a holder, and is entitled to demand delivery from the carrier. Under a special endorsement, only the named endorsee can become a holder, and only that person can demand delivery from the carrier or endorse the bill of lading to another party so as to make it a holder. Thus, the special endorsement better protects the interests of the parties from thieves and forgers than a blank endorsement.

A carrier under a negotiable bill of lading is required to obtain the original bill of lading prior to releasing the goods. If the carrier does not obtain the original bill of lading, it will be held liable to the shipper for misdelivery. The negotiable bill of lading is used in the documentary sale described below, and is required for CIF and CFR contracts, as well as the letter of credit transaction.

(2) On board bills of lading and received-for-shipment bills of lading. Shippers and carriers often refer to an "on board" bill of lading. An "on board" or "loaded" bill of lading is issued once the goods have been loaded on board the vessel. The document gives some assurance that the goods described in the bill of lading are underway to the buyer. A received-for-shipment bill of lading, on the other hand, is issued by a carrier only upon having received goods for transport. There is usually a time delay between the delivery of goods to the carrier and their being loaded on board ship. Suppose a buyer who is required to pay for a received-for-shipment bill of lading for bananas being shipped from Thailand to the United States. The buyer has no guarantee that the bananas will not be sitting on the sun-parched dock for several weeks waiting to be loaded. Thus most sales contract will require the seller tender on board bill of lading.

(3) Clean bills of lading and foul bills of lading. A "clean" bill of lading is one that has no clause or notation on the face of the bill indicating visible or possible defects in the packaging or condition of the goods. Otherwise the bill is "foul" (claused) and will detail the shortfalls or damage to goods observed. In most sales contracts the buyer will require the seller tender a clean bill of lading. A foul or claused bill of lading is normally unacceptable to third parties. However, such a clause or notation may be added on the bill only at the time the goods are loaded. Later clauses or notations will have no effect, and the bill will be treated as if it were "clean".

(4) Multimodal bills of lading. Multimodal bills of lading, also named combined transport bills of lading or through bills of lading, are used when the carrier agrees to transport and deliver the goods to their final destination using connecting carriers such as railroads, trucks, and air carriers so that the bill of lading governs all of the links of transportation.

(5) Electronic bills of lading. Technology is transforming society and shipping industry, the use of electronic bill of lading is increasing. An electronic bill of lading (eBOL or eB/L) is the legal and functional equivalent of a paper bill of lading. Compared with a paper bill of lading, an electronic bill of lading has a number of advantages, e.g. it can be sent around the world instantly, hugely lowering the administrative burden of trade. Any amendments or corrections required can be made far more efficiently and cost effectively. However, the difficulties mainly lie in how to guarantee the authenticity and confidentiality of negotiable electronic bills of lading. The use of an electronic trading system does lead to other risks such as hacking, systems collapse, e-theft and viruses.

1.1.2 International Conventions Governing Bills of Lading

Regulation of the terms of a bill of lading or the relationship between the carrier and its customers is the subject of four international conventions: the Hague Rules, the Hague–Visby Rules, the Hamburg Rules and the Rotterdam Rules. All cover contracts of transport and bills of lading, but have different approaches and are progressively more customer-oriented.

The Hague Rules (*International Convention for the Unification of Certain Rules of Law Relating to Bills of Lading*) were adopted in 1924, and established uniform basic duties of the carrier and shipper for the transport of goods covered under a bill of lading. These rules represent an international effort to achieve uniformity of bills of lading, and thus were intended to reduce the uncertainties concerning the liabilities of ocean carriers. The Hague Rules preclude contractual exculpatory clauses in bills of lading, providing the carrier is liable for its failure to use due diligence in providing a seaworthy ship before or at the beginning of the voyage, and the carrier is also responsible for properly loading, storing and carrying the goods. The Hague Rules provide considerable protection to the carrier by setting forth 17 defenses against carrier and carrier liability, and limit liability to a minimum of £100 per package or customary freight unit. A detailed discussion will be made in the part of carrier's liability and immunities. Virtually every trading nation of the world today has incorporated them into its national law.

The Hague–Visby Rules or the Visby Amendment (*Protocol to Amend the International Convention for the Unification of Certain Rules of Law Relating to Bills of Lading*) was adopted in 1968 and amended the Hague Rules; thus, they are referred to as the Hague–Visby Rules. The Hague–Visby Rules addressed certain issues that had arisen under the Hague Rules, such as the broadness of the carrier defenses and the inadequacy of the $500 per package provision in light of multimodal transportation and containerized packaging. The Hague–Visby Rules define the term "package" to include containerized cargo, increase the per package liability to 666.67 units of account or 2 units of account per kilogram, whichever is higher. The unit of account mentioned here is the special drawing right (SDR) as defined by the International Monetary Fund. But if the shipper has declared a higher value for the goods before shipment or the damage resulting from the carrier's intent or recklessness, the abovementioned per package liability limit shall not be entitled to the carrier.

The Hamburg Rules (*United Nations Convention on the Carriage of Goods by Sea*), adopted in 1978, serve as major departure from the Hague Rules and Hague–Visby Rules, because the Hamburg Rules substantially decrease carrier's defenses and increase carrier's potential liability. The Hamburg Rules eliminate many defenses from the 17 defenses provided in the previous conventions. For example, under the Hamburg Rules, the carrier is no longer immune from the loss or damage resulting from errors in navigation and management of the ship; the Hamburg Rules increase carrier's liability limit to 835 units of account per package or other shipping unit or 2.5 units per kilogram of gross weight of the goods, whichever is higher. The Hamburg Rules include liability for on deck cargo and shipments without a bill of lading for the first time (these items are specifically excluded by the prior conventions). The Hamburg Rules were drafted by the United Nations to serve the interests of cargo owners and shippers in developing countries. However, the rules are strongly opposed by developed countries, which have large carrier fleets. Therefore, the Hamburg Rules have not been as widely adopted as the Hague Rules, and a number of the adopting states are developing and/or land-locked states.

On December 11, 2008, the UN General Assembly adopted the Convention on Contracts for the International Carriage of Goods Wholly or Partly by Sea, known as **the Rotterdam Rules**. The Rotterdam Rules aim to replace the Hague Rules, the Hague–Visby Rules and the Hamburg Rules and that it will achieve uniformity of law in the field of international maritime transport. The Rotterdam Rules will extend and modernize the existing international rules relating to contract of transport of goods by sea. The Rotterdam Rules significantly increase carrier's liability limits and protection for cargo interests. For example, the Rotterdam Rules apply to door-to-door transportation, instead of the tackle-to-tackle coverage of the previous related conventions; the limit on the carrier's liability is increased to 875 SDRs "per package or other shipping unit" or 3 SDRs per kilogram of gross weight of the goods lost or damaged, whichever is the higher (unless the nature and value of the goods have been declared by the shipper and shown on the transport document); the Rotterdam Rules extend the carrier's obligation to provide a seaworthy vessel to the entire voyage and potentially render the carrier liable for the actions of so-called "maritime performing parties", including sub-carriers, stevedores and terminals. Further, under the Rotterdam Rules, carriers will no longer be able to defend a claim arising from the negligent navigation of the ship, and cargo owners may have a choice of jurisdictions in which to bring a claim. The Rotterdam Rules will enter into force one year after "the twentieth instrument of ratification, acceptance, approval or accession". However, only four countries have ratified the Rotterdam Rules to date.

To date, the international conventions regulating the bill of lading and transport of goods by sea include the Hague Rules, the Hague–Visby Rules, and the Hamburg Rules. The Rotterdam Rules are drafted to bring international uniformity to the law of transport of goods by sea, and to make the law of this area appropriate to the modern age of containerized and intermodal transportation of goods. However, before the Rotterdam Rules come into force, more countries are needed to finish their signature and ratification.

Some countries have chosen one set of rules to apply as their national law. Although China is not a contracting state to any of the above Conventions, the *Maritime Law of the People's Republic of China*, which took effect as of July 1, 1993, does incorporate some rules (e.g. rules on carrier liability and immunities) of the Hague Rules and draw on the other Conventions.

English law is based on the Hague–Visby Rules. The United States has notonly enacted the Hague Rules into its domestic law as the *Carriage of Goods by Sea Act* (COGSA) in 1936, but also has non-conforming pre-COGSA legislation (the Harter Act) in force. The Harter Act governs liability for cargo between the vessel owner or carrier and the shipper in the domestic trade. COGSA, derived from the Hague Rules, applies to every bill of lading or document of title that evidences a contract for the transport of goods by sea to or from a U.S. port, but does not automatically apply to solely domestic bills of lading. COGSA—this Act governs the liability of a carrier from the time goods are loaded onto the ship until the time the cargo is unloaded. COGSA does not apply to losses that occur prior to loading or after discharge from the vessel, during which the Harter Act applies. Thus it is commonly said that COGSA applies from "tackle to tackle". However, COGSA does permit the shipper and the carrier to extend the application of it beyond such period of "tackle to tackle". In international transport of goods by sea, virtually all bills of lading issued in the United States provide that they are controlled by COGSA. But Article 7 of the *Uniform Commercial Code* (UCC) governs the intrastate transfer of the bill of lading. This multiplicity of statutes governing the terms of bills of lading and their use, conflicting concepts and rules can often be expected.

1.1.3 Carriers Duties and Immunities under a Bill of Lading

The law governing the ocean carrier's liability for damage or loss to cargo is rooted in the history of transportation and trade. As goods moved across the seas, they were under the exclusive control of the ship's captain for months at a time. Shippers had no way of proving that goods were lost or destroyed as a result of a natural disaster, the negligence of the carrier, or from the crew's pilferage or theft. As a result, the early maritime law of England held carriers to be liable for all loss or damage to cargo in their possession. At the international level, the Hague Rules provide the carrier's liabilities under a bill of lading.

Article 3 of the Hague Rules provides the carrier's duties or liabilities under a bill of lading. It requires a carrier to exercise due diligence before or at the beginning of the voyage in:

(1) Making the ship seaworthy.

(2) Properly manning, equipping, and supplying the ship.

(3) Making the holds, refrigerating, and cool chambers, and other parts of the ship in which goods are carried, fit and safe for their reception, transport, and preservation.

(4) Properly and carefully loading, handling, stowing, carrying, keeping, caring for, and discharging the goods carried.

The carrier is liable for damage to cargo resulting from its failure to use due diligence before or at the beginning of the voyage to make the ship seaworthy. This duty has been called assurance of seaworthiness. A vessel is seaworthy if it is reasonably fit to carry the cargo it has undertaken to carry on the intended voyage. The standard of seaworthiness includes a number of factors: the type of ship, the condition and suitability of the ship's equipment, the competence of its crew, the type of cargo being carried and the manner in which it is stowed, the weather (i.e. Was the ship prepared for the types of weather expected?), and the nature of the voyage. The carrier must also properly load, store, and carry the goods. For example, the ship's holds must not be in such a condition that causes moisture damage to the goods through condensation. Cargo should not be stowed in a manner that causes it to shift and be crushed. Cargo shall not be exposed to rain and seas, etc.

The above provisions under the Hague Rules have been widely incorporated into national law. For example, much similar provisions can be found in Articles 46–48 of the *Maritime Law of the People's Republic of China* and COSGA in the United States.

Most courts strictly enforce this obligation. For example, in *Riverstone Meat Co. Pty., Ltd. v. Lancashire Shipping Co. Ltd.*, goods were damaged by water due to the negligent work of a shipfitter employed by a ship repair company. The court held that the carrier had failed to use due diligence in making the ship seaworthy.

Case III-6

Riverstone Meat Co. Pty., Ltd. v. Lancashire Shipping Co. Ltd.

[1961] 1 Lloyd's Rep. 57 (H.L.)

Facts

On May 7, 1953, 150 cases of canned ox tongue, the property of Riverstone

Meat Co. Pty. Limited, were shipped in good order and condition on board the MUNCASTER CASTLE at Sydney under a bill of lading of that date for transport to London. It was provided by the bill of lading that it should have effect subject to the Hague Rules. The MUNCASTER CASTLE experienced heavy weather during a voyage from Australia to London. On July 16, 1953, four days after the beginning of the discharge in London, sea water was discovered in the No. 5 lower hold in which 113 cases of the goods were found to be damaged thereby. Through inspection, the reason was found to be leakage covers over storm valves. These covers had been replaced before the vessel's prior voyage from the U.K. to Australia, but the court found that the securing nuts had been improperly fitted. The replacement of the covers and fitting of the nuts was carried out by a fitter employed by a firm of ship-repairers who were instructed by the superintendent of owners' managers.

Issue

Were the shipowners liable to cargo losses for fitter's (ship-repairers' employee) negligence? Put another way, had shipowners proved that they had exercised the due diligence to make the ship seaworthy required by the Hague Rules? What is the amount of damages to which an injured party is entitled for breach of contract?

Decision

The case was finally appealed to the House of Lords. The House of Lords decided that the exercise of due diligence required from a shipowner under Article 3 of the Hague Rules covered not only the shipowners, their employees and servants, but also their sub-contractors and agents, whether independent or not. Therefore, the House of Lords decided that the ship-repairers and their negligent employee fell into the second category. On this basis, the shipowners were held liable.

However, on the other hand, a carrier is exempt, under the Hague Rules, from liability for damages that arise from a variety of perils:

(1) errors in the navigation or in the management of the ship;

(2) fire, unless caused by the actual fault of the carrier;

(3) perils, dangers, and accidents of the sea or other navigable water;

(4) act of god (a natural disaster);

(5) act of war;

(6) act of public enemies;

(7) legal seizures of the ship;

(8) quarantine restrictions;

(9) an act or omission of the shipper or owner of the goods;

(10) labor strikes or lockouts;

(11) riots and civil commotions;

(12) saving or attempting to save life or property at sea;

(13) an inherent defect, quality, or vice of the goods that causes wastage in bulk or weight or other damage or loss;

(14) insufficiency of packing;

(15) inadequate marking of goods or containers;

(16) latent defects in ship or equipment (which might render the ship seaworthy) that were not discoverable by due diligence; and

(17) any other cause arising without the actual fault of the carrier and without the fault or negligence of the agents or servants of the carrier, but the burden of proof shall be on the person claiming the benefit of this exception.

These immunities are narrowly construed. If cargo is damaged and the damage falls within one of the immunities, the carrier will nonetheless be responsible if the underlying cause was the result of the carrier's failure to exercise due diligence in carrying out its fundamental duties provided in Article 3 of the Hague Rules. For example, among the above listed situations in which a carrier is not liable for damage or cargo, one of the most important is that the carrier is not liable for errors in navigation or mismanagement of the ship caused by the master, mariner, pilot, or the crew of the carrier. That is, even the error in navigation or mismanagement of the ship is caused by the actual fault of the carrier or carrier's crew, the carrier will not be liable for any loss of or damage to the goods arising from such an error. This immunity shows great partiality to the carrier, thus often criticized by shippers or cargo owners. Thus in practice some courts have held carriers liable for their crew's negligence by reasoning that a crew errs in navigating or managing a ship is not competent, and a ship is not seaworthy without a competent crew. As a result, carriers can be held liable despite the protection they receive from the defense. The (17) clause of the immunities serves as a catch-all clause covering any other cause arising without the actual fault of the carrier or its agents and crew. However, the carrier must prove that neither the actual fault of the carrier itself nor the actual fault or neglect of its agents and crew contributed to the loss or damage to the cargo.

1.1.4 Other Questions

Time Limitations. Claims for loss or damages have to be lodged within a year after the goods were or should have been delivered. The claim may be initiated by filing suit or by commencing arbitration proceedings.

Third Party Rights (Himalaya Clauses). The Hague Rules apply only to the carrier and the party shipping goods under a bill of lading. Third parties, including officers, crew members, agents, and stevedores, who help in the transport of the goods, but who are not the parties to the transport-of-goods contract contained in the bill of lading, normally have no contractual right to claim the liability limits established by the Hague Rules. To extend the liability limits of the conventions to these individuals, many carriers add a clause to their bills of lading known as a "Himalaya Clause". This clause purports to extend to third parties the carrier's immunities established by the Hague Rules. These clauses are valid in some courts (e.g., the United States), but unenforceable in others (e.g., the United Kingdom).

1.2 Charterparties

Shippers who need to hire entire ships to carry their goods are not subject to the above rules governing common transport. They are, rather, "charterparties". A "charterparty" (CP) is a contract for the hire of an entire ship for a particular voyage or a set of period of time. Oil, sugar, ores, coal and other bulk commodities are almost always shipped under such contracts. The ship can be hired in two forms: non-demise CPs, whereby the shipowner provides the vessel and crew, and demise CPs whereby the shipowner furnishes the vessel only.

The Hague Rules, the Hague–Visby Rules and the Hamburg Rules do not apply to charterparties, unless a bill of lading issued by the shipowner comes into the hands of a third party. The shipper (or charterer) and the shipowner are free to set the terms governing the transport of goods in their contract. And commonly they use standardized contracts drafted by various conferences and nongovernmental organizations. These standard contracts include Uniform General Charter (Gencon) drafted by the Baltic and International Maritime Conference (BIMCO) and Chamber of Shipping Australian Grain Charter (Austral).

◆ **Voyage Charterparties**

A voyage charterparty involves the employment of a ship and its crew for the transport of goods from one place to another. Under this contract, the owner provides the ship at a named port at a specified time to carry the goods to an agreed destination. The charterer provides a full cargo and arranges for its loading at an agreed upon time. If the charterer provides less than a full load, the shipowner will charge "dead freight" for the amount of the deficiency. If the shipowner fails to arrive at the named port for loading at the specified time, the charterer will commonly be able to terminate the contract by citing a cancellation clause in the contract. If the charterer keeps the ship lying idle too long for loading or unloading, the shipowner will charge "demurrage". The obligation to pay the demurrage will be secured by a lien on the cargo, which any holder of the corresponding bill of lading will have to pay off before taking delivery.

◆ **Time Charterparties**

A time charterparty involves the employment of a vessel for a stated period of time. Questions of dead freight and demurrage do not arise because the charterer must pay for the use of the ship whether or not it is carrying a cargo. The charterer has the right to direct the ship to proceed to wherever it is needed. Usually, the only limitation on this right is the charterer's promise to engage only in lawful trades, to carry only lawful goods, and to only direct the ship to safe ports. If the shipowner attempts to interfere with the charterer's use of the ship, he will commit a breach of the charterparty.

◆ **Charterparties and Bills of Lading**

The shipowner will commonly issue the charterer a bill of lading when goods are loaded on board, whereas between the two parties the bill will only be a receipt for goods and a document of title. However, where the bill is transferred by the charterer to a third party by endorsement, the Hague Rules will apply and the contract between the shipowner and the third party will be governed by the bill of lading.

2 Transport of Goods by Air

The liability of air carriers for loss of or damage to cargo and baggage as well as the bodily injury or death of passengers is governed by a host of international conventions and national laws. The governing international conventions are collectively called "Warsaw Regime". This regime consists of the Warsaw Convention 1929, its subsequent Protocols and the Montreal Convention 1999, which enters into force since 2003. The focus of the Warsaw Convention 1929 was on the protection of air carriers, while the newer Montreal Convention 1999 generally modernized the law, including issuing tickets and air waybills electronically, and eliminated many of the criticisms of the older treaty. However, the Warsaw Convention 1929 will continue to be effective until more nations ratify the new treaty.

2.1 The Warsaw Convention 1929

The Warsaw Convention 1929 sets uniform rules governing the transport of international cargo, baggage as well as passengers. It governs the form of air waybills, passenger tickets, and baggage claim receipts, defining the liability of airlines for injuries to passengers and damage or loss of their baggage or cargo. It also provides a uniform limitation on the liability of an air carrier to both shippers and passengers. It sets the limitation on air carriers' liability for a passenger at 125,000 francs (gold value), and 250 francs (gold value) per kilo of cargo/baggage. In recent years, many people came to believe that these limits were inequitable and unfair. The limitation will apply where the shipper has not declared a higher value for the goods on the air waybill. And such a limitation does not apply if the shipper has declared the goods to be of higher value on the air waybill and paid an additional fee.

The application of the liability limits is illustrated in the following case:

Williams Dental Company (Plaintiff) shipped 50 ounces of dental gold and equipment to Sweden Aboard Air Express International (Defendant), an air carrier. The Plaintiff's employee checked, packaged and sealed the gold in a pail. When the shipment was delivered to the buyer in Sweden, it was found that the seals on the pail were broken and the gold was missing. On the air waybill the Plaintiff declared a special value for the entire shipment of $23,474, and declared separately a value of $21,680 for the gold. Plaintiff sued to recover the $23,474, while Defendant claimed that its liability would be limited to $1,262 under the Warsaw Convention. In this case the court finally decided that since the shipper (Plaintiff) has declared a higher value for the missing gold, the liability limits provided in the Warsaw Convention would not apply and the Plaintiff was entitled to get the recovery of $21,680, neither the amount of $1,262 nor $23,474.

2.2 The Montreal Convention 1999

The most important change to air transportation law in recent decades occurred with the adoption of the *Montreal Convention for the Unification of Certain Rules for International Carriage by Air* (1999), referred to as the Montreal Convention 1999. It now replaces the outdated Warsaw Convention in those countries where ratified it (the Warsaw Convention remains in effect in others). Now the Montreal Convention had been ratified by more than one hundred countries and regions, including Canada, China, Mexico, Japan, the

European Union, the United States and others. The Montreal Convention 1999 modernizes the provisions on issuing tickets, baggage claims, and air waybills and provides for the use of electronic documents. It also eases the restrictions on recovering damages from airlines for loss to baggage or cargo, or for bodily injuries or death to passengers. It also includes provisions for compensating passengers for flight delays. Like the Warsaw Convention, the Montreal Convention 1999 applies only to passengers ticketed for international travel. Specifically, Article 1 states that the Convention applies "to all international transport of persons, baggage and cargo by aircraft." The Montreal Convention 1999 does not apply to a passenger who is ticketed for domestic travel solely within one country or between two countries not party to the Convention.

The Montreal Convention 1999 sets up a two-tiered liability system for death or bodily injuries of passengers: the carrier is strictly liable for 113,100 SDRs, and the carrier is liable for the proven damages above 113,100 SDRs unless it can show (1) either the damages were not due to its negligence or the negligence of its agents; (2) the damages was solely due to the negligence or wrongful acts of third parties. It means that the carrier is strictly liable for all damage from death or bodily injury not exceeding 113,100 SDRs per passenger. Strict liability means that the carrier is liable without regard to fault. In addition, the carrier is presumed to be liable for all proven damages above 113,100 SDRs, with no limit on the amount, unless it can show that the damage were not due to its or its employees' negligence. Therefore, the "fault" of the carrier is only a factor for damages above the 113,100 SDR level.

Under the Montreal Convention 1999, the air carrier is liable for the damage or loss of the cargo upon condition that the event, which caused such damage or loss took place during the transport by air. An air carrier is liable for losses of cargo under its control, but not exceeding 19 SDRs per kilogram, unless the shipper has declared a higher value on the air waybill and paid an additional fee if required. However, the carrier is not liable if it proves that the damage to or loss of the cargo resulted from one or more of the following:

(1) Inherent defect, quality or vice of that cargo;

(2) Defective packing of that cargo performed by a person other than the carrier or its servants or agents;

(3) An act of war or an armed conflict; and

(4) An act of public authority carried out in connection with the entry, exit or transit of the cargo.

The liability of the air carrier in the case of loss or delay to baggage on board an aircraft or under its control is limited to 1,131 SDRs for each passenger, unless the passenger has declared a higher value and paid any additional fees required (but in no case greater than the actual value of the baggage).

Travelers will appreciate the new provisions of the Montreal Convention 1999, which make airlines liable for delays in transporting passengers, baggage, or cargo. However, the carrier is not liable if it proves that it and its servants and agents took reasonable measures to avoid the damage or that it was impossible for it or them to take such measures. Liability for delays is limited to 4,694 SDRs per passenger.

On February 28, 2005, the Standing Committee of the Tenth National People's Congress of PRC ratified the Montreal Convention 1999 and this Convention has been binding on China as of July 1, 2005. However, this Convention only applies to international transport of cargo, luggage and passenger by air. For the domestic transport, the Civil Aviation Law and relevant regulations will apply. *Regulations on Liability Limits of Air Carriers in Domestic Carriage by Air* was issued by the General Administration of Civil Aviation of PRC on March 28, 2006. These Regulations increase the air carrier's liability limits from RMB 70,000 yuan to RMB 400,000 yuan for the death and bodily injury of passengers. For the damage or loss of the luggage or the cargo, the limits are RMB 100 yuan per kilo.

Up to now countries including Canada, China, Japan, Mexico, New Zealand, and the United States have ratified the Montreal Convention 1999 and more countries are expected to be contracting states to this Convention. For those countries not ratified this Convention, but contracting states to the Warsaw Convention 1929, they will still be bound by the latter Convention in regulating international transport of goods, luggage and passengers.

3 Transport of Goods by Rail and Road

3.1 Transport of Goods by Rail

Rail transportation is one of the oldest forms of modern transport. Even today, it is used by hundreds of millions of people around the world. Transport of goods by rail is suitable for bulky goods sent over long distances. The cost-effectiveness of the method increases when the journey is longer, especially in Continental Europe where there are many high-speed services. A problem with transport of goods by rail is the need for transshipment, although this can sometimes be avoided for consignments large enough to use "swap body" containers, i.e. self-contained trailers on their own wheels that can be exchanged between vehicle cabs, as opposed to "flat" trailers on to which containers have to be loaded. The entire swap body can be uncoupled from a cab, rolled on to a train for long haul rail transport, and rolled off and attached to another cab at its final destination.

The China-Europe Railway Express is a landmark project of the China-proposed Belt and Road Initiative. In recent years, the railway has achieved great accomplishments in terms of its rail freight volumes. For example, as of early November, 2020, there have been more than 10,000 trains. Compared with the mode of transportation by sea and by air, the China-Europe Railway Express is to become a more competitive and cost-effective transport mode. The international transport of goods by rail may play a more important role in China.

For the faciliation and regulation of international transport by rail, there are nine agreements concluded within the framework of OSJD①:

- *Agreement on the International Passenger Transport by Rail* (SMPS);
- *Agreement on the International Goods Transport by Rail* (SMGS);
- *Agreement on the International Passenger Tariff* (MPT);
- *Agreement on the International Railway Transit Tariff* (MTT);
- *Agreement on the Uniform Transit Tariff* (ETT);
- *Agreement on Rules for the Use of Coaches in International Traffic* (PPW);
- *Agreement on Rules for the Use of Wagons in International Traffic* (PGW);
- *Agreement on the Accounting Rules in International Transport of Passengers and Goods by Rail*; and
- *Agreement on Organizational and Operational Aspects of Combined Transportation between Europe and Asia.*

The major OSJD agreements are the *Agreement on the International Goods Transport by Rail* (SMGS) and the *Agreement on the International Passenger Transport by Rail* (SMPS).

① The OSJD (Organization for Cooperation between Railways) is an international organization established at the Railway Transport Ministers Conference on June 28, 1956 in Sofia (the Republic of Bulgaria). The key objective of OSJD is the development of international cargo and passenger transportation, the creation of a common railway transport area in the Euro-Asian Region, increasing competitiveness of transcontinental railway routes and contributing to technological progress, scientific and technical cooperation in the field of railway transport.

The *Agreement on the International Passenger Transport by Rail* (SMPS) entered into force on November 1, 1951, and undergoes revision from time to time. Major contracting parties to SMPS are Azerbaijan, China, Democratic People's Republic of Korea, Georgia, Kazakhstan, Kyrgyzstan, Mongolia, Russian Federation, Tajikistan, Turkmenistan, Uzbekistan and Vietnam. The SMPS Agreement consists of 9 chapters and 45 articles. There are also two technical appendices. Besides, there is an accompanying document entitled SMPS Manual that contains comments and explanatory notes for the application of the Agreement.

Chapter I "Basic Provisions" defines the overall subject of the Agreement to establish the rules of international transport of passengers, baggage and cargo baggage. The chapter covers the scope of application of the Agreement, main terms used in the text and overall responsibilities involved into the process of international transport of passengers by rail.

Chapter II "Transport of Passengers" describes the main transport document for passenger transport (ticket) and its additional elements; conditions of ticket validity, categories of seats in trains and rules of changing the seat category. It also covers the provisions related to travel of children, ticket inspections, transport of baggage and pets, defines items forbidden for transport as hand baggage, amendment of the passenger itinerary, and sequences of train delay and cancellation.

Chapter III "Transport of Baggage" establishes baggage allowance for passengers, defines items allowed and not allowed to be carried as baggage, sets up the rules for acceptance and release of baggage by the carrier, packaging and marking, declaration of baggage value, and terms of delivery.

Chapter IV "Transport of Cargo Baggage" contains rules for cargo baggage of very close nature to those applied for baggage and set out in Chapter III thereof: items allowed and not allowed to be carried as cargo baggage, rules for acceptance and release of cargo baggage by the carrier, packaging and marking, declaration of value of cargo baggage, terms of delivery, and obstacles for transport and release of cargo baggage.

Chapter V "Transport Charges" defines the rules on using tariffs for calculation of transport charges and sets the procedures for payment and refund of transport charges.

Chapter VI "Carrier Liability" covers the issues of joint liability of railways, liability for harm to passenger's health or life, as well as carrier's liability in cases of delay in delivery, full or partial loss or damage to baggage/cargo baggage.

Chapter VII "Liabilities of Passenger, Sender and Recipient of Baggage or Cargo Baggage" defines the scope of liability of the captioned actors.

Chapter VIII "Claims" sets up the procedures for claims submission and limitation period.

Chapter IX "General Provisions" refers to the obligation to comply with customs rules and regulations and applicable national legislation in the course of international passenger transport. It also covers the status of the SMPS Manual, procedures for publishing amendment of the Agreement and Manual, and on administering the implementation of the Agreement by OSJD bodies.

Appendix 1 is entitled "Items under the Monopoly of Postal Authorities", and Appendix 2 is the "List of the Railway Undertakings for Claim Submission and Handling".

The *Agreement on the International Goods Transport by Rail* (SMGS) entered into force on November 1, 1951, and undergoes revision from time to time. The major contracting parties to SMGS are Azerbaijan, China, Democratic People's Republic of Korea, Georgia, Islamic Republic of Iran, Kazakhstan, Kyrgyzstan, Mongolia, Russian Federation, Tajikistan, Turkmenistan, Uzbekistan and Vietnam. The SMGS Agreement structurally consists of the main agreement and 22 appendices. Besides, there is an accompanying document entitled SMGS Manual that contains comments and explanatory notes for the application of the Agreement. The main agreement consists of 8 chapters and 41 articles.

Chapter I "Basic Provisions" defines the main subject of the Agreement to establish direct international freight rail traffic between the railways of the contracting parties. The chapter also covers the scope of application of the Agreement and provisions related to duties of railways to carry goods, items not allowed for transport or allowed for transport on special conditions and special conditions for certain types of transport.

Chapter II "Conclusion of the Contract of Transport" covers the issuing of the consignment note, acceptance of goods for transport, calculation of goods' weight and quantity, declared value of goods, responsibility for the validity of the data in the consignment note; tariffs and calculation of transport charges and fines; rules for the terms of goods delivery.

Chapter III "Performance of the Contract of Transport" covers the matters of payment of transport charges, release of goods to the consignee, issuing of commercial acts and carrier's right of retention.

Chapter IV "Amendment of the Contract of Transport" includes provisions on the procedure for amending the contract of rail transport and special provision for the cases of when obstacles to release of goods to the consignee occur.

Chapter V “Liability of Railways” establishes provisions on joint liability of railway carriers, overall principles related to limitation of carrier’s liability, rules of limitation of liability in cases of shortage of goods, limitations of compensation by carriers in cases of full or partial loss, damage, and delayed delivery of goods. It also describes the rules of payment of compensation and accruing interest on the amount of compensation payable.

Chapter VI “Claims and Actions” covers the procedures for submitting claims and actions, sets the limitation periods and the rules of defining jurisdiction for legal proceedings.

Chapter VII “Payments” contains the rules of payment settlement, including the cases of reimbursement of compensation paid by the railway carriers.

Chapter VIII “General Provisions” covers the issues of currency for the calculation of amounts of payments, status of the SMGS Manual, procedures for amendment of the Agreement and Manual, and on administering the implementation of the Agreement by OSJD bodies.

The appendices to the SMGS Agreement, which are referred to in the relevant articles of the main body of the Agreement, cover various specific aspects of international rail transport of goods: Appendix 1 “Items under the Monopoly of Postal Authorities”; Appendix 2 “Rules of Transport of Dangerous Goods”; Appendix 3 “Rules of Transport of Goods Accompanied by the Representatives of Consignor or Consignee”; Appendix 4 “Rules of Transport of Perishable Goods”; Appendix 5 “Loading Dimensions”; Appendix 6 “Stickers and Marks on Consignments, Wagons, Containers and Consignment Notes”; Appendix 7 “Rules of Transport of Road Vehicles and Tractors”; Appendix 8 “Rules of Transport of Containers”; Appendix 9 (reserved); Appendix 10 “Rules of Transport of Private and Rented Wagons”; Appendix 11 “Rules of Transport of Goods in Transport Packets”; Appendices 12 and 13 (contain a number of templates and operating instructions for SMGS consignment note, railway memorandum bills and other transport documents accompanying goods); Appendix 14 “Rules of Stowage and Fastening of Goods in Wagons and Containers”; Appendices 15–18 (contain templates of documents related to international rail transport); Appendix 19 (indicates official names and contacts of the railway undertakings for claim submission and handling); Appendix 20 (provides a template of claim for delayed delivery); Appendix 21 “Rules of Transport of Combinations of Road Vehicles, Road Vehicles, Trailers, Semi-trailers and of Demountable Road Vehicle Bodies”; and Appendix 22 “Handbook on CIM/SMGS Common Consignment Note”.

Since entering into force in 1951, both SMGS and SMPS Agreements have undergone multiple regular revisions. The amendments to the Agreements are being proposed, discussed and agreed by the OSJD Commission on Transport Law. The current round of SMGS revision commenced in 2005 and included, among other important updates of the SMGS Agreement, many of which were aimed at harmonization of some of its provisions with the relevant provisions of COTIF. The current efforts in the revision of SMPS Agreement also pursue the target to make it more compatible to COTIF.

The first international convention concerning the transport of goods by rail dates from the year 1890. It created an administrative union as per the prevailing rules of international law with a permanent secretariat, the Central Office for International Carriage by Railway, headquartered in Berne, Switzerland. On May 1, 1985, the ***Convention concerning International Carriage by Rail*** of May 9, 1980 (COTIF) entered into force and this led to formation of the Intergovernmental Organisation for International Carriage by Rail (OTIF). After significant modifications to COTIF that were brought about by the Vilnius Protocol of June 3, 1999 (Protocol 1999), the amended convention entered into force on July 1, 2006. The objectives of the convention are to promote, improve and facilitate international traffic by railway. The COTIF 1999 consists of:

- Base convention that has seven subheadings containing 45 articles that cover scope, structure and functioning, finances, arbitration, modification procedure and final provisions;
- Protocol on the privileges and immunities of the Intergovernmental Organisation for International Carriage by Rail (OTIF) having 14 articles;
- Protocol of June 3, 1999 for the modification of the *Convention concerning International Carriage by Rail* (COTIF) of May 9, 1980 (Protocol 1999) having seven articles; and
- Appendices including their annexes.

Uniform rules for international carriage by rail are contained in the seven Appendices to COTIF. They are briefly discussed below. Appendix A Uniform Rules Concerning the Contract of International Carriage of Passengers by Rail (CIV). Some important provisions are applicable to contracts for transport of rail passengers where the place of departure and place of destination are situated in two different member states; applicable to whole of the infrastructure unless reservation at the time of accession; applicable to consensual contract (no obligation); applicable to international transport being subject to single contract that includes transport by road or inland waterway. Appendix B Uniform Rules

Concerning the Contract of International Carriage of Goods by Rail (CIM). Some Carriage provisions are applicable to whole of the rail infrastructure unless reservations to scope are made at accession; are applicalble to transport by road or inland waterway in internal traffic of a member state as a supplement to transfrontier transport by rail; applicable to consensual contract (no obligation to carry) and Consignment Note (*prima facie* evidence of Carriage). Appendix C Regulation Concerning the International Carriage of Dangerous Goods by Rail (RID). The regulations apply to international transport of dangerous goods by rail on territory of RID contracting member states; transport complementary to transport by rail to which CIM Uniform Rules are applicable; activities referred to by the Annex to this Regulation. Appendix D Uniform Rules Concerning Contracts of Use of Vehicles in International Rail Traffic (CUV). These uniform rules apply to bilateral or multilateral contracts concerning the use of railway vehicles as means of transport for transport in accordance with CIV and CIM uniform rules; questions on liability in case of loss of or damage to a vehicle, limitation of actions, and forums for settlement of disputes. Appendix E Uniform Rules Concerning the Contract of Use of Infrastructure in International Rail Traffic (CUI). These rules apply to any contract of use of railway infrastructure for international transport as per CIV and CIM uniform rules; liability of infrastructure manager for bodily loss or damage, loss of or damage to property and pecuniary loss to the carrier during the use of infrastructure; period of limitation (three years from the day of loss or damage to the infrastructure). Appendix F Uniform Rules Concerning the Validation of Technical Standards and the Adoption of Uniform Technical Prescriptions Applicable to Railway Material Intended to be Used in International Traffic (APTU) lays down the procedure for validation of technical standards and the adoption of uniform technical prescriptions for railway material intended to be used in international traffic. Appendix G Uniform Rules Concerning the Technical Admission of Railway Material Used in International Traffic (ATMF) lays down the procedure for the admission of railway vehicles and other railway material for admission to circulation or use in international traffic.

3.2 Transport of Goods by Road

Transport of goods by road offers door-to-door collection and delivery of goods. There is no need for transshipment, thus reducing handling costs and pilferage losses. In international sales, transport of goods by road is often an integral part of transportation by sea or by air. Problems with road transport are its vulnerability to bad weather, limited load sizes, and the fact that lorries often return empty.

The *Convention on the Contract for the International Carriage of Goods by Road* (CMR) is a United Nations convention that was signed in Geneva on May 19, 1956. The CMR standardizes the terms of the contract of transport, the liability of the carrier and the form of documentation to be used concerning transportation of cargo by road. It has been ratified by the majority of European states. As of 2021, it has been ratified by 44 states.① The CMR consignment note, also called the CMR transport letter, regulates the transport of goods of any kind, by trucks. Liability for damage caused during transport is also regulated by the CMR consignment letter. CMR is intended exclusively for the transport of goods by road, container and modular superstructures are not considered vehicles. The CMR consignment letter is used when loading and unloading are in different countries. At least one of these countries must be a CMR member. This is true regardless of the seat or the citizenship of the parties.② The CMR consignment note draws up three original copies, one of which (proof of receipt) is for the consignor, the second one (proof of delivery) is for the carrier and the third one is for the consignee.

According to Article 5 and Article 6 of the CMR, the CMR consignment note must contain the following data: (1) the place and date of its drawing up; (2) the name and address of the consignor; (3) the name and address of the carrier; (4) the place and date of receipt of the goods and the place where they are to be delivered; (5) the name and address of the consignee; (6) the nature of the goods and the type of packaging; (7) the number of packages, special markings and their numbers; (8) the gross weight or the quantity of the goods; (9) the expenses related to the transport (transport price, additional expenses, customs duties and other expenses incurred from the conclusion of the contract until the release); (10) the necessary instructions for customs formalities and others; (11) the

---

① The current contracting countries are Albania, Armenia, Austria, Azerbaijan, Belarus, Belgium, Bosnia and Herzegovina, Bulgaria, Croatia, Cyprus, Czech Republic, Denmark, Estonia, Finland, France, Georgia, Germany, Greece, Hungary, Islamic Republic of Iran, Ireland, Italy, Kazakhstan, Kyrgyzstan, Latvia, Lebanon, Lithuania, Luxembourg, Malta, Mongolia, Montenegro, Morocco, Netherlands, Norway, Poland, Portugal, Moldova, Romania, Russian Federation, Serbia, Slovakia, Slovenia, Spain, Sweden, Switzerland, Tajikistan, The Former Yugoslav Republic of Macedonia, Tunisia, Turkey, Turkmenistan, Ukraine, United Kingdom and Uzbekistan.

② Article 1 of the CMR states: "This Convention shall apply to every contract for the transport of goods by road in vehicles for reward, when the place of taking over of the goods and the place designated for delivery, as specified in the contract, are situated in two different countries, of which at least one is a contracting country, irrespective of the place of residence and the nationality of the parties."

indication that the transport is subject to the arrangements established by this Convention and any other contrary provision.

If applicable, the consignment note must also contain the following: (1) prohibiting transshipment; (2) expenses that the sender takes over; (3) the total amount of money to be paid for the release of the goods; (4) the declared value of the merchandise and the amount representing the special interest in the issue; (5) the sender's instructions to the carrier regarding the insurance of the goods; (6) the agreed time frame in which the shipment is to be carried out; (7) the list of documents delivered to the carrier. If a situation is not sufficiently regulated by the CMR, it is applicable in addition to national legislation. Annexes A and B contain the technical requirements for road transport, i.e. the conditions under which dangerous goods, when authorized for transport, may be carried internationally, as well as uniform provisions concerning the construction and operation of vehicles carrying dangerous goods.

4 Multimodal Transport of Goods

When the transport of goods is accomplished by using more than one mode of transport, it is multimodal transport of goods, in which the goods are transported between various transshipment points by sea, air, rail, road or inland waterway. Nowadays, there is a growing tendency, where most of the shipments are carried under multimodal transport contract, with the involvement of at least two different modes of transport. Within the multimodal transport system, the use of containers, roll-on/roll-off vehicles, and barges has reduced risk and saved money and time, with the support of information technology and innovative transport management. On the other hand, the multimodal transport system has brought some legal chaos. It was a new urgency to answer to the questions like who to sue (actual carrier or freight forwarder or contracting carrier) if the delivery is delayed or goods are lost or damaged, where to sue, time limit for initiating action, the basis of the liability and so on. For example, in multimodal transport of goods, the multimodal transport operator (MTO) is a person who concludes a multimodal transport contract and assumes responsibility for the performance of the contract as a carrier. The combined transport document or the multimodal bill of lading is a single contract between the shipper and the operator who in turn contracts with each of carriers involved. Thus the multimodal transport operator becomes responsible for the transport of goods throughout the time of their shipment. However, in through transport contract, the carrier shall contract as the shipper's agent only and liable for any loss or damage between the port of loading and the port of discharge, but not for other parts of the transport, even though the freight for the whole transport was collected by him.

For the absence of any uniform convention, currently, provisions of some unimodal conventions are dealing with multimodal transport, for example Article 31 of Warsaw Convention for air transport, for rail COTIF-CIM 1999 and Article 2 of CMR Convention. However, *Geneva Convention on International Multimodal Transport of Goods* (MT Convention) 1980 was drawn up by UN to introduce a set of uniform rules. This MT Convention introduced a modified uniform liability system. It provides two limitations for unlocalized damages. Firstly, if multimodal transport involves transport by sea or by inland waterway, MTO will be liable for 920 SDRs per package or other shipping unit, or 2.75 SDRs per kg, whichever is the higher. This figure is about 10% higher than Hamburg Rules and about 20% higher than Hague–Visby Rules. Secondly, if multimodal transport does not involve transport by sea or by inland waterway, the limitation amount is raised to a higher level of 8.33 SDR per kg (same as CMR amount). However, the limits of liability will be determined by reference to any applicable international convention or mandatory national law which provides a higher limit of liability than that of the 1980's MT Convention for localized loss. Articles 18 and 19 of MT Convention clearly apply a network-like system by derogating the principle of a unitary system. Moreover, as an improvement in this area, MTO will be liable for delay regardless of the stage of occurrence delay, therefore, there is no need of proving for the claimant the leg where the delay occurred. This MT Convention system did not solve all the significant problems. For example, mode of transport has not been defined, hence, it is not clear whether it is restricted to the vehicle (e.g. ship, plane), the medium (e.g. sea, air) or, both. Nonetheless, to some extent, this MT Convention system makes the area of multimodal transport complex. As the Convention is seen overly consignor-friendly, it has not attracted the required number of signatures to come into force and parties of combined transport need to come up with the solution of their problems.

Though multimodal transport of goods is very sophisticated, the legal infrastructure governing it is not that much. To any multimodal transport contract, different transport conventions are possibly applicable which create further confusion in using the appropriate convention in resolving legal disputes between contracting parties, resulting in waste of a huge amount of money. Till now, no general acceptance has obtained through mandatory convention or private voluntary rules, or by any uniform or network proposals. Nonetheless, the best solution is to abolish individual conventions by introducing a uniform one, which can be applied for all multimodal transport contracts. This may take a long time to introduce such one, but in the long run, costs and many current problems can be solved.

5 Marine Cargo Insurance

As for the transportation of goods, the insuring of goods is also an essential element of international business. The risks of damage or loss of goods possibly occur at every time of the transportation, particularly during ocean shipments, which are lengthier and more dangerous. Sometimes the damage or loss of the goods arising from these risks is tremendous that may weep out all the profits from the business. In the previous chapter we have discussed the allocation of risks between the seller and the buyer in international sales. If damage or loss does occur, the party (perhaps the holder of the bill of lading) bearing the risk will surely seek to shift its financial burden to an insurer. Sellers, buyers, and even banks that finance international sales may also want to be certain that their interests in the goods can be fully protected by insurance.

5.1 Types of Losses

Usually marine insurance policies cover several different types of loss: (1) total losses, (2) general average losses, and (3) partial or particular average losses.

Total losses include actual total losses and constructive total losses. The former refers to the situations in which the goods are totally lost or due to the damage to them failing to serve their intended purpose. The latter refers to the circumstances under which the repairing costs for the damaged goods plus extra freights will possibly exceed the value of the goods themselves. For the total losses, the insurer will compensate. For the constructive total losses, the insured has options: (1) claiming for total losses or (2) claiming for partial losses. If the insured chooses the first option, he must dispatch notice of abandonment to the insurer. Otherwise, he is deemed to claim for partial losses.

General average is an important concept in maritime transport. The word "average" in maritime law means loss. General average arises when extraordinary expenses or losses are incurred in saving the vessel or its cargo from danger at sea. Everyone of an interest in the ship and the cargo benefits from the general average. Each must then contribute, in proportion to the value of their interests, to restoring the party who suffered the loss or damage, or who incurred the expense. This is called a "general average contribution", an ancient principle of maritime law. Under this rule, if A's cargo is damaged or sacrificed in the process of saving the ship, and B's cargo is saved as a result, B and shipowner must contribute to A for the loss. A's claim is a general average. Similarly the owners of cargo that is thrown overboard to save a sinking ship may have a general average claim against those whose cargo was thereby saved. The principle of general average contribution also applies when a carrier incurs extraordinary expenses in rescuing, saving or repairing an endangered ship.

In order to prove a general claim, the claimant must show that: (1) the ship, cargo, and crew were threatened by a common danger; (2) the danger was real and substantial; (3) the cargo or ship was voluntarily sacrificed for the benefit of the cargo and the ship. Or put it in another way, the sacrifice must be extraordinary, and any following damages from the sacrifice is also considered to the general average cost. The sacrifice is made intentionally, any accidents that occur are not considered as general average. There must be a peril to the ship voyage, the captain has to ascertain that the peril is real and not made up. Actions resulting in general average must be for the common safety, not for the safety of part of the property involved.

As an effort to develop commonly accepted principles of general average, the York–Antwerp Rules were completed. The latest version was agreed to in 2004. The York–Antwerp Rules are not treaties or conventions, however, the Rules have achieved widespread acceptance by maritime industry and have been incorporated into most of the modern bills of lading. The York–Antwerp Rules 2004 provide rules for sacrifices, expenditure and contribution of general average. Some rules for sacrifices in the York–Antwerp Rules are: Jettison of Cargo; Loss or Damage by Sacrifices for the Common Safety; Extinguishing Fire on Shipboard; Cutting away Wreck; Voluntary Stranding; Damage to Machinery and Boilers; Cargo, Ship's Materials and Stores Used for Fuel; Damage to Cargo in Discharging; Loss of Freight. Some rules for expenditure in the York–Antwerp Rules are: Salvage Remuneration; Expenses lightening a Ship when Ashore, Consequent Damage Expenses of Port of Refuge; Wages and Maintenance of Crew and Other Expenses Bearing up for and in a Port of Refuge; Temporary Repairs. It is noted that expenditure or loss that is indirect such as demurrage charges, pollution cleaning charges, cargo delay loss is not included as expenditure in the York–Antwerp Rules.

All parties affected by the sacrifice have to be notified. Then, an average adjuster is appointed to calculate the cost of general average and make a statement. It is important that average adjusters act impartially because they are not only entrusted to determine cost but also to sift through claims and resolve disputes. Surveyors are appointed to assess the damages to the vessel and cargo, they have skills that differentiate themselves from average adjustors because they determine a nominal value to the damage cost. Average adjustors rely on the sea protest report, prepared by the vessel's captain, to determine events that lead to the declaration of general average. This report also helps adjustors investigate the captain's action after the sacrifices are made. Average bonds are distributed to the cargo owners involved to establish a mutual understanding between shipowner, insurance adjustors and cargo owners that all cargo details are shared without reservation to assist in the adjustments. The average bond also serves as notice to cargo owners that they are obligated to contribute to general average. General average guarantee is also another document ensuring that the cargo owner will contribute to general average. The cargo in the inflicted vessel will only be released to the cargo owner if this document is signed. Shipowners have to fulfill their obligations spelled out in the bills of lading, in order to justify a general average claim. For example, if the shipowner did not fulfill the obligation to maintain the vessel's seaworthiness to an acceptable degree, any extraordinary events and sacrifices may be determined by the adjustors as negligence of the shipowner. Cargo owners also have to fulfill their obligations per the terms of bills of lading. In a shipment normally there are two or more parties involved, it is important to determine who is the actual cargo owner before laying the responsibility of general average contribution to them. Once the cargo owners are determined, they hold the responsibility to contribute to general average. In this case, they will be the signatory of the general average bond and general average guarantee.

There are two key variables that determine the cargo owners' contribution: the contributory value of each stakeholder, and the total damage cost due to general average. In simple terms, contributory value is the percentage of value each stakeholder contributes to the total value of the adventure. Once the cost of salvaging the vessel, jettisoning the cargos, putting out fires, floating the vessel, barging or berthing on a port of refuge, has been summed up by the average adjustors, all stakeholders will contribute an amount that is proportionate to the contributory value. Here is an example in the ACME Pet Food Ltd cargo owner's perspective.

Cost of Sacrifice and Expenditure	USD 50,000,000
Sum of Value of Vessel Voyage	USD 500,000,000
ACME Pet Food Ltd Cargo C.I.F Value	USD 1,000,000
Contributory Value	USD 1,000,000 / USD 500,000,000 = 2%
ACME Pet Food Ltd Responsibility	USD 50,000,000 × 2% = USD 100,000

In this simplified example, ACME Pet Food Ltd will have to pay $ (USD) 100,000 in order to release the cargo, as the average bond and general average guarantee terms of agreement.①

Ordinarily general average contribution will be covered by insurance. If not, however, the ship's crew will hold the goods belonging to a shipper until the contribution is paid. Although total losses and general average losses are ordinarily covered by the insurance policy, special problems result from partial or particular average losses. A **particular average loss** is a partial loss to the insured's cargo. Many insurance polices limit the insurer's liability for particular average losses. A policy designed as free of particular average (FPA) will not cover any partial losses. A policy FPA, followed by certain specified losses, for example, "FPA fire" will not pay for any partial losses of that nature. As such, the "FPA fire" will not pay for partial losses to the cargo due to fire.

5.2 Types of Marine Insurance Policies

Marine insurance is available either as a special cargo policy covering a single shipment or as an open cargo policy that insures all the cargo shipped by an exporter during a particular time period.

An open policy offers the convenience and protection of covering all shipments, whether by truck, rail, air or vessel, by the shipper of certain types of goods to certain destination and over specified routes. With an open cargo policy, the exporter is authorized to issue a certificate of insurance in a form provided by the insurance company. However, the insurance company must be notified as soon as possible after shipment under an open cargo policy. These certificates are negotiable and are transferred along with the bill of lading to the importer or the holder of the bill of lading. The form of the insurance certificate is determined by the parties or the bank under a letter of credit sale. And the

---

① See Kelvinsee, *General Average – A Simplified Explanation*, Max Freight Forwarders (30 September 2021), https://maxfreights.com/general-average/.

insurance certificate only states the main provisions on the face side of an insurance policy such as the insured goods, name of the insured, premium, etc. Those provisions on the reverse side relating to the rights and obligations of the insured and the insurer are omitted. If a party is obligated to purchase insurance for an isolated sale, he can purchase a special cargo policy covering the single sale. Parties involved in an isolated shipment often arrange to have their goods covered by the open cargo policy of a freight forwarder or customs broker.

5.3 Types of Coverage

Marine cargo insurance may be the most traditional and the most developed business of insurance. It is available for virtually any type of risk, for any cargo, destined for almost any port. The limitations are the willingness of the insurer to undertake the risk and the price.

◆ **The Perils Clause**

The perils clause covers the basic risks of an ocean voyage. Examples of perils that cover are fire, jettison, shipwreck, stranding, etc. But not every event that can cause the damage to goods is covered by the perils clause. Neither the loss due to unseaworthiness of the vessel nor loss from explosion or pilferage is covered. In fact, the perils clause only covers losses of the goods while at sea.

◆ **A Specially to Cover Clause**

A shipper who desires additional coverage beyond the perils clause can purchase a specially to cover clause from the insurance company at an extra charge. For instance, loss resulting from explosion or pilferage is not generally covered in a standard perils clause, but insurance to cover it can be obtained in the form of an explosion clause. Similarly additional coverage can also be purchased to protect against the risks of theft, pilferage and non-delivery (T.P.N.D.), rain fresh water damages, shortage, contamination, odor, rust, etc. To help the insured to reasonably choose proper additional coverage, many insurers have offered specially designed import-export insurance packages for shippers of perishable foodstuffs, steel and other products.

◆ **All Risks Coverage**

An all risks policy covers all the above risks except those specially excluded in the policy. Such risks specially excluded usually include damage from acts of war, damage or loss from delay in reaching destination, or damage resulting from strikes and civil commotion. If the above risks specially excluded from all risks coverage are desired by the insured, the insured will have to purchase them separately from the insurer. For example, under CIF terms, the seller is not expected to purchase insurance against war risk. However, if the buyer desires the war risk insurance, the parties will have to agree on the price separately from the marine insurance provisions and purchase the war risk insurance additionally from the insurer. The rates for war risk insurance are relatively stable in peacetime, but dramatic fluctuations are usually expected almost daily in times of war.

Chapter Summary

The international transport of goods is deemed to be an integral part of international sales from business perspective. However, a set of independent governing rules do have been developed in the form of conventions and national laws. Modes of transportation by sea, air, rail, road and multimodal transportation are available for international transport of goods. However, the greatest portion of trade in the world today still moves on sea. The contract of transport between shippers and carriers is set forth in a bill of lading or a charterparty. As a receipt of goods, the evidence of contract and a document of title, bills of lading play an important role in international transport of goods as well as international payment. Before the new convention—the Rotterdam Rules takes its effect, the Hague Rules 1924, together with the Hague–Visby Rules 1968 and the Hamburg Rules 1978, is the main convention governing the ocean carrier's duties and immunities under bills of lading. Under the Hague Rules 1924, the carrier's primary obligation is to provide a seaworthy ship. With this prerequisite, the carrier enjoys 17 exemptions from liability including errors in navigation and management of ship, fire, Act of God, etc. The Hague Rules 1924 was incorporated into the COGSA in the U.S., and the Maritime Law of PRC also has drawn greatly on the Hague Rules 1924.

The major OSJD legal documents governing the international transport of goods by rail are the *Agreement on the International Goods Transport by Rail* (SMGS) and the *Agreement on the International Passenger Transport by Rail* (SMPS). The *Convention concerning International Carriage by Rail* (COTIF) aims to promote, improve and facilitate international traffic by railway in European Continent. The *Convention on the Contract for the International Carriage of Goods by Road* (CMR) standardizes the terms of the contract of transport, the liability of the carrier and the form of consignment note to be used concerning transportation of cargo by road. Though multimodal transport of goods is very sophisticated, no uniform conventions govern the multimodal transport contract. Different conventions on transport of air, sea, rail or road may apply in resolving disputes arising from multimodal transport contracts.

In cases where the carrier is held liable for the loss or damage to cargo, such losses usually fall on the insurers of the cargo and vessel. Under the principle of general average contribution, a carrier can assert a general average claim against the owners of the cargo demanding them or their insurers contribute to the expenses incurred in saving a vessel from a common danger perils on the sea. The shippers, in order to shift the burden of loss or damage to their goods, usually need to purchase insurance. Marine insurance policies are complex contracts. Shippers must exercise due caution in choosing sufficient coverage insuring their goods for transport by sea.

Exercises

I. True or False Statements

1. In international sales, a clean, onboard and negotiable bill of lading will generally be required.

2. The original consignee may endorse an order bill of lading either in blank by a bare signature of the endorser or by a special endorsement.

3. Under the Hague Rules 1924, the ocean carrier will not be held liable for the damage or loss caused by the ocean carrier's actual fault.

4. China has ratified the Montreal Convention 1999, and its domestic carriage of cargo, luggage and passengers by air is also governed by the Montreal Convention 1999.

5. The Rotterdam Rules has replaced the Hague Rules, the Hague–Visby Rules and the Hamburg Rules and achieved uniformity of law in the field of international maritime transport.

6. The terms in the bill of lading issued by the ocean carrier is the conclusive contractual terms between the shipper and the carrier.

7. The Hague Rules limit carrier's liability to £100 per package or customary freight unit. The limits apply even if the shipper has declared higher value for the goods.

8. Under the Montreal Convention, the air carriers will not be liable for the damage from passengers' death or bodily injury if the air carriers can prove the damage was not due to their fault.

9. No bill of lading will be issued when the goods are transported under a charterparty.

10. The Warsaw Convention 1929 has been substituted by the Montreal Convention

1999, and thus ceased to be binding on its contracting states.

II. Chapter Questions

1. What are the legal functions a bill of lading serves? Give your understanding of these functions.

2. How many types of bills of lading used in international sale? What are the usual circumstances under which they are used?

3. Explain the process of the international transport of goods. What are the potential risks for the seller and the buyer during the process?

4. Compare the major changes in the provisions of the Hague Rules, the Hague–Visby Rules and the Hamburg Rules.

5. What are the basic duties of ocean carriers under bills of lading regulated by the Hague Rules?

6. To decide the seaworthiness of the ship provided by the ocean carrier, what factors should be taken into account?

7. How do you understand the Himalaya Clause established in the United States?

8. What will regulate the obligations of shipper and shipowner under a charterparty?

9. What is your understanding on general average and the principle of general average contribution? Give an example to illustrate them.

10. What is the air carrier's liability for the death and bodily injury for passengers under the Montreal Convention 1999?

III. Case Problems

Usually, a Himalaya clause will be placed within the bill of lading or such other transportation contract. By such a clause, the carrier or shipper attempts to extend liability limitations which benefit himself, to others who are employed to assist in the transportation such as stevedores or longshoremen. The Himalaya Clause arises as the result of a decision of the English Court of Appeal in the case of *Adler v. Dickson (the Himalaya)*. Read the case and try to answer the questions:

1. According to Justice Denning, does the law permit a carrier to stipulate an exemption clause in the bill of lading for goods or the passenger ticket not only for himself but also for those who engage in carrying out the contract?

2. Can Mrs Adler claim damages against the Master and the Boatswain? Why or why not?

Adler v. Dickson (the Himalaya)

[1955] 1 QB 158

Facts

In June, 1952, Mrs. Adler decided to go for a cruise upon the P. & O. Steamship "Himalaya". She travelled first-class and paid £188 for the trip. In return the Steamship Company issued her with a first-class passage ticket by virtue of which she joined the ship at Southampton and sailed on the cruise. On July 16, 1952, the ship reached Trieste and Mrs Adler went ashore. A gangway was placed horizontally from the ship to a gantry on the quay. She went ashore across that gangway. When she returned to the ship, she was walking along the gangway and suddenly the gangway came adrift from the gantry. She was thrown onto the wharf below, a distance of 16 feet, and suffered severe injuries, including a broken leg, broken pelvis, and broken ribs. The passenger ticket contained a non-responsibility clause exempting the carrier, so she claimed damages against the Master and the Boatswain of the ship alleging that they were negligent. They denied this and said that the gangway was properly placed and secured and that the cause of the accident was that there was an exceptionally violent gust of wind which suddenly blew the ship.

Lord Justice Denning

We must assume for the purposes of the argument that the Master and the Boatswain were personally guilty of negligence and are *prima facie* liable in tort for their wrongdoing. The question is whether they are protected by the exemption clause. It is an important question, because the Steamship Company say that, as good employers, they will stand behind the Master and Boatswain and meet any damages or costs that may be awarded against them. They say that if Mrs Adler's claim is admissible, it means that a way has been found of getting round the exemption clause which no one has ever thought of before.

I pause to say that, if a way round has been found, it would not shock me in the least. I am much more shocked by the extreme width of this exemption clause which exempts the Company from all liability for any acts, default or negligence of their servants under any circumstances whatsoever to the passenger. And this exemption is imposed on the passenger by a ticket which is said to constitute a contract but which she has no real opportunity of accepting or rejecting. It is a standard printed form upon which the Company insist and from which they would not depart in favor of any individual passenger. The effect of it is that, if the passenger is to travel at all, she must travel at her own risk. She is not even given the option of traveling at the Company's risk on paying a higher fare. She pays the highest fare, first-class, and yet has no remedy against the Company for negligence. Nearly 100 years ago Mr. Justice Blackburn in a memorable Judgment said that a condition exempting a carrier wholly from liability for the neglect and default of their servants was unreasonable. I think so.

I can imagine that some lawyers would decide in Mrs. Adler's favor out of hand and for a reason which appears at first sight both simple and sufficient. It is this: The Master and Boatswain were not parties to the contract of carriage and cannot therefore claim the benefit of the exemption clause in it, because no one can enforce a contract to which he was not a party. And if that decision was right, it concludes the case in Mrs. Adler's favor. Mr. Mocatta has, however, urged us to say that that decision was wrong. It is, he says, inconsistent with the decision of the House of Lords in the case of which was not cited to the Court. He says further that, in the case of carriage of goods by sea, it is well established that the Master and crew are entitled to the protection of the exemption clauses, and that there is no reason why they should not also be so entitled in the carriage of passengers.

This is a serious argument which makes it necessary for us to consider the cases on carriage of goods. They undoubtedly show that when a carrier issues a bill of lading for goods, the exception clauses therein ensure for the benefit, not only of the carrier himself, but also for the benefit of the shipowner, the Master, the stevedores and any other persons who may be engaged in carrying out the services provided for by the contract. Such persons are not parties to the contract of carriage, but nevertheless when they are rendering their services, they are protected by the exceptions contained therein; this is so, even though the clauses are not expressed to be made for their benefit, at any rate, not in so many words. It follows that if they are guilty of negligence in rendering their services and are sued in tort, they can nevertheless rely on the exceptions to relieve them from liability. These propositions have been established in England, in Australia and in the United States of America.

There was much discussion before us as to the true principle underlying these propositions... It seems to me that there was only one contract, namely, the contract evidenced by the bill of lading. The reason why the stevedores and others are protected is because, although they were not parties to the contract, nevertheless they participated in the performance of it, and the exception clause was made for their benefit whilst they were so performing it. And they have a sufficient interest to entitle them to enforce it. Their interest lies in this: they participated insofar as it affected them and can take those benefits of it which appertain, to their interest therein. It is one of those cases—by no means rare—where a third person is entitled to enforce a contract made for his benefit. Such being the rule in respect of carriage of goods, the question is whether a similar rule applies to the carriage of passengers? In principle it clearly does...

My conclusion therefore is that, in the carriage of passengers as well as of goods, the law permits a carrier to stipulate for exemption from liability not only for himself but also for those whom he engages to carry out the contract, and this can be done by necessary implication as well as by express words. When such a stipulation is made, it is effective to protect those who render services under the contract, although they were not parties to it, subject however to this important qualification: the injured party must assent to the exemption of those persons. His assent may be given expressly or by necessary implication.

In all cases where the wrongdoer has escaped it will be found that the injured party assented expressly or by necessary implication to forego his remedy against him. In the case of goods it is not difficult to infer an assent because the owner of the goods habitually insures them against loss or damage in transit. If the carrier is protected by an exemption clause, so should his servants be, leaving the owner to recover against the insurance company. In the case of passengers, however, it is not so easy to infer an assent.

Applying those principles to the present case, the important thing to notice is that the Steamship Company only stipulated for exemption from liability for themselves. They did not in terms stipulate for exemption for their servants or agents, and I see no reason to imply any such exemption. The servants or agents are therefore not excused from the consequences of their personal negligence. In any case, even if the Company intended that the stipulation should cover their servants, nevertheless I see nothing whatever to suggest that Mrs. Adler knew of their intention or assented to it. Suppose a steward on a liner were to strike a passenger or falsely to imprison her, or injure her by some willful misconduct, then albeit it was done in the course of his employment, he could not claim the protection of the clause, for the simple reason that the passenger never agreed to his being exempted. She could sue the steward personally, even though her remedy against the Company was barred. So also if the steward is negligent in the course of his employment, for there is no difference in principle between the cases.

The passenger has not agreed to forego his remedy against the actual wrongdoer and can still pursue it.

The result in my opinion is that Mrs Adler can pursue her claim against the Master and the Boatswain without being defeated by the exemption clause. I think the appeal should be dismissed.

Disposition

The appeal will be dismissed with costs.

IV. Reading Material

On December 11, 2008, the UN General Assembly adopted the Convention on Contracts for the International Carriage of Goods Wholly or Partly by Sea (the Rotterdam Rules). This Convention, although does not come into effect yet, will replace the Hague Rules, the Hague–Visby Rules and the Hamburg Rules and will achieve uniformity of law in the field of maritime carriage. The following is an extract of this Convention on obligations and liability of carriers. Read and compare with the Hague Rules.

Chapter 4 Obligations of the carrier

Article 11 Carriage and delivery of the goods

The carrier shall, subject to this Convention and in accordance with the terms of the contract of carriage, carry the goods to the place of destination and deliver them to the consignee.

Article 12 Period of responsibility of the carrier

1. The period of responsibility of the carrier for the goods under this Convention begins when the carrier or a performing party receives the goods for carriage and ends when the goods are delivered.

2. (a) If the law or regulations of the place of receipt require the goods to be handed over to an authority or other third party from which the carrier may collect them, the period of responsibility of the carrier begins when the carrier collects the goods from the authority or other third party.

(b) If the law or regulations of the place of delivery require the carrier to hand over the goods to an authority or other third party from which the consignee may collect them, the period of responsibility of the carrier ends when the carrier hands the goods over to the authority or other third party.

3. For the purpose of determining the carrier's period of responsibility, the parties may agree on the time and location of receipt and delivery of the goods, but a provision in a contract of carriage is void to the extent that it provides that:

(a) The time of receipt of the goods is subsequent to the beginning of their initial loading under the contract of carriage; or

(b) The time of delivery of the goods is prior to the completion of their final unloading under the contract of carriage.

Article 13 Specific obligations

1. The carrier shall during the period of its responsibility as defined in article 12, and subject to article 26, properly and carefully receive, load, handle, stow, carry, keep, care for, unload and deliver the goods.

2. Notwithstanding paragraph 1 of this article, and without prejudice to the other provisions in chapter 4 and to chapters 5 to 7, the carrier and the shipper may agree that the loading, handling, stowing or unloading of the goods is to be performed by the shipper, the documentary shipper or the consignee. Such an agreement shall be referred to in the contract particulars.

Article 14 Specific obligations applicable to the voyage by sea

The carrier is bound before, at the beginning of, and during the voyage by sea to exercise due diligence to:

(a) Make and keep the ship seaworthy;

(b) Properly crew, equip and supply the ship and keep the ship so crewed, equipped and supplied throughout the voyage; and

(c) Make and keep the holds and all other parts of the ship in which the goods are carried, and any containers supplied by the carrier in or upon which the goods are carried, fit and safe for their reception, carriage and preservation.

Article 15 Goods that may become a danger

Notwithstanding articles 11 and 13, the carrier or a performing party may decline to receive or to load, and may take such other measures as are reasonable, including unloading, destroying, or rendering goods harmless, if the goods are, or reasonably appear likely to become during the carrier's period of responsibility, an actual danger to persons, property or the environment.

Article 16 Sacrifice of the goods during the voyage by sea

Notwithstanding articles 11, 13, and 14, the carrier or a performing party may sacrifice goods at sea when the sacrifice is reasonably made for the common safety or for the purpose of preserving from peril human life or other property involved in the common adventure.

Chapter 5 Liability of the carrier for loss, damage or delay

Article 17 Basis of liability

1. The carrier is liable for loss of or damage to the goods, as well as for delay in delivery, if the claimant proves that the loss, damage, or delay, or the event or circumstance that caused or contributed to it took place during the period of the carrier's responsibility as defined in chapter 4.

2. The carrier is relieved of all or part of its liability pursuant to paragraph 1 of this article if it proves that the cause or one of the causes of the loss, damage, or delay is not attributable to its fault or to the fault of any person referred to in article 18.

3. The carrier is also relieved of all or part of its liability pursuant to paragraph 1 of this article if, alternatively to proving the absence of fault as provided in paragraph 2 of this article, it proves that one or more of the following events or circumstances caused or contributed to the loss, damage, or delay:

(a) Act of God;

(b) Perils, dangers, and accidents of the sea or other navigable waters;

(c) War, hostilities, armed conflict, piracy, terrorism, riots, and civil commotions;

(d) Quarantine restrictions; interference by or impediments created by governments, public authorities, rulers, or people including detention, arrest, or seizure not attributable to the carrier or any person referred to in article 18;

(e) Strikes, lockouts, stoppages, or restraints of labor;

(f) Fire on the ship;

(g) Latent defects not discoverable by due diligence;

(h) Act or omission of the shipper, the documentary shipper, the controlling party, or any other person for whose acts the shipper or the documentary shipper is liable pursuant to article 33 or 34;

(i) Loading, handling, stowing, or unloading of the goods performed pursuant to an agreement in accordance with article 13, paragraph 2, unless the carrier or a performing party performs such activity on behalf of the shipper, the documentary shipper or the consignee;

(j) Wastage in bulk or weight or any other loss or damage arising from inherent defect, quality, or vice of the goods;

(k) Insufficiency or defective condition of packing or marking not performed by or on behalf of the carrier;

(l) Saving or attempting to save life at sea;

(m) Reasonable measures to save or attempt to save property at sea;

(n) Reasonable measures to avoid or attempt to avoid damage to the environment; or

(o) Acts of the carrier in pursuance of the powers conferred by articles 15 and 16.

4. Notwithstanding paragraph 3 of this article, the carrier is liable for all or part of the loss, damage, or delay:

(a) If the claimant proves that the fault of the carrier or of a person referred to in article 18 caused or contributed to the event or circumstance on which the carrier relies; or

(b) If the claimant proves that an event or circumstance not listed in paragraph 3 of this article contributed to the loss, damage, or delay, and the carrier cannot prove that this event or circumstance is not attributable to its fault or to the fault of any person referred to in article 18.

5. The carrier is also liable, notwithstanding paragraph 3 of this article, for all or part of the loss, damage, or delay if:

(a) The claimant proves that the loss, damage, or delay was or was probably caused by or contributed to by (i) the unseaworthiness of the ship; (ii) the improper crewing, equipping, and supplying of the ship; or (iii) the fact that the holds or other parts of the ship in which the goods are carried, or any containers supplied by the carrier in or upon which the goods are carried, were not fit and safe for reception, carriage, and preservation of the goods; and

(b) The carrier is unable to prove either that: (i) none of the events or circumstances referred to in subparagraph 5(a) of this article caused the loss, damage, or delay; or (ii) it complied with its obligation to exercise due diligence pursuant to article 14.

6. When the carrier is relieved of part of its liability pursuant to this article, the carrier is liable only for that part of the loss, damage or delay that is attributable to the event or circumstance for which it is liable pursuant to this article.

Article 18 Liability of the carrier for other persons

The carrier is liable for the breach of its obligations under this Convention caused by the acts or omissions of:

(a) Any performing party;

(b) The master or crew of the ship;

(c) Employees of the carrier or a performing party; or

(d) Any other person that performs or undertakes to perform any of the carrier's obligations under the contract of carriage, to the extent that the person acts, either directly or indirectly, at the carrier's request or under the carrier's supervision or control.

Article 19 Liability of maritime performing parties

1. A maritime performing party is subject to the obligations and liabilities imposed on the carrier under this Convention and is entitled to the carrier's defences and limits of liability as provided for in this Convention if:

(a) The maritime performing party received the goods for carriage in a Contracting State, or delivered them in a Contracting State, or performed its activities with respect to the goods in a port in a Contracting State; and

(b) The occurrence that caused the loss, damage or delay took place: (i) during the period between the arrival of the goods at the port of loading of the ship and their departure from the port of discharge from the ship; (ii) while the maritime performing party had custody of the goods; or (iii) at any other time to the extent that it was participating in the performance of any of the activities contemplated by the contract of carriage.

2. If the carrier agrees to assume obligations other than those imposed on the carrier under this Convention, or agrees that the limits of its liability are higher than the limits specified under this Convention, a maritime performing party is not bound by this agreement unless it expressly agrees to accept such obligations or such higher limits.

3. A maritime performing party is liable for the breach of its obligations under this Convention caused by the acts or omissions of any person to which it has entrusted the performance of any of the carrier's obligations under the contract of carriage under the conditions set out in paragraph 1 of this article.

4. Nothing in this Convention imposes liability on the master or crew of the ship or on an employee of the carrier or of a maritime performing party.

Article 20 Joint and several liability

1. If the carrier and one or more maritime performing parties are liable for the loss of, damage to, or delay in delivery of the goods, their liability is joint and several but only up to the limits provided for under this Convention.

2. Without prejudice to article 61, the aggregate liability of all such persons shall not exceed the overall limits of liability under this Convention.

Article 21 Delay

Delay in delivery occurs when the goods are not delivered at the place of destination provided for in the contract of carriage within the time agreed.

Article 22 Calculation of compensation

1. Subject to article 59, the compensation payable by the carrier for loss of or damage to the goods is calculated by reference to the value of such goods at the place and time of delivery established in accordance with article 43.

2. The value of the goods is fixed according to the commodity exchange price or, if there is no such price, according to their market price or, if there is no commodity exchange price or market price, by reference to the normal value of the goods of the same kind and quality at the place of delivery.

3. In case of loss of or damage to the goods, the carrier is not liable for payment of any compensation beyond what is provided for in paragraphs 1 and 2 of this article except when the carrier and the shipper have agreed to calculate compensation in a different manner within the limits of chapter 16.

Article 23 Notice in case of loss, damage or delay

1. The carrier is presumed, in absence of proof to the contrary, to have delivered the goods according to their description in the contract particulars unless notice of loss of or damage to the goods, indicating the general nature of such loss or damage, was given to the carrier or the performing party that delivered the goods before or at the time of the delivery, or, if the loss or damage is not apparent, within seven working days at the place of delivery after the delivery of the goods.

2. Failure to provide the notice referred to in this article to the carrier or the performing party shall not affect the right to claim compensation for loss of or damage to the goods under this Convention, nor shall it affect the allocation of the burden of proof set out in article 17.

3. The notice referred to in this article is not required in respect of loss or damage that is ascertained in a joint inspection of the goods by the person to which they have been delivered and the carrier or the maritime performing party against which liability is being asserted.

4. No compensation in respect of delay is payable unless notice of loss due to delay was given to the carrier within twenty-one consecutive days of delivery of the goods.

5. When the notice referred to in this article is given to the performing party that delivered the goods, it has the same effect as if that notice was given to the carrier, and notice given to the carrier has the same effect as a notice given to a maritime performing party.

6. In the case of any actual or apprehended loss or damage, the parties to the dispute shall give all reasonable facilities to each other for inspecting and tallying the goods and shall provide access to records and documents relevant to the carriage of the goods.

Chapter 3
Law and Banking Practice of International Payment

Learning Objectives
(1) Having some ideas of potential risks seller and buyer may face in the international payment
(2) Getting to know the advantages and disadvantages of different modes of international payment
(3) Understanding the transaction process of collection and letter of credit
(4) Understanding the difference between documentary letter of credit and standby letter of credit
(5) Having a deep understanding of the principle of independance, fraud exception and the rule of strict compliance under the UCP 600

Like international transport of goods, international payment is also an integral part of international sale of goods. And an independent set of rules and trade customs have been developed to regulate and facilitate international payment.

1 Modes of International Payment

Unlike most domestic sales transactions, in a cross-border sale of goods the exporter (seller) and the importer (buyer) may not have previously dealt with one another; or each may know nothing about the other, or the other's national legal system. Where the parties are strangers, these risks are significant, possibly overwhelming. Since they operate at a distance from each other, seller and buyer cannot concurrently exchange the goods for the payment funds without the help of third parties. The seller does not know: whether the buyer is creditworthy or trustworthy; whether information received on these subjects from the buyer's associates and bankers is reliable; whether exchange controls will hinder movement of the payment funds; how great the exchange risk is if payment in buyer's currency is permitted; and what delays may be involved in receiving payment from the buyer. On the other hand, the buyer does not know: whether the seller can be trusted to ship the goods if the buyer prepays; whether the goods shipped will be of the quantity and quality as required in the contract; whether the goods will be shipped by an appropriate carrier and properly insured; whether the goods may be damaged in transit; whether the seller will provide the buyer sufficient ownership documentation covering the goods (e.g., a bill of lading) to allow the buyer to claim them from the carrier; whether the seller will provide the documentation necessary to satisfy export control regulations and import customs and valuation regulations (e.g., country of origin certificates, and inspection certificates); and what delays may be involved in receiving possession and use of the goods in the buyer's location.

Therefore appropriate modes of payment are needed to distribute and reduce these potential risks to a considerable degree.

◆ **Remittance**

It is a mode of international payment under which the buyer in international sale will voluntarily make payment to the seller via banks. The process is usually as follows: the buyer entrusts a local bank (buyer's bank) to make the payment, the payment will then be forwarded to the seller through a seller's bank. Such a mode of payment is simple and cost-saving, however it will be agreed on by the parties only where the seller has great trust in the buyer, especially in the creditworthiness of the buyer.

By using the mode of remittance, if the buyer's bank transfers the instruction of payment to the seller's bank by mail, it is called mail transfer (M/T); if the instruction of payment is transferred by telegraph, then the payment is telegraphic transfer (T/T); where the buyer purchases a banker's draft and transfer the draft to the seller, the payment will be demand draft (D/D).

◆ **Collection**

Under this mode of payment the seller issues a draft appointing the buyer to be payer (drawee) and then forwards the draft (or together with some other documents) to banks and entrusts banks to collect payment for the sale of goods from the buyer. There are two types of collection: clean collection and documentary collection. In the event of a clean collection, only draft will be used in the process, while under a documentary collection the other documents including commercial invoice, bill of lading, insurance policy will be required. Compared with clean collection, documentary collection provides a safer alternative for payment, and therefore more often used in the international payment. The parties might indicate their desire for a documentary collection by specifying it in payment terms of the international sales contract.

Typically, the documentary collection works like this: the seller places the goods in the hands of a carrier and receives a bill of lading in return. The seller presents the bill of lading to the bank for collection (the seller's bank). Along with the bill of lading, the seller will include other essential documents such as a commercial invoice, and a certificate of origin, which may be required by customs regulations in the buyer's country. Other documents may be required as well, depending on the needs of the parties or the regulations on import and export of their countries. The draft and documents are accompanied by a collection letter that provides instructions from the seller on such matters as who is responsible for bank collection charges, what to do in the event the buyer dishonors the draft, and instructions for remittance of the proceeds back to the seller. The seller's bank forwards the draft and documents to a buyer's bank, also called collecting bank, with instructions that documents can be released to the buyer only upon payment of the draft. The collecting bank negotiates the documents to the buyer upon payment of the draft, and remits the money back to the seller's bank. Finally the seller can get the payment from the seller's bank. In this process the banking institutions serve as intermediaries between seller and buyer to handle the exchange of documents for payment.

There are two types of documentary collection: **document against payment (D/P)** and **document against acceptance (D/A)**. When D/P is used, the buyer shall not obtain the bill of lading and other documents until he has made the payment to the collecting bank. When D/A is used, the collecting bank will hand over the shipping documents to the buyer only upon the acceptance of the draft. However, D/A requires a time draft must be prepared. Comparatively speaking, D/A may pose greater potential risks to the seller. For example, the buyer may refuse to pay the draft or has declared to be insolvent when the draft is mature.

As for the rules governing the collection there is *Uniform Rules for Collection* (URC 522) published by the ICC. This version was published in 1995 and came into effect in the international trade practice on January 1, 1996. URC 522 are codification of international customs and usages in international payment, they are binding when the parties to a contract agree to apply them or do not expressly exclude the application of them. In fact, URC 522 have achieved wide acceptance in international trade practice.

◆ Letter of Credit

Ideally the seller would prefer not to release the title to the goods until it is certain that he will be paid. The buyer, on the other hand, would want to postpone payment until it is assured that the goods required by the sales contract are no longer subject to the seller's possession. In order to reconcile these conflicting objectives and reduce the risks involved in an international sale of goods transaction, the parties may arrange for payment under a letter of credit. Letters of credit are flexible commercial instruments adaptable to a broad range of commercial uses. Evidence exists that early forms of letters of credit were used in Renaissance Europe and in ancient Greece and Egypt. Today, almost all large banks can issue a letter of credit, although in practice most are issued by a small number of the world's largest banks. Letters of credit can be either domestic or international. They can be used in transactions for the sale of goods or services or to guarantee performance of other business obligations (e.g. the standby letter of credit). They are the most common form of payment for the international sale of goods. The details concerning the letter of credit will be discussed later in this Chapter.

To sum up, major modes of payment used in international transactions are as follws:

Exhibit III-3

Major Modes of Payment

remittance	telegraphic transfer (T/T) mail transfer (M/T) remittance by banker's demand
negotiable instruments	promissory note check bill of exchange or draft
collection	D/P (document against payment) D/A (document against acceptance)
letters of credit	

2 The Bill of Exchange

2.1 Negotiable Instruments

In the previous discussion, the draft has been mentioned from time to time. It is a specialized negotiable instruments commonly used to expedite foreign money payments in many types of international transactions. The negotiable instruments can serve two purposes: (1) they act as a substitute for money; and (2) they act as a financing or credit device. Although it is beyond the scope of this Chapter to offer a thorough discussion on the law of negotiable instruments, an overview understanding of the negotiable instruments, especially the draft is essential to the study of international trade law.

◆ **Bill of Exchange**

It is often called a draft. The word "draft" is more frequently used in the U.S. law and banking practice, while the term "bill of exchange" is more frequently used outside the United States, particularly in England. In this Chapter the term of draft and the term of bill of exchange are used as the equivalent of each other. The origin of the bill of exchange lies in the history of the merchants. As merchants began to buy and sell goods in the markets of distant cities, they sought a safer means of transferring money than by carrying it in their caravans. They invented a wiser method to make the payment. It might have worked like this: assume Merchant A delivered goods to Merchant B in a distant city, who became indebted to A for the purchase. Later Merchant A desired to purchase goods from Merchant C. Merchant A could pay Merchant C by writing a piece of paper—an order addressed by A to B to pay that amount of money to C. Since nineteenth century, the practice has been widely recognized and improved by the modern law of countries. A bill of exchange is a **three-party instrument that is an unconditional written order by one party that orders the second party to pay money to a third party**. Three primary parties are involved in a bill of exchange: (1) drawer—the party who writes the order; (2) drawee—the party who must pay the money stated in the draft (payer); (3) payee—the party who receives the money from a draft.

Two types of bill of exchange or draft are often used in international payment: sight draft and time draft. **Sight draft** is a draft that is to be paid upon presentation or demand. It is also called demand draft. **Time draft** is a draft due at future date or after a specified period of time. The time draft requires a procedure of acceptance by the drawee. Typically the acceptance is done by stamping the date and the word "accepted" across the face of draft, together with the name and signature of the drawee. The acceptance indicates the drawee's unconditional obligation to pay the draft on the date due. A draft payable at "sixty days after date" is payable by the drawee sixty days after the original date of the instrument. A draft payable at "sixty days sight" means that it is due to be paid sixty days after the date of the acceptance. Thus the time draft can provide the seller and the buyer with a mechanism for financing the international sale. Considering the difference in its negotiation, there are order bill of exchange and bearer bill of exchange. The former is payable to a specific payee, while the bearer bill of exchange that is payable to the holder, not specific payee. The order bill of exchange must be negotiated through proper endorsement and the bear bill of exchange may be negotiated just by delivery.

◆ **Check**

It is drawn on a financial institution (the drawee) and is payable on demand. Primary parties involved in a check is also three parties: drawer, drawee and payee. Drawer is the customer who has the checking account and writes the check. Drawee is the financial institution where the drawer has his or her account. Payee is the party to whom the check is written. Obvious differences between a check and a draft are (1) the drawee under a check is always the financial institutions, and (2) the check must be paid on demand, no "time check" exists. In the civil law countries like Germany and France, check is not regarded as a kind of negotiable instruments, which is covered by a specialized law rather than by their law of negotiable instruments.

◆ **Promissory Note**

It is a two-party negotiable instrument that is an unconditional written promise by one party to pay money to another party. Unlike the draft and the check, only two primary parties are involved in a promissory note: drawer and payee. Drawer is the party who makes the promise to pay (borrower). Payee is the party to whom the promise to pay is made (lender). Promissory note should be distinguished from an IOU (e.g. "IOU Adam Brown, $100"). In a promissory note there is "a promise to pay" and it is an undertaking to pay more than a mere acknowledgement of an existing debts.①

Exhibit III-4

A Sample of Draft

One hundred and twenty (120) days after date ________

PAY TO THE ORDER OF ____________ US $ _____________ US DOLLARS.

FOR VALUE RECEIVED AND CHARGE TO THE ACCOUNT OF Hank's Bank, 100 Elkhorn Road, Sun Valley, Idaho 83353

____

Michael Martin

① The form of these negotiable instruments follows the requirements under UCC. Under the law of negotiable instruments of civil law countries, including China, the form is substantially the same except the words of "Bill of Exchange", "Check" and "Promissory Note" must appear on the face of these instruments.

Exhibit III-5

A Sample of Check

January 3, 2017

PAY TO THE ORDER OF *Greg Cheeseman* US $1,000.00 *One Thousand and no/100* US DOLLARS

SECURITY PACIFIC NATIONAL BANK, 4929 Wilshire Blvd. Los Angeles, CA 90010

Florence Cheeseman

Exhibit III-6

A Sample of Promissory Note

January 3, 2017

1. PARTIES

"Borrower" means each person signing at the end of this Note, and the person's successors and assign. "Lender" means THE BIG SKY CORPORATION and its successors and assigns.

2. BORROWER'S PROMISE TO PAY; INTEREST

On demand, the undersigned promises to pay the order of Lender at its office in Missoula, Montana, the sum of Ten Thousand Dollars, with interest from date at the rate of 10% per annum until paid. Principal and interest are paid in lawful money of the United States.

Paul Brown (seal)

Borrower

Among the negotiable instruments, the bill of exchange is more complex and frequently used in international business. Therefore, some special attention should be paid to the bill of exchange.

2.2 Laws Governing the Bill of Exchange

Though until the middle of the seventeenth century, bills of exchange were governed by a single international law, the lex mercatoria, the rise of national laws brought about differences in the rules governing bills of exchange. Currently there is no uniform legal system governing the bills of exchange across the world.

In 1882 England enacted the *Bills of Exchange Act of 1882*. Today this law continues in force in the United Kingdom. And in the United States the bill of exchange or draft now falls within the province of UCC (Article 3 Commercial Papers). The German law of negotiable instruments was enacted in 1871 and France incorporated its law of negotiable instruments into the French Commercial Code of 1807. On the European continent, there were calls throughout the latter half of the nineteenth century for the creation of an international negotiable instruments law. Finally in 1907, a conference convened at Hague to draw up a convention. A draft was agreed to in 1912, but its ratification was interrupted by the World War I. After World War I, the League of Nations then organized a series of conferences to update the 1912 draft. In 1930, three *Geneva Conventions on the Unification of the Law Relating to Bills of Exchange* (ULB) were signed. In the following year, two additional *Geneva Conventions on the Unification of the Law Relating to Checks* (ULC) were also signed. Now the ULB and ULC have been ratified by most European continental countries as well as China, Japan, and some Latin American countries. Following the ULB and ULC, China has promulgated its Negotiable Instruments Law, being effective as of January 1, 1996. However, the Anglo-American common law countries have not ratified the ULB or ULC.

Efforts have been made in drafting a truly international convention governing bills of exchange. The UNCITRAL produced a text called the Convention on International Bills of Exchange and International Promissory Notes in May 1988, and was approved by the UN General Assembly open for ratification. Though only ten states must ratify the Convention before it will come into effect, until 1999 only Guinea and Mexico had ratified the Convention, and it seems unlikely that it will be effective anytime soon.

2.3 Formal Requirements of the Bill of Exchange

There are strict and formal requirements for the bill of lading. Under ULB, a bill of exchange/draft must be: (1) an unconditional order in writing; (2) addressed by one person to another; (3) signed by the person giving it; (4) that the addressee pay on demand or at a fixed determinable future time; (5) a sum certain in money; (6) to or to the order of a specified person, or to a bearer; (7) the date and place of issuing the instrument; (8) of the words "bill of exchange" on the face of the instrument. A bill of exchange which does not conform to any of the above requirements will make the instrument invalid and dishonored. Under the Anglo-American laws governing the bills of exchange, the items (7) and (8) are not required. The bill of exchange cannot be conditioned on the performance of some other obligation. The reason for this is basic to the nature of negotiability of bills of exchange. If a holder of a bill of exchange has to determine whether a collateral obligation had or had not been fulfilled, the negotiability and the use of bills of exchange will be greatly reduced. A bill of exchange must be payable in money, which must be for a definite sum. Usually the parties to bills of exchange will routinely define their money obligations by referring to money units of account such as the European Union's euro.

For example, the bills of exchange containing any of the following statements are deemed to be invalid: (1) "ABC Corp. promises to pay $100,000 to the order of Johnson provided the helicopter sold meets all contractual specifications." (2) "Payable to the order of Ray Rodes 6 months after the death of Alber Olds." (3) "I wish you would pay to the order of Merry Smith $500 on Oct. 20." The statement of "provided the helicopter sold meets all contractual specifications" indicates the instrument is not an "unconditional order", "the death of Alber Olds", though will come in the future, surely is not a fixed determinable future time, and the expression of "I wish" or the like does not indicate an order.

2.4 Negotiation of the Bill of Exchange

◆ Negotiation

It is the transfer of an instrument from one party to another so that the transferee (holder) takes legal rights in the instrument. The rights that a holder acquires depend on the manner in which the instrument was negotiated and the governing law. The correct **manner of negotiation** depends on whether the instrument is bearer or order instrument. Order bill of exchange is payable to a specific payee, often containing the words of "pay to the order of Co. A" or "pay to Francis Madero". Order bill of exchange is negotiated by endorsement and delivery. While the bearer bill of exchange that is payable to the holder, not specific payee, often contains the words of "pay the bearer" or the signature of the last endorsee. Bearer bill of exchange is negotiated by delivery alone.

◆ Endorsements

An endorsement refers to the act of writing down signatures with or without additional statements on the back of the negotiable instrument. When endorsed, the amount of money stated in the bill of exchange is indivisible, i.e. a bill of exchange must be transferred as a whole, partial negotiation of the sum of payment is not allowed. There are **special endorsements** and **blank endorsements**. In blank endorsements, only the signature of the endorser appears on the instrument, for example, "(signed) Jane Austin". In special endorsements, the signatures of both the endorser and the endorsee appear, for instance, "Pay to William Kaiser (signed) Jane Austin (signed)". Sometimes the endorser would add some statements to limit the rights of subsequent holders, for example, "pay to William Kaiser, without recourse, (signed) Jane Austin". Such endorsements are called qualified endorsements. Or "Pay to William Kaiser only, (signed) Jane Austin", which will prohibit further endorsements. This kind of endorsements is restrictive endorsements. **Restrictive endorsements** limit the rights of subsequent holders in some way, such as conditioning payment on the occurrence of a specified event, or making the endorsee a collection agent, or making the instrument payable only to a particular person, or requiring the endorsee to pay the proceeds to the endorser or to some third party. A **qualified endorsement** states that the endorser does not guarantee that the instrument will be accepted or paid.

By putting his signature on the bill of exchange, the endorser will be held secondarily liable to the subsequent holders for guaranteeing the acceptance or payment of the bill of exchange except that the endorsement is a restrictive or qualified one. That is, when the bill of exchange is dishonored by the drawee, the last holder has the right to require the endorser to reimburse the stated amount and relevant expenses of the bill of exchange. However, the holder must take three steps before he can seek recourse from the endorser or endorsers. First, the bill of exchange must contain all necessary endorsements and must be timely presented at the place required. Second, the bill of exchange must be protested. In other words, a formal certification of dishonor must be issued by a person authorized to certify dishonor by the law, for example, a notary public. Third, a notice must be given to the endorser or endorsers. Any endorser who receives such a notice must notify his immediate endorser. Under the UCC, the notice has to be given within three business days, and under ULB, the requirement is two business days. Any form of notice is sufficient so long as it identifies the bill of exchange and states that the instrument has been dishonored.

◆ Excuses Drawers Can Use to Avoid Paying Off a Bill of Exchange

When a bill of exchange is properly negotiated, drawers must pay the person presenting the instrument for payment. The excuses that drawers can use for not paying are those contained in the ULB. Anyone who acquires a bill of exchange by negotiation is a holder who is entitled to payment from the drawer. There are only three excuses available to the drawer: (1) that the possessor is not a holder because he did not acquire title through an uninterrupted series of endorsements, (2) that the holder acquired the instrument in bad faith, and (3) that the holder acquired the instrument through gross negligence.

3 Documentary Letters of Credit

3.1 Use of the Documentary Letter of Credit

A transaction of international sales typically involves at least three contracts: the sales contract between buyer and seller, the transport contract, and the letter of credit contract by which the sale is financed. The use of the letters of credit as a tool to reduce payment risk has grown substantially over the past decade. Letters of credit accomplish their purpose of facilitating international trade by substituting the credit of the bank for that of the buyer. Electronic communication has taken over some aspects of letters of credit practice, but not others. They dominate the issuance process in bank-to-bank communications, and are sometimes used by applicants to stimulate the issuance process.

This part covers two types of letters of credit: documentary letters of credit and standby letters of credit. The discussion starts with this type, because documentary letters of credit are used in international sales. And in business letters of credits are generally referred to documentary letters of credits, thus in the following text the expression of letters of credit or credits are equivalents to documentary letters of credit.

The letter of credit is defined as a contract-conditional undertaking by a bank, issued in accordance with the instructions of the applicant (the buyer), in favor of the beneficiary (the seller) wherein the bank promises to pay, accept, or negotiate the beneficiary's draft up to the amount of the contract price within the prescribed time limit, upon the beneficiary's presentation of stipulated documents. Letters of credit can be revocable or irrevocable. A revocable letter of credit can be withdrawn at any time without prior notification to the beneficiary. An irrevocable letter of credit, once established with the beneficiary, can only be altered with the consent of the beneficiary. A credit is irrevocable even if there is no indication to that effect.

In a letter of credit transaction, the promise of an internationally recognized bank is substituted for that of the buyer. As long as the seller complies with all requirements in the letter of credit, such as tendering the documents called in the letter of credit (usually including bill of lading, draft, insurance policy, commercial invoice and other collateral documents) within the time allowed, the seller has more assurance of being paid than in any other mode of payment except by receiving cash in advance.

The use of the letter of credit in international payment is as follows:

If the sales contract requires the payment to be made by letter of credit: At first, there will be a contract between the buyer and the buyer's bank (**issuing bank**). The buyer initiates the contract by applying to his own bank for the issuance of a letter of credit in favor of the seller (beneficiary), and thereby agrees to reimburse the issuing bank for payment of drafts presented with certain shipping documents (such as bills of lading) specified in the terms and conditions of the letter. Thus the issuing bank undertakes the payment obligation to the seller (the beneficiary). If the seller requires an obligation of a bank in the seller's jurisdiction, the letter of credit must be confirmed by a seller's bank (**confirming bank**). The buyer's bank (issuing bank) will forward its letter of credit to the seller through another bank, the seller's bank, which is usually a correspondent bank to the buyer's bank. By merely indicating "we confirm this credit", the seller's bank (confirming bank) makes a direct promise to the seller that it will assume the same obligation and liability as the issuing bank, and pay the contract price to the seller, if the seller presents the required documents to it.[①] If no confirmation of the credit is required by the sales contract, buyer's bank can forward the letter of credit through a "notifying bank" or an "**advising bank**", which is near the seller. These banks act as the agents of the issuing bank and have only a duty to communicate the terms of the credit accurately. They are not obligated to the seller, but will take the documents and forward them to the buyer's bank for collection purposes only.[②] The issuing bank communicates the issuance of the letter of credit to the seller's bank, via the confirming or advising bank. The confirming bank or advising bank then informs the seller of the issuance of the letter of credit.

Upon receiving the letter of credit, the seller will prepare the necessary documents according to the letter of credit. For example, the seller will send the goods to the carrier,

---

① Confirmation of a letter of credit must be bargained for and specified in the sales contract.

② There are many other categories of banks, which may be involved in the letters of credit transaction. Any bank which is authorized to pay against the documents is a "**nominated bank**", whether it also undertakes an obligation to pay or not. A bank, which is a nominated bank and has given value for the document is a "**negotiating bank**".

which issues a negotiable bill of lading as a combination receipt and contract. The seller now has the complete set of documents needed, and takes these documents to the seller's bank, which (as a confirming bank) is obligated to pay the seller the contract price upon presentation of the documents. To obtain payment, the seller attaches a "draft" to the documents; in the letter of credit the banks have promised to honor such a draft. If a "demand draft" is used, the confirming bank will pay the amount immediately, usually by crediting the seller's account either in the seller's bank or in some other bank designated by the seller. In the event that the draft is a "time draft" (e.g. "pay thirty days after sight"), the confirming bank need not pay upon presentment of the draft and documents, but it must "accept" the time draft when it is presented. This "acceptance" creates an obligation on confirming bank that it will pay at the later time stated in the draft.

In return for the bank's payment, the seller will endorse both the draft and the negotiable bill of lading to the seller's bank and transfer the other documents to it. The seller's bank, in turn, will endorse and will forward the draft, with the required documents attached to the buyer's bank. It thus, presents the draft (with the accompanying documents) to the buyer's bank for payment. The buyer's bank is obligated under the letter of credit to honor the draft and to reimburse the seller's bank if the documents attached to the draft are conforming. Since there is already a correspondent relationship between the two banks, the buyer's bank will credit the seller's bank's account with the amount of the draft.

The buyer's bank then advises the buyer that the documents have arrived and that payment is due. Since the buyer and the buyer's bank usually have an established relationship, the usual course of events will be for the bank to be authorized to charge the amount of the draft to the buyer's bank account, and to forward the documents to the buyer. If the buyer has arranged for credit from the buyer's bank, the credit will be advanced when the draft and documents arrive. If there was not an established relationship between the buyer and its bank, the buyer would be required to pay or to arrange sufficient credit for the draft before the documents were released to it. As the draft and documents are forwarded from the seller to the seller's bank to the buyer's bank to the buyer, each of these parties will endorse the bill of lading to the next party.

Once the buyer has paid, or arranged to pay, the buyer's bank will obtain possession of the bill of lading and only then will it be entitled to obtain the goods from carrier. Note that the buyer has effectively paid for the goods while they were at sea, long before their arrival. In fact, the buyer was bound to pay for the goods as soon as the draft and required documents were presented to the seller's bank. If the goods failed to arrive the buyer must look to its insurance certificate for protection and reimbursement.

3.2 The Governing Rules: UCP 600

Although there are national laws governing letters of credit, the *Uniform Customs and Practice for Documentary Credits* (commonly called "UCP") published by the ICC is the most important rule governing letters of credit across the world. UCP is the codification of international trade customs and usages on bankers' dealing with letters of credit, offering a rather uniform and detailed manual of operations for banks. The UCP does not purport to be law, however, it is incorporated by reference in most international letters of credit.

The ICC published the first version of UCP in 1993, and has published a revision of the UCP about every ten years. The latest version is the sixth revision of the rules called UCP 600. It is the fruit of more than three years of work by the International Chamber of Commerce's (ICC) Commission on Banking Technique and Practice. The UCP 600, came into effect on July 1, 2007. **UCP 600 applies to** "any documentary credit, including, to the extent to which they may be applicable, any standby letter of credit, when the text of the credit expressly indicates that it is subject to these rules. They are binding on all parties thereto unless expressly modified or excluded by the credit" (Article 1 of UCP 600) . And a letter of credit must state the following terms: (1) the bank with which it is available or whether it is available with any bank; (2) whether it is available by sight payment, deferred payment, acceptance or negotiation; (3) the draft available drawn on the applicant; (4) an expiration date for presentation; (5) the place for presentation.[①]

Though UCP 600 reduces the number of articles from 46 in UCP 500 to 39, it is a leaner set of rules than UCP 500. The new edition contains major changes that letter of credit practitioners will need to know. Among them are new sections on definitions and interpretations, replacement of the term "reasonable time" with a maximum of five banking days for examining documents and re-drafted transport articles aimed at resolving confusion over the identification of carriers, masters and agents. Also available along with UCP 600 is an updated version of International Standard Banking Practice for the Examination of Documents under Documentary Credits, commonly called ISBP. The ISBP is a checklist of items document checkers need to look for when examining documents presented under letters of credit. Since it was first published in 2003, the ISBP has been an indispensable companion to the UCP. The updated version, ICC Publication 681, aligns

---

① See Article 6 of UCP 600.

the ISBP with the changes in UCP 600. Worldwide interest in the new UCP has been evidenced in dozens of well-attended seminars on the rules that have been held on several continents. The response of practitioners has been positive, with many commenting on the enhanced clarity and precision of the text.

3.3 Basic Legal Principles

UCP 600 has established two basic legal principles of the letter of credit. One is the Principle of Independence and the other is the Rule of Strict Compliance.

3.3.1 The Principle of Independence

The Principle of Independence, sometimes also called the autonomy of letters of credit, is intended to secure the wide use of letter of credit in the international payment. Generally it means that the bank's obligations under the letter of credit are independent of the buyer's and seller's obligations under the contract for the sale of goods. Such a principle is embodied in Article 4 of UCP 600. It states: "A credit by its nature is a separate transaction from the sale or other contract on which it may be based. Banks are in no way concerned with or bound by such contract, even if any reference whatsoever to it is included in the credit. Consequently, the undertaking of a bank to honor, to negotiate or to fulfill any other obligation under the credit is not subject to claims or defenses by the applicant resulting from its relationships with the issuing bank or the beneficiary. A beneficiary can in no case avail itself of the contractual relationships existing between banks or between the applicant and the issuing bank. An issuing bank should discourage any attempt by the applicant to include, as an integral part of the credit, copies of the underlying contract, proforma invoice and the like." Article 5 of UCP 600 furthers the Principle of Independence by stating: "Banks deal only with documents, and not with the goods or any issues concerning performance of the sale contract."

That is to say, the issuing and conforming banks will perform its obligations of payment if the beneficiary (the seller) performs its obligations i.e. presenting the documents as required by the irrevocable letter of credit, regardless of whether those obligations fulfill the sales contract obligations or not, even the issuing bank or the confirming bank is notified there is a breach of sales contract committed by the seller. In the event of a breach of sales contract committed by the seller, the proper redressing way for the buyer is to seek remedies for breach of contract from the seller.

Case III-7

Maurice O'Meara Co. v. National Park Bank of New York

239 N.Y. 386, 146 N.E. 636 (1925)

Facts

National Park Bank issued a letter of credit to the beneficiary, Ronconi & Millar, covering the shipment of 1,322 tons of newsprint paper in 72½-inch and 36½-inch rolls to test 11–12, 32 lbs, and delivery to be made in December 1920 and January 1921. When Ronconi & Millar's invoice and draft were presented to the bank, the documents described the paper as was required in the letter of credit. However, the bank refused payment because it had no opportunity to test the tensile strength of the paper. Ronconi & Millar transferred their rights to collect payment to Maurice O'Meara, a financial institution, who brought this action to collect the full amount of the drafts. Maurice O'Meara claims that the issuing bank had no right to test or inspect the paper.

Reasoning

According to Judge Mclaughlin, the letter of credit … was in no way involved in or connected with the contract for the purchase and sale of the paper between the buyer and the seller. The bank's obligation was to pay sight drafts when presented if accompanied by genuine documents specified in the letter of credit. Whether the paper was what the buyer contracted to purchase did not concern the bank and in no way affected its liability National Park Bank's obligation to pay the beneficiary's drafts submitted under its letter of credit. If the paper when delivered did not correspond to what had been purchased, either in weight, kind or quality, the purchaser had his remedy against the seller for damages.

Decision

Therefore the defendant, National Park Bank, could not withhold payment of the drafts even if it believed that the paper was not of the weight, kind, or quality as ordered. Defendant also had no right to demand testing of the paper or to inspect it prior to payment.

To this Principle of Independence there is one well-established exception. This exception provides that **fraud** on the part of the seller/beneficiary brought to the issuing bank's attention before it has paid out against tender of apparently conforming documents discharges the bank's absolute obligation to pay.

This exception was established in the United States in *Sztejn v. Henry Schroder Banking Corporation.*

Case III-8

Sztejn v. Henry Schroder Banking Corporation

31 N.Y.S. 2d 631 (1941)

Background and Facts

The Plaintiff contracted with Transea, an Indian company, for the purchase of hog bristles. The Plaintiff contracted with Schroder Banking Corporation, a U.S. bank, for the issuance of irrevocable letter of credit providing: Schroder will pay once the shipment is made, and when the commercial invoice and bill of lading made out to the order of Schroder is presented. Then the letter of credit was delivered to Transea through banking channels. Transea filled 50 cases with cow hair and other worthless rubbish and procured bill of lading from the ship company and obtained the invoice, showing the shipment of 50 cases of hog bristles ordered by the Plaintiff. The documents and the draft were presented to Schroder by the Chartered Bank of India, acting as agent for Transea. The Plaintiff filed a complaint that Transea filled the 50 boxes with worthless junk to defraud, seeking to refrain the issuing bank from paying on the letter of credit.

Justice Shientag

It is well established that a letter of credit is independent of the primary contract of sale between the buyer and the seller. The issuing bank agrees to pay upon presentation of documents, not goods. It would be a most unfortunate interference with business transactions if a bank before honoring drafts drawn upon it was obligated or even allowed to go behind the documents, at the request of the buyer, and enter into controversies between the buyer and the seller regarding the quality of the merchandise shipped. Of course, the application of this doctrine presupposes that the documents accompanying the draft are genuine and conform in terms to the requirements of the letter of credit. However, I believe that a different situation is presented in the instant action. This is not a controversy between the buyer and the seller concerning a mere breach of warranty regarding the quality of the merchandise; on the present motion, it must be assumed that the seller has intentionally failed to ship any goods ordered by the buyer. In such a situation, where the seller's fraud has been called to the bank's attention before the drafts and documents have been presented for payment, the principle of the independence of the bank's obligation under the letter of credit should not be extended to protect the unscrupulous seller. It is true that even though the documents are forged or fraudulent, if the issuing bank has already paid the draft before receiving notice of the seller's fraud, it will be protected if it exercised reasonable diligence before making such payment. However, in the instant action Schroder has received notice of Transea's active fraud before it accepted or paid the draft...

The distinction between a breach of warranty and active fraud on the part of the seller is supported by authority and reason. As one court has stated: "Obviously, when the issuer of a letter of credit knows that a document, although correct in form, is, in point of fact, false or illegal, he cannot be called upon to recognize such a document as complying with the terms of a letter of credit. No hardship will be caused by permitting the bank to refuse payment where fraud is claimed, where the merchandise is not merely inferior in quality but consists of worthless rubbish, where the draft and the accompanying documents are in the hands of one who stands in the same position as the fraudulent seller, where the bank has been given notice of the fraud before being presented with the drafts and documents for payment, and where the bank itself does not wish to pay pending an adjudication of the rights and obligations of the other parties..."

Accordingly, the defendant's motion to dismiss the supplemental complaint is denied.

Decision

The court held in favor of the plaintiff and enjoined the bank's payment.

Coincidently, Justice Cardozo's dissenting opinion in *Maurice O'Meara Co. v. National Park Bank of New York* became the majority opinion in 1941.[①] The fraud exception was incorporated into Article 5 of the UCC, but the UCP 600 has no provisions concerning the fraud exception. The newly revised Article 5-109 with a title of "Fraud and

① Cardozo stated in that case: "I dissent from the view that, if [the issuing bank] chooses to investigate and discovers thereby that the merchandise is not in truth the merchandise which documents describe, it may be forced by the delinquent seller to make payment of the price irrespective of its knowledge."

Forgery" states:

"(a) If a presentation is made that appears on its face strictly to comply with the terms and conditions of the letter of credit, but a required document is forged or materially fraudulent, or honor of the presentation would facilitate a material fraud by the beneficiary on the issuer or applicant:

(1) the issuer shall honor the presentation, if honor is demanded by (i) a nominated person who has given value in good faith and without notice of forgery or material fraud, (ii) a confirmer who has honored its confirmation in good faith, (iii) a holder in due course of a draft drawn under the letter of credit which was taken after acceptance by the issuer or nominated person, or (iv) an assignee of the issuer's or nominated person's deferred obligation that was taken for value and without notice of forgery or material fraud after the obligation was incurred by the issuer or nominated person; and

(2) the issuer, acting in good faith, may honor or dishonor the presentation in any other case.

"(b) If an applicant claims that a required document is forged or materially fraudulent or that honor of the presentation would facilitate a material fraud by the beneficiary on the issuer or applicant, a court of competent jurisdiction may temporarily or permanently enjoin the issuer from honoring a presentation or grant similar relief against the issuer or other persons."

From the proceeding provision, we can see that the application of fraud exception under the UCC is narrowly defined and applied. Its application is subject to a lot of limitations such as "materially fraudulent", good faith holder of the draft, etc.

As for the fraud exception, the law of China has expressed in a much clearer way. *Provisions on Adjudicating the Disputes Arising from Letters of Credit* were issued by the Supreme People's Court of China and came into effect on January 1, 2006. Article 8 thereof provides four situations in which a fraud under a letter of credit transaction shall be deemed to exist: (1) the beneficiary forged the documents or tendered the documents containing fraudulent information; (2) the beneficiary intentionally failed to deliver the goods or deliver the worthless goods; (3) the beneficiary and the applicant or a third party colluded to tender fraudulent documents based on fictional underlying transaction; (4) other situations in which a fraud under the letter of credit was committed.

When discovering any of the above situations and irreparable harm may arise from the fraud, the issuing bank, the applicant or the other parties having an interest in the letter of credit transaction, may petition to the competent court for suspending the payment under the letter of credit. The court order for suspending the payment under the letter of credit shall be rendered within 48 hours and come into force upon its rendering (Article 9 and Article 12). However, in the event a fraud under the letter of credit has been proved, the payment under the letter of credit shall not be suspended in any of the following circumstances: (1) a nominated person has made the payment in good faith according to the instruction from the issuing bank; (2) a nominated person has in good faith honored the draft drawn under the letter of credit; (3) the confirming bank had performed its duty of payment under the letter of credit in good faith; or (4) the negotiating bank had negotiated the draft drawn under the letter of credit in good faith.

3.3.2 The Rule of Strict Compliance

Since banks may only deal with the documents rather than the goods or services related to the letter of credit, in determining whether the documents submitted by the beneficiary are in order on their face, a bank under the obligation for payment, which may be the issuing bank, the confirming bank or a nominated bank, is entitled to apply the so-called Rule of Strict Compliance. In other words, the bank may reject documents that do not strictly comply with the terms specified in the letter of credit.

◆ The Standard for Examination of Documents

Article 14 of UCP 600 provides the standard for examination of documents. "Data in a document, when read in context with the credit, the document itself and international standard banking practice, need not be identical to, but must not conflict with, data in that document, any other stipulated document or the credit." And "In documents other than the commercial invoice, the description of the goods, services or performance, if stated, may be in general terms not conflicting with their description in the credit." That is to say, data in documents are not required to be identical but no conflict is endured. And the primary document for describing the goods in a documentary sale transaction is the commercial invoice. **The description in the commercial invoice must be specific and correspond with the description in the credit; descriptions in all other documents can be "in general terms not conflicting with" the description in the credit.** Thus, where a credit called for "100% acrylic yarn" and the invoice merely stated "imported acrylic yarn," the credit was not satisfied, even though the packing list stated "100% acrylic yarn". As for the addresses of the parties, Article 14 states: "When the addresses of the beneficiary and the applicant appear in any stipulated document, they need not be the same as those stated in the credit or in any other stipulated document, but must be within the same country as the respective addresses mentioned in the credit. Contact details (telefax, telephone, email and the like) stated as part of the beneficiary's and the applicant's address will be disregarded. However, when the address and contact details of the applicant appear as part of the consignee or notify party details on a transport document they must be as stated in the credit."

Many of the cases which litigate issues concerning the strict compliance of documents seem to revolve around discrepancies in transportation terms. Express conditions in the credit that loading, presentment or other acts must be performed by a certain time will be strictly enforced. So also, a discrepancy in the location of shipment or delivery will fail to comply with the terms of a credit. A credit calling for "Full Set Clean on Board Ocean Bills of Lading" is not satisfied by a tender of "truckers bills of lading", even though evidence was presented that the bills of lading were in customary Mexican form and that Mexican truckers did not specify on the bill of lading that the goods were "on board." Nor is the "Full Set Clean on Board Bills of Lading" requirement satisfied by air waybills, even though air delivery may be preferable. Recent cases often involve typographical errors. When the letter of credit mistakenly identified the beneficiary as Sung Jin Electronics, while the documents were correctly addressed to Sung Jun Electronics, the banks were allowed to refuse payment. But this decision has been criticized by practicing lawyers as being "too narrow".[①]

◆ Period for Documents Examination

Banks including a nominated bank, a confirming bank, and the issuing bank shall each have **a maximum of five banking days following the day of presentation to determine if a presentation is complying**. The presentation of required documents must be made by or on behalf of the beneficiary not later than 21 calendar days after the date of shipment, but in any event not later than the expiration date of the credit. For the presented documents not required by the letter of credit, the banks may just disregard them or return them to the beneficiary.

◆ Notice Procedures for the Dishonor

When an issuing bank, a confirming bank or a nominated bank determines that a presentation is complying, it must honor the payment under the letter of credit. However, when a nominated bank, a confirming bank, or the issuing bank determines that a presentation does not comply, it may refuse to honor or negotiate. Sometimes the

---

① See Hanil Bank *v.* Pt. Bank Negara Indonesia (Persero) (S.D.N.Y. 2000).

discrepancies between documents and the requirements of the letter of credit may be trivial or typographical, and the applicant—buyer may want the payment made and the goods delivered, despite the discrepancy. Thus before deciding to dishonor, an issuing bank may in its sole judgment, send **a waiver of the discrepancies** to the applicant (the buyer). About 90% of the time that they are consulted by the issuing bank, applicants will in fact waive the discrepancies discovered by the bank. Thus, the system of honoring will continue to work.

When a nominated bank, a confirming bank, if any, or the issuing bank decides to refuse to honor or negotiate, it must give a single **notice** to that effect to the presenter. The notice must state: (1) that the bank is refusing to honor or negotiate; (2) each discrepancy in respect of which the bank refuses to honor or negotiate; (3) that the bank is holding the documents pending further instructions from the presenter; or that the issuing bank is holding the documents until it receives a waiver from the applicant and agrees to accept it, or that the bank is returning the documents; or that the bank is acting in accordance with instructions previously received from the presenter. The notice must be given by telecommunication, or, if that is not possible, by other expeditious means no later than the close of the fifth banking day following the day of presentation. After providing the notice, banks may return the documents to the presenter at any time.

If the issuing bank, the confirming bank, or the nominated bank dishonors the credit, and refuses to pay when the documents are presented, the dishonor may be rightful or wrongful. If there truly are discrepancies between the specifications in the credit and the documents actually presented (and they are not waived), the banks are entitled to dishonor, although they must follow the above notice procedures specified in the UCP 600 to protect themselves. If the issuer dishonors a presentation of documents which do comply strictly to the letter of credit, that is a wrongful dishonor. It is also a breach of one or more contracts. First, it is a breach of the letter of credit contract, for which the beneficiary will have a cause of action. Second, it may be a breach of the credit application agreement between the applicant and the issuer for which the applicant may have a cause of action. The applicant's right to sue the issuer for wrongful dishonor would arise out of the credit application agreement, and would be analyzed under ordinary contract law. It would also depend upon the terms of the credit application agreement, which might or might not include a clause disclaiming liability of the issues for wrongful dishonor.

◆ **Disclaimers of Banks**

The banks enjoy some disclaimers under the UCP 600. **First,** the bank is not liable for "the effectiveness of documents". A bank assumes no liability or responsibility for the form, sufficiency, accuracy, genuineness, falsification or legal effect of any document, or for the general or particular conditions stipulated in a document; nor does it assume any liability or responsibility for the description, quantity, weight, quality, condition, packing, delivery, value or existence of the goods, services or other performance represented by any document, or for the good faith or acts or omissions, solvency, performance or standing of the consignor, the carrier, the forwarder, the consignee or the insurer of the goods or any other person. **Second,** the bank is not liable for the consequences resulting from transmission and translation problems of documents. A bank assumes no liability for the consequences arising out of delay, loss in transit, mutilation or other errors arising in the transmission of any messages or delivery of letters or documents, when such messages, letters or documents are transmitted or sent according to the requirements stated in the credit, or when the bank may have taken the initiative in the choice of the delivery service in the absence of such instructions in the credit. If a nominated bank determines that a presentation is complying and forwards the documents to the issuing bank or confirming bank, whether or not the nominated bank has honored or negotiated, an issuing bank or confirming bank must honor or negotiate, or reimburse that nominated bank, even when the documents have been lost in transit between the nominated bank and the issuing bank or confirming bank, or between the confirming bank and the issuing bank. And a bank assumes no liability or responsibility for errors in translation or interpretation of technical terms and may transmit credit terms without translating them. **Third,** *force majeure* exemption. A bank assumes no liability for the consequences arising out of the interruption of its business by acts of God, riots, civil commotions, insurrections, wars, acts of terrorism, or by any strikes or lockouts or any other causes beyond its control. A bank will not, upon resumption of its business, honor or negotiate under a credit that expires during such interruption of its business. **Fourth,** disclaimer for acts of an instructed party. A bank utilizing the services of another bank for the purpose of giving effect to the instructions of the applicant does so for the account and at the risk of the applicant. An issuing bank or advising bank assumes no liability or responsibility should the instructions it transmits to another bank not be carried out, even if it has taken the initiative in the choice of that other bank.[①]

---

① See Articles 34–37 of the UCP 600.

4 Standby Letters of Credit

Although like the documentary letters of credit, standby letters of credit are also mechanisms for allocating risks among parties in commercial transactions, great differences exist between the two types of letters of credit.

The functions of a standby letter of credit differ substantially from those of the documentary letter of credit. The standby letters of credit can be used to ensure the repayment of a loan. For example, a subsidiary of a U.S. company operating in Mexico that borrows money from the local bank can require a standby letter of credit from a U.S. bank. The standby letter of credit would allow it to draw against the credit, should the subsidiary default on its obligations. However, most standby letters of credit are used not in sale-of-goods transactions, but as guaranties of performance under a service contract, or construction contract.

Unlike a documentary letter of credit in which the beneficiary of the credit is the seller, a standby letter of credit is issued in favor of the buyer to guarantee the seller's performance. Therefore, the standby letter of credit is primarily a risk-shifting device, with the advantage of providing the beneficiary (the buyer) with easy access to funds in case of a default of performance by the seller, much as if the seller had left a cash deposit with the beneficiary.

The documentary letter of credit usually requires the beneficiary (the seller) present some documents strictly complying with the credit, however, under a standby letter of credit the issuing bank is required to honor a demand for payment upon receiving a signed statement by the beneficiary (the buyer) that the seller has not performed the contract. Because all that is required for the beneficiary to receive payment is a statement that a default has occurred, a standby letter of credit is sometimes called a suicide credit. Under suicide credits payable upon unilateral demands, the account party's exposure may be enormous and the legal protection against arbitrary demands is limited to the fraud exception. Thus standby letters of credit tend to rely more heavily on the good faith of the parties than the documentary letters of credit. To protect an account party (the seller) under a suicide credit from an unfair demand by the beneficiary, many attorneys will require the beneficiary's request for payment be accompanied by an independent confirmation of the account party's default by a third party.

Standby letters of credit are also governed by the UCP 600 now, and are governed by the same rules as those applicable to documentary letters of credit "to the extent they may be applicable".[①] Standby letters of credit share the principle of independence under the documentary letters of credit. The bank's obligations under the letter of credit are independent of the buyer's and seller's obligations under the underlying contract. Banks deal with documents but not with the performance of the underlying contract. The bank does not and cannot investigate the allegation of the seller's nonperformance or delay payment in order to investigate the validity of the allegation. The bank cannot assert any defenses, except fraud, which the seller may have against the beneficiary. Typically standby letters of credit are not supported by funds on deposit with the bank, because the bank does not anticipate having to pay out on them and the seller simply guarantee that the bank will be reimbursed if it is forced to pay out on the standby letter of credit. Thus due to their contingent nature, standby letters of credit are more risky to a bank than documentary letters of credit.

Some legal commentators question whether the principle of independence under the documentary letters of credit rules should be applied to standby letters of credit, since the standby letters do not assure an exporter about payment for goods to be shipped, but serve principally a non-payment function to assure an importer (beneficiary) about payment if an exporter (the account party) does not supply goods, services or raw materials. However, the text of UCP 600 makes it clear that the drafters are intended to cover standby letters of credit and apply the principle of independence to such bank obligations.

Chapter Summary

This Chapter discusses some legal issues involved in the different modes of international payment. These modes of payment are designed to balance and reduce the payment risk and delivery risk between the seller and the buyer in international sales. Documentary collection can help you better understand the documentary sale and their assurance for the payment and delivery of goods. The negotiability of the draft and the trade financing function of time draft make it the primary instrument for effectuating payment in international transactions. As the most important kind of negotiable instruments, the draft is widely used in documentary collections and documentary letters of credit as well. Documentary letters of credit are not bank guarantees, but assurance to

① See Article 1 of UCP 600.

the seller of payment, if the seller complies with all the terms and conditions stated in the letter of credit.

Across the world the UCP (the most updated version is UCP 600) is the most prominent governing rules for letters of credit transactions. Courts in most countries rely on the UCP to interpret the rights of the parties to a letter of credit. Under the principle of independence, a letter of credit transaction is separate from the underlying sales transactions between the seller and the buyer. The issuing bank, the confirming bank or a nominated bank shall not invoke any of the defenses arising from the underlying sales contract to delay or refuse to pay. However, after the examination of the documents presented by the seller within five banking days, the bank may duly dishonor the payment where a discrepancy has been found and a notice has been made following the procedures of UCP 600. Standby letters of credit, although mainly governed by the same rules as the documentary letters of credit, are substantially different schemes. Standby letters of credit are guarantees of the seller's performance to the buyer. The buyer is the beneficiary and the beneficiary is entitled to payment upon presentation of a signed statement by the beneficiary that the seller has not performed his obligations under the contract.

Although most of the discussion has focused on transactions involving in the sale of goods, the same legal concepts and rules discussed also apply to the payment in many other different types of transactions, including the international transfer of technologies and the international trade in services.

Exercises

I. True or False Statements

1. Direct payment by buyers such as M/T, T/T and D/D is the simplest mode of international payment and no bank is involved in the process of payment.

2. Documentary collections and documentary letters of credit belong to the documentary sale where documents of a bill of lading and a draft are often used.

3. Drafts, checks and promissory notes are all written and unconditional orders to pay a sum of money.

4. *Convention on the Unification of the Law Relating to Bills of Exchange and Promissory Notes* (ULB) is the internationally uniform rules governing the bill of exchange.

5. An advising bank is a bank that independently promises that it will pay, accept, or negotiate a letter of credit when the documents specified in the credit are presented to it

and the other terms and conditions of the credit have been complied with.

6. According to the rule of strict compliance, data in the documents must be identical to the requirements of the letter of credit.

7. Fraud is a well-established exception to the principle of independence under the UCP 600.

8. Fraud exception was confirmed by some national laws such as the UCC and the law of China, but the UCP 600 has no provisions concerning fraud exception.

9. Banks including a nominated bank, a confirming bank, and the issuing bank shall each have a maximum of seven banking days following the day of presentation to determine if a presentation is complying.

10. Upon finding discrepancies, the issuing bank must send a waiver of discrepancy to the applicant of the letter of credit under UCP 600.

II. Multiple Choices

1. Which of the following statements is correct about the negotiable instrument?

> One hundred and twenty (120) days after date October 30, 2020
>
> PAY TO THE ORDER OF ABC Corporation U.S.$ 100,000 ONE HUNDRED THOUSAND U.S. DOLLARS.
>
> FOR VALUE RECEIVED AND CHARGE TO THE ACCOUNT OF Hank's Bank, 100 Elkhorn Road, Sun Valley, Idaho 83353
>
> Michael Martin

A. It may be tranferred by mere delivery.

B. The drawer is Hank's Bank.

C. It is a sight draft.

D. The payee may not be ABC Corporation.

2. Which of the following statements is not the formal requirements for a bill of exchange under the *Convention on the Unification of the Law Relating to Bills of Exchange and Promissory Notes*?

A. an unconditional order in writing

B. addressed by one person to another and signed by the person giving it

C. the addressee pays on demand or at a fixed determinable future time

D. a sum certain in money

E. to or to the order of a specified person, or to a bearer

F. the date and place of issuing the instrument

G. the words “bill of exchange” on the face of the instrument

H. the perfomance of some obligations

3. How would you respond to each of the following discrepancies?

Situation 1 The L/C calls for shipment of “1000 bed pillows, size 20×26 in”. The commercial invoice shows shipment of “1000 bed pillows, size 20×26 in”, but the B/L describes the shipment as “1000 pillows”.

Situation 2 The L/C calls for shipment of 1000 kilograms. The commercial invoice and other stipulated documents show shipment of an equal amount in pounds.

A. Both constitute discrepancies and refuse to pay.

B. Only Situation 1 constitutes discrepancy and refuses to pay.

C. Only Situation 2 constitutes discrepancy and refuses to pay.

D. Neither constitutes discrepancies and should make payment.

4. Under the relevant laws of China, in the event a fraud under the letter of credit has been proved, the payment under the letter of credit shall not be suspended in the following circumstances, except that ________ .

A. A nominated bank has made the payment in good faith according to the instruction from the issuing bank.

B. A nominated bank has in good faith honored the draft drawn under the letter of credit.

C. The confirming bank had performed its duty of payment under the letter of credit in good faith.

D. The advising bank had forwarded the the letter of credit to the issuing bank.

5. For the legal nature of the letter of credit, which of the following statements is more convincing for the legal relationship between the issuing bank and the beneficiary?

A. an agency contract

B. a third-party beneficiary contract

C. a new type of legal relationship

D. a sales contract

III. Chapter Questions

1. How do you understand the importance of the draft in international payment?

(Consider the financing function of drafts and its role in the documentary sale and the documentary credit.)

2. How many categories of banks are involved in letter of credit transactions?

3. Suppose you (the buyer) are involved in an international sale of goods and the letter of credit is used as a tool of payment. If you hope to be protected from the potential fraud committed by the seller, what should you do?

4. In case of discovering a discrepancy, how will the issuing bank act if the rules of UCP 600 apply?

5. What are the two basic principles for handling the letters of credit under the UCP 600?

6. Under the laws of China what are the provisions on the fraud exception to the principle of independence in letter of credit transactions?

7. How do you understand the standard for examination of documents stated in Article 14 of UCP 600?

8. Under what circumstances will the banks not be held liable under a letter of credit?

9. How do you understand the statement "a standby letter of credit is sometimes called as a suicide credit"?

10. Make a brief comparison between documentary letters of credit and standby letters of credit.

IV. Reading Material

The International Standard Banking Practice for the Examination of Documents under Documentary Credits (ISBP), i.e. ICC Publication 745, has evolved into a necessary companion to the UCP for determining compliance of documents with the terms of letters of credit. ISBP does not amend UCP 600. It explains how the practices articulated in UCP 600 are applied by documentary practitioners. Thus the ISBP and the UCP should be read in their entirety and not in isolation. It is, of course, recognized that the law in some countries may compel a different practice than those stated in ISBP.

The following is an extract of the International Standard Banking Practice for the Examination of Documents under Documentary Credits (ISBP) subject to UCP 600. Read and improve your understanding about the UCP 600.

The application and issuance of the credit

1) The terms of a credit are independent of the underlying transaction even if a credit

expressly refers to that transaction. To avoid unnecessary costs, delays, and disputes in the examination of documents, however, the applicant and beneficiary should carefully consider which documents should be required, by whom they should be produced and the time frame for presentation.

2) The applicant bears the risk of any ambiguity in its instructions to issue or amend a credit. Unless expressly stated otherwise, a request to issue or amend a credit authorizes an issuing bank to supplement or develop the terms in a manner necessary or desirable to permit the use of the credit.

3) The applicant should be aware that UCP 600 contains articles such as 3, 14, 19, 20, 21,23, 24, 28(i), 30 and 31 that define terms in a manner that may produce unexpected results unless the applicant fully acquaints itself with these provisions. For example, a credit requiring presentation of a bill of lading and containing a prohibition against transhipment will, in most cases, have to exclude UCP 600 sub-article 20(c) to make the prohibition against transhipment effective.

4) A credit should not require presentation of documents that are to be issued or countersigned by the applicant. If a credit is issued including such terms, the beneficiary must either seek amendment or comply with them and bear the risk of failure to do so.

5) Many of the problems that arise at the examination stage could be avoided or resolved by careful attention to detail in the underlying transaction, the credit application, and issuance of the credit as discussed.

Abbreviations

6) The use of generally accepted abbreviations, for example, "Ltd." instead of "Limited", "Int'l" instead of "International", "Co." instead of "Company", "kgs" or "kos." instead of "kilos", "Ind" instead of "Industry", "mfr" instead of "manufacturer" or "mt" instead of "metric tons"—or vice versa—does not make a document discrepant.

7) Virgules (slash marks "/") may have different meanings, and unless apparent in the context used, should not be used as a substitute for a word.

Certifications and declarations

8) A certification, declaration or the like may either be a separate document or contained within another document as required by the credit. If the certification or declaration appears in another document which is signed and dated, any certification or declaration appearing on that document does not require a separate signature or date if the certification or declaration appears to have been given by the same entity that issued and

signed the document.

Corrections and alterations

9) Corrections and alterations of information or data in documents, other than documents created by the beneficiary, must appear to be authenticated by the party who issued the document or by a party authorized by the issuer to do so. Corrections and alterations in documents which have been legalized, visaed, certified or similar, must appear to be authenticated by the party who legalized, visaed, certified etc., the document. The authentication must show by whom the authentication has been made and include the signature or initials of that party. If the authentication appears to have been made by a party other than the issuer of the document, the authentication must clearly show in which capacity that party has authenticated the correction or alteration.

10) Corrections and alterations in documents issued by the beneficiary itself, except drafts, which have not been legalized, visaed, certified or similar, need not be authenticated. See also "Drafts and calculation of maturity date".

11) The use of multiple type styles or font sizes or handwriting in the same document does not, by itself, signify a correction or alteration.

12) Where a document contains more than one correction or alteration, either each correction must be authenticated separately or one authentication must be linked to all corrections in an appropriate way. For example, if the document shows three corrections numbered 1, 2 and 3, one statement such as "Correction numbers 1, 2 and 3 above authorized by XXX" or similar, will satisfy the requirement for authentication.

[...]

Language

23) Under international standard banking practice, it is expected that documents issued by the beneficiary will be in the language of the credit. When a credit states that documents in two or more languages are acceptable, a nominated bank may, in its advice of the credit, limit the number of acceptable languages as a condition of its engagement in the credit.

Mathematical calculations

24) Detailed mathematical calculations in documents will not be checked by banks. Banks are only obliged to check total values against the credit and other required documents.

Misspellings or typing errors

25) A misspelling or typing error that does not affect the meaning of a word or

the sentence in which it occurs, does not make a document discrepant. For example, a description of the merchandise as "mashine" instead of "machine", "fountan pen" instead of "fountain pen" or "modle" instead of "model" would not make the document discrepant. However, a description as "model 123" instead of "model 321" would not be regarded as a typing error and would constitute a discrepancy.

Multiple pages and attachments or riders

26) Unless the credit or a document provides otherwise, pages which are physically bound together, sequentially numbered or contain internal cross references, however named or entitled, are to be examined as one document, even if some of the pages are regarded as an attachment. Where a document consists of more than one page, it must be possible to determine that the pages are part of the same document.

27) If a signature or endorsement is required to be on a document consisting of more than one page, the signature is normally placed on the first or last page of the document, but unless the credit or the document itself indicates where a signature or endorsement is to appear, the signature or endorsement may appear anywhere on the document.

Originals and copies

28) Documents issued in more than one original may be marked "Original", "Duplicate", "Triplicate", "First Original", "Second Original", etc. None of these markings will disqualify a document as an original.

29) The number of originals to be presented must be at least the number required by the credit, the UCP 600, or, where the document itself states how many originals have been issued, the number stated on the document.

30) It can sometimes be difficult to determine from the wording of a credit whether it requires an original or a copy, and to determine whether that requirement is satisfied by an original or a copy.

For example, where the credit requires:

a) "Invoice", "One Invoice" or "Invoice in 1 copy", it will be understood to be a requirement for an original invoice.

b) "Invoice in 4 copies", it will be satisfied by the presentation of at least one original and the remaining number as copies of an invoice.

c) "One copy of Invoice", it will be satisfied by presentation of either a copy or an original of an invoice.

31) Where an original would not be accepted in lieu of a copy, the credit must prohibit an original, e.g., "photocopy of invoice—original document not acceptable in lieu

of photocopy", or the like. Where a credit calls for a copy of a transport document and indicates the disposal instructions for the original of that transport document, an original transport document will not be acceptable.

32) Copies of documents need not be signed.

33) In addition to UCP 600 article 17, the ICC Banking Commission Policy Statement, document 470/871(Rev), titled "The determination of an 'Original' document in the context of UCP 500 sub-Article 20(b)" is recommended for further guidance on originals and copies and remains valid under UCP 600. The content of the Policy Statement appears in the Appendix of this publication, for reference purposes.

Shipping marks

34) The purpose of a shipping mark is to enable identification of a box, bag or package. If a credit specifies the details of a shipping mark, the documents mentioning the marks must show these details, but additional information is acceptable provided it is not in conflict with the credit terms.

35) Shipping marks contained in some documents often include information in excess of what would normally be considered "shipping marks", and could include information such as the type of goods, warnings as to the handling of fragile goods, net and/or gross weight of the goods, etc. The fact that some documents show such additional information, while others do not, is not a discrepancy.

36) Transport documents covering containerized goods will sometimes only show a container number under the heading "Shipping marks". Other documents that show a detailed marking will not be considered to be in conflict for that reason.

Signatures

37) Even if not stated in the credit, drafts, certificates and declarations by their nature require a signature. Transport documents and insurance documents must be signed in accordance with the provisions of UCP 600.

38) The fact that a document has a box or space for a signature does not necessarily mean that such box or space must be completed with a signature. For example, banks do not require a signature in the area titled "Signature of shipper or their agent" or similar phrases, commonly found on transport documents such as air waybills or road transport documents. If the content of a document indicates that it requires a signature to establish its validity (e.g., "This document is not valid unless signed" or similar terms), it must be signed.

39) A signature need not be handwritten. Facsimile signatures, perforated signatures,

stamps, symbols (such as chops) or any electronic or mechanical means of authentication are sufficient. However, a photocopy of a signed document does not qualify as a signed original document, nor does a signed document transmitted through a fax machine, absent an original signature. A requirement for a document to be "signed and stamped", or a similar requirement, is also fulfilled by a signature and the name of the party typed, or stamped, or handwritten, etc.

40) A signature on a company letterhead paper will be taken to be the signature of that company, unless otherwise stated. The company name need not be repeated next to the signature.

41) Documents may be titled as called for in the credit, bear a similar title, or be untitled.

For example, a credit requirement for a "Packing List" may also be satisfied by a document containing packing details whether titled "Packing Note", "Packing and Weight List", etc., or an untitled document. The content of a document must appear to fulfil the function of the required document.

42) Documents listed in a credit should be presented as separate documents. If a credit requires a packing list and a weight list, such requirement will be satisfied by presentation of two separate documents, or by presentation of two original copies of a combined packing and weight list, provided such document states both packing and weight details.

43) The tenor must be in accordance with the terms of the credit.

a) If a draft is drawn at a tenor other than sight, or other than a certain period after sight, it must be possible to establish the maturity date from the data in the draft itself.

b) As an example of where it is possible to establish a maturity date from the data in the draft, if a credit calls for drafts at a tenor 60 days after the bill of lading date, where the date of the bill of lading is 12 July 2007, the tenor could be indicated on the draft in one of the following ways:

i. "60 days after bill of lading date 12 July 2007", or

ii. "60 days after 12 July 2007", or

iii. "60 days after bill of lading date" and elsewhere on the face of the draft state "bill of lading date 12 July 2007", or

iv. "60 days date" on a draft dated the same day as the date of the bill of lading, or

v. "10 September 2007", i.e. 60 days after the bill of lading date.

c) If the tenor refers to xxx days after the bill of lading date, the on board date is deemed to be the bill of lading date even if the on board date is prior to or later than the date of issuance of the bill of lading.

d) UCP 600 article 3 provides guidance that where the words “from” and “after” are used to determine maturity dates of drafts, the calculation of the maturity commences the day following the date of the document, shipment, or other event, i.e., 10 days after or from March 1 is March 11.

e) If a bill of lading showing more than one on board notation is presented under a credit which requires drafts to be drawn, for example, at 60 days after or from bill of lading date, and the goods according to both or all on board notations were shipped from ports within a permitted geographical area or region, the earliest of these on board dates will be used for calculation of the maturity date. Example: the credit requires shipment from European port, and the bill of lading evidences on board vessel “A” from Dublin August 16 and on board vessel “B” from Rotterdam August 18. The draft should reflect 60 days from the earliest on board date in a European port, i.e., August 16.

f) If a credit requires drafts to be drawn, for example, at 60 days after or from bill of lading date, and more than one set of bills of lading is presented under one draft, the date of the last bill of lading will be used for the calculation of the maturity date.

44) While the examples refer to bill of lading dates, the same principles apply to all transport documents.

Maturity date

45) If a draft states a maturity date by using an actual date, the date must have been calculated in accordance with the requirements of the credit.

46) For drafts drawn “at XXX days sight”, the maturity date is established as follows:

a) in the case of complying documents, or in the case of non-complying documents where the drawee bank has not provided a notice of refusal, the maturity date will be XXX days after the date of receipt of documents by the drawee bank.

b) in the case of non-complying documents where the drawee bank has provided a notice of refusal and subsequent approval, at the latest XXX days after the date of acceptance of the draft by the drawee bank. The date of acceptance of the draft must be no later than the date the issuing bank accepts the waiver of the applicant.

47) In all cases the drawee bank must advise the maturity date to the presenter. The calculation of tenor and maturity dates, as shown above, would also apply to credits designated as being available by deferred payment, i.e., where there is no requirement for a draft to be presented by the beneficiary.

Banking days, grace days, delays in remittance

48) Payment must be available in immediately available funds on the due date at the place where the draft or documents are payable, provided such due date is a banking day in that place. If the due date is a non-banking day, payment will be due on the first banking day following the due date. Delays in the remittance of funds, such as grace days, the time it takes to remit funds, etc., must not be in addition to the stated or agreed due date as defined by the draft or documents.

Part IV Law of International Trade in Services

Learning Objectives
(1) Getting to know the fundamentals of international trade in services
(2) Having a command of types of intellectual property rights recognized under international conventions and the laws of China
(3) Understanding the international intellectual property organizations and treaties relating to the protection and transfer of intellectual property
(4) Having a deep understanding of intellectual property licensing
(5) Grasping the rules that govern the transfer of intellectual property

The services sector is the fastest-growing sector of the world economy, providing more than 60% of global output and, in many countries, an even larger share of employment. Over the past 20 years, trade in services has become the most dynamic segment of world trade, growing more quickly than trade in goods. Developing countries and transition economies have played an increasingly important role in this area, increasing their share in exports of world services from a quarter to one-third over this period.

It should be underscored that services account for a larger share of world trade than suggested by traditional statistics. Trade in services also contribute to global value chains in two ways: First, services are disaggregated and traded as separate "tasks", thus creating global value chains. Second, services play a role of enablers in making global values chains in goods operational and smooth. Today, manufacturing companies rely on many service inputs that are embodied in their exports of goods and in value-added terms services represent half of the value of world trade. Take automobile industry as an example. The U.S. automobile industry has a great variety of inputs from different service sectors, whether domestic or foreign, including research and development services, design services, advertising services, data processing services and insurance services. Taken together, the contribution of services to a manufactured car can be as high as 30%. Thus, services are an integral part of global production networks. Therefore, when we discuss international business law, we should not ignore rules governing international trade in services.

1 Introduction to International Trade in Services

The previous chapters in Part III have focused on discussing the legal framework for trade in goods. However, trade in services do have some special features that distinguish itself from trade in goods.

◆ Features of Trade in Services

Trade in services, by its nature, is different from trade in goods. First, services are intangible, invisible, and perishable, and usually require simultaneous production and consumption. Trade in goods involves transactions of tangible products, no matter manufactured products, raw materials or agricultural products. In merchandise trade, tangible goods are produced, stored, moved and consumed at different places and times. Unlike goods, services cannot be stored and moved around for later consumption. Unlike goods that can be shipped, the provision of services, in many cases, requires the presence of service suppliers (proximity). For example, we need to go to the barber shop to have our hair cut. When we feel sick, we need to see doctor in person. Doctor will have face-to-face conversation with us and use medical devices to figure out the problems. Therefore, the supply of many services is possible only through the simultaneous physical presence of both producer and consumer. Second, a tangible border exists in the case of trade in goods. As a result, countries can collect tariffs at the border, and use tariffs as a means of protection for its domestic production. Such border does not exist in the case of trade in services, however. The only way for a country to protect its domestic services industries is to impose regulations on the product (services) or product providers (service suppliers). Thus, the approach under the GATT to negotiate tariffs to liberalize trade cannot be transplanted to services trade liberalization. Third, many services industries are highly regulated, due to certain market failures (such as information asymmetry). This feature makes it a daunting task for trade negotiators to identify barriers to services trade. Therefore, liberalization of trade in services must follow a different approach from that of trade in goods. Based on the features of trade in services, it is understandable that in many instances, in order to be commercially meaningful, liberalization of trade in services must extend to cross-border movements of the consumer, the establishment of a commercial presence within a market, or the temporary movement of the service provider himself. That is the reason why international rules define trade in services through different modes of supply.

◆ **Definition of Trade in Services**

The World Trade Organization's *General Agreement on Trade in Services* (hereinafter as GATS) entered into force in 1995, as the first and only multilateral agreement governing international trade in service. It was created in the wake of the "growing importance of trade in services for the growth and development of the world economy", aimed at "the expansion of such trade". The notion of "services" is not explicitly defined in the GATS or elsewhere in the WTO law and jurisprudence. However, Article I:2 of GATS defines "trade in services" as the supply of a service in four different "modes of supply": ①

(1) Mode 1 covers services supplied from one country to another (for example, call center services or online medical services). It is service per se moving across borders.

(2) Mode 2 covers consumers or firms making use of a service in another country (for example, Chinese tourists traveling abroad or Chinese students studying overseas).

(3) Mode 3 covers a foreign company setting up subsidiaries or branches to provide services in another country (such as Disney that had opened an entertainment park in Shanghai or a British bank setting up a branch in Beijing).

(4) Mode 4 covers individuals travelling from their own country to supply services in another (for example, a consultant travelling abroad to provide an IT service or a woman providing baby care overseas).

In the past, many services can only be commercialized through physical proximity of suppliers and consumers. However, with rapid and innovative technology development, many services can be transported through fast-speed internet. Just take this online course as example. Traditionally, teachers need to deliver a course through face-to-face communication in a physical classroom. In recent years, online courses have gained exponential popularity. Both teachers and students gradually acknowledge that high-quality education services can be achieved without physical presence. Especially, during the Covid-19 period, education services, financial services and entertaining services have partly transformed from off-line approach to online approach, presenting a promising

---

① These modes of supply are not of definitional value only but are important for the listing of specific commitments for different sectors and subsectors. See Mira Burri, *Trade in Services Regulation in the Data-Driven Economy*, 12 Trade, Law and Development 208, 213 (2020).

market for mode 1. Hence, it is evident that in a digital era mode 1 is more promising. At the same time, we have to admit that some sectors of services in nature cannot be supplied remotely, such as constructions and maritime transportation services.

◆ **Services Sectors**

International trade in services covers a great variety of services sectors, ranging from business and professional services to transport services. Though sectors listed in Exhibit IV-1 all belong to international trade in services, it should be stressed that, services sectors are highly differentiated from each other, and even within the same services sector, quality of a service may vary from one service provider to another. For the main services sectors, see Exhibit IV-1.

Exhibit IV-1

Main Services Sectors

Business and professional services, including:
- Accountancy services
- Advertising services
- Architectural and engineering services
- Computer and related services
- Legal services

Communication services
- Audiovisual services
- Postal and courier services
- Telecommunications

Construction and related services
Distribution services
Educational services
Energy services
Environmental services
Financial services
Health and social services
Tourism services
Transport services

2 International Protection of Intellectual Property

Intellectual property is considered to play a major role in international trade in services. Intellectual property is the key source of services imports and exports including the software publishing, motion picture and video, financial services, science R&D, and management and technical consulting industries. Right holders may authorize the use of technologies, trademarks, and entertainment products that they own to entities in foreign countries, resulting in revenues through royalties and license fees.

2.1 Fundamentals of Intellectual Property Rights

Intellectual property refers to creation of the human mind, and in essence, useful information or knowledge. Intellectual property rights are legal rights granted by governments to encourage innovation and creative output by ensuring that creators reap the benefits of their inventions or works. They may take forms such as copyrights, trademarks, patents, trade secrets, or geographical indications. Through intellectual property rights, governments grant a temporary legal monopoly to innovators by giving them the right to limit or control the use of their creations by others. Intellectual property rights may be traded or licensed to others, usually in return for fees and/or royalty payments.

Regardless of the categories, intellectual property is a creature of national law. International law does not create it, although it does establish rules and guidelines for its uniform definition and protection, and it sets up ways that make it easier for owners to acquire rights in different countries. National laws are also important in establishing the rules for assigning and licensing intellectual property. Before discussing the international transfer of intellectual property, this Chapter shall begin with the fundamentals of intellectual property rights.

2.1.1 Copyrights

Copyrights belong to the authors of any work that can be fixed in a tangible medium for the purpose of communication, such as literary, dramatic, musical or artistic works; sound recordings; films; radio and television broadcasts; computer programs.[①] Article 3 of *Copyright Law of the People's Republic of China*[②] provides that the term "work" in this Law includes, among other things, work of literature, art, natural sciences, social sciences, engineering and technology, which are created in any of the following forms: (1) written works; (2) oral works; (3) musical, dramatic, quyi, choreographic and acrobatic works; (4) works of fine arts and architecture; (5) photographic works; (6) cinematographic works and works created by a process analogous to cinematography; (7) graphic works

---

① See Ray August, *International Business Law: Texts, Cases and Readings*, Higher Education Press, 2002, p.469.

② *Copyright Law of the People's Republic of China* was promulgated in 1990 and three amendments have been made respectively in 2001, 2010 and 2020.

such as drawings of engineering designs and product designs, maps and sketches, and model works; (8) computer software; and (9) other intellectual property in line with the characteristics of the work. Unlike patents or trademarks, copyright arises automatically upon the creation of work, and there is no registration process. To be entitled to ownership of the work, the author shall be required to produce original and dated evidence of the creation of the work, prove his/her authorship and the first publication of the work in a country. As for the requirements for a work to be protected by copyright, the Copyright Law and related regulations of China provide: (1) it should be the expression of ideas or feelings; (2) it should be original; (3) it should be able to be reproduced in material form. Oral works can receive copyright protection because they can be reproduced by writing or recording.

Copyrights can date back to the fifteenth century. It is recorded that the first known copyright was issued by the Duke of Milan in 1481, granting the exclusive right to print a work to the printer of a local history. The first true copyright act, which protected authors without their having to obtain an individual grant from their states, was enacted in England in 1709. Later similar statutes appeared in Spain, the United States, France and Germany. In 1886, 10 countries including Belgium, Britain, France, Germany, Italy, Spain, and Switzerland, signed *Berne Convention for the Protection of Literary and Artistic Works* (the Berne Convention) at Berne, Switzerland. It is by far the most influential copyright convention. Today most of the states in the world have ratified this Convention including China, U.K. and the United States.①

Theoretically a copyright is classified into **pecuniary rights and moral rights**. The "pecuniary rights" inherent in a copyright allow an author to exploit a work for economic gain. In particular, this includes the right to reproduce the work, the right to distribute the work, and (depending on the nature of the work) the right of public performance. Whereas moral right is an author's personal rights to keep others from tampering with his works. The three basic moral rights are: (1) the right to object to distortion, mutilation or modification, (2) the right to be recognized as the author, and (3) the right to control public access to the work. In a few countries there is the fourth moral right: the right to correct or retract a work. Moral rights are not recognized in the copyright laws of the common law legal system such as the U.K. and the United States. They claim that the author can bring an action against the distortion, mutilation or modification of his/her work according to contract law and tort law. Considering such a difference in legal systems around the

① Later in this Chapter the Berne Convention will be discussed in more details.

world, the *Agreement on Trade-Related Aspects of Intellectual Property Rights* (TRIPS Agreement) requires WTO members to comply with provisions of the Berne Convention with one significant exception: member states are not required to grant moral rights to authors. Thus it seems that the authors in the common law countries will continue to do without moral rights, despite the provisions in the Berne Convention and the practice in most of the other states.

A copyright applies only within the territory of the state granting it. About the duration for which copyrights may be granted, the TRIPS Agreement sets the minimum time period of **the life of author plus 50 years**. Some WTO members provide for longer terms of duration for personal works. For example, Germany, Austria, Switzerland and the United States grant protection for 70 years after the mortality of the author. Spain grants protection for the life of author plus 60 years.

2.1.2 Patents

Patents are "a statutory privilege granted by the government to inventors, and to others deriving their rights from the inventor, for a fixed period of years, to exclude other persons from manufacturing, using or selling a patented **product** or from utilizing a patented **method** or **process**".[①]

There are two basic reasons why governments grant patents. One is that patents are a confirmation of the private property rights of the inventor. The second is that a patent is a grant of a special monopoly, which prevents others from utilizing the patentee's invention without his consent, to encourage invention and industrial development across the state. Sometimes these purposes are at odds with each other. On the private side are the inventor's claim for recognition and economic advantage. On the public side, there is not only the interests of the government in promoting economic development but also the social benefits in encouraging intervention, as well as the desire of consumers to purchase goods at reasonable price. Some legal writers have suggested that the function of the patent law is, therefore, to reconcile and satisfy the whole scheme of public and private interests pressing for recognition.

◆ Inventions That Qualify for Patent Protection

To acquire a patent, an inventor must show (depending on the country issuing the

---

① See *The Role of Patents in the Transfer of Technology to Developing Countries*, UN Doc. Sales No. 65. II. B.1, 1964, p.9.

patent) that a new product, method or process has **novelty**, **inventiveness**, and **industrial utility**. Novelty means that no other inventor can have obtained a patent for the same invention. The invention has not been made available to the public anywhere in the world by written or oral description, by use or in any other way. Sometimes "great minds think alike"—two or more inventors may reach the invention at the same time and each file a patent application. Under such circumstances the rule of "early coming, early serving" will apply in order to avoid granting the same patent to two patentees. That is, the early application is deemed to be the prior invention when considering the novelty of the latter application. Inventiveness means that the idea underlying an invention cannot have been obvious at the time the invention was made to a person having ordinary skill in the art. Here "a person having ordinary skill in the art" has been described as "a skilled technician who is well acquainted with workshop technique and who has carefully read all the relevant literature. He is supposed to have an unlimited capacity to assimilate the contents of, it may be, scores of specifications but to be incapable of a scintilla of invention."[①] Industrial utility means that the product or process is one that can be used in industry or commerce (capable of industrial application). Just by this nature can patents be expected to stimulate the economic development of a country.

Disputes about the existence of novelty, inventiveness, and industrial utility can come up at different times in the life of a patent. These disputes most commonly arise while the inventor's application is being reviewed by the patent office of a country, during the appeal of a denial, during a revocation or cancellation hearing, or during an infringement suit.

The patent application process varies from country to country. In some countries, it begins with a simple review of the application form to see if it is complete; in others, it starts with an extensive search of domestic and foreign materials to determine if the product or process is both novel and inventive. The next step is to publish notice of the application. In most countries the notice has to include all of the information contained in the inventor's application. The reason for doing this is to give interested third parties the opportunity to oppose the application. In developing countries, it also serves as a substitute for an examination of novelty and inventiveness by a patent office.

◆ Inventions Excluded from Patent Protection (Non-patentability)

Besides inventions that do not meet the above basic qualifications for a patent, the TRIPS Agreement allows countries to deny patents, if it wishes, to (1) diagnostic,

---

① Clive M. Schmitthoff & David A. G. Sarre, *Mercantile Law*, Stevens & Sons, 1984, p.610.

therapeutic, and surgical methods for the treatment of humans and animals; (2) plants and animals other than microorganisms and plant varieties, and (3) essentially biological processes for the production of plants or animals. The TRIPS Agreement allows a WTO member to deny a patent to an inventor in order to protect the lives or health of humans, animals, or plants or to protect the environment from serious injury. Besides, the Agreement also allows the WTO member to deny a patent to an inventor in order to protect the order of the public or morality.① In conformity with the TRIPS Agreement, *Patent Law of the People's Republic of China* provides that two types of inventions cannot receive patent protection: (1) illegal inventions, and (2) non-patentable subject matters. The "illegal inventions" refer to the inventions whose purpose is contrary to the laws, the public policy or public interests. The non-patentable subject matters include: scientific discoveries, rules and methods of mental activities, methods of diagnosis or treatment of disease, new varieties of animals and plants, and substances by means of nuclear fission.

◆ **Duration of Patents**

The TRIPS Agreement sets the minimum duration of patents at 20 years. The 20-year duration is followed by almost all WTO members.

2.1.3 Trademarks

Trademarks are used by merchants and others to identify themselves and their products from similar goods or services supplied by others. Now trademarks have become one of the core factors in the competitiveness of enterprises. In the broad sense, there are different kinds of trademarks. (1) A **trademark**, in common sense, is any word, name, symbol, or device or any combination thereof adopted and used by a manufacturer or merchant to identify his goods and distinguish them from those manufactured or sold by others. (2) A **trade name** is the name of the manufacturer who is commercialing the brand. (3) A **service mark** is a mark used in the sale or advertising of services to identify the services of one person and distinguish them from the services of another. (4) **Collective marks** are used by members of an association, the collective or cooperative organization to identify their products or services to their members. (5) A **certification mark** is a mark used exclusively by a licensee or franchisee, to indicate that a product meets certain standards. Among the above kinds of trademarks, it should be noted that a trademark is different from a trade name. Once a trade name was used to denote any mark descriptive

---

① See Article 27, Para. 2 and Para. 3 of the TRIPS Agreement.

of a good or service, but today, it is also a company business name. For example, "P&G" is a trade name for "P&G Inc.", and "PANTENE" is one of the trademarks of its products. A related concept to trademarks is the geographic indication. The geographic indication acts to protect the quality and reputation of a distinctive product originated in a certain region; however, the benefit does not accrue to a sole producer, but rather the producers of a product originating from a particular region. Geographic indications are generally sought for agricultural products, or wines and spirits.

◆ Acquiring Trademarks

Trademarks are acquired in two ways: by use and by registration. In either case, a person claiming a trademark must show that it does not infringe on any other mark and that it is distinctive. Distinctive means that the mark is such that it will distinguish the goods or services with which it is connected from other similar goods.

◆ The Term of Registered Trademarks

The TRIPS Agreement requires that members of the WTO protect trademarks for terms of at least seven years. Also, it provides for trademarks to be renewable indefinitely. Under the *Trademark Law of the People's Republic of China*, the duration term for a trademark is 10 years and renewable. ①

◆ Trademark Infringement

Trademarks have several functions. From the perspective of an owner, a trademark is the fortune and the right to put a product, with this mark, into circulation. From the viewpoint of a consumer, a trademark serves to designate the origin or source of a service, indicate a particular standard of quality, protect the consumer from confusion and help the consumer to make a purchase decision among the various similar products or services.

Trademark infringement is the unauthorized use of a trademark or service mark on or in connection with goods and/or services in a manner that is likely to cause confusion about the source of the goods and/or services. Trademark law seeks to prevent others from intentionally or unintentionally infringing on the owner's mark. A trademark owner who believes its mark is being infringed may file a civil action to a competent court. The user may defend its use of a similar mark on the basis that such use will not create confusion in the consumers, either through the unrelated nature of the goods or markets or their geographic distance apart.

---

① *Trademark Law of the People's Republic of China* was promulgated in 1982, and four amendments have been made respectively in 1993, 2001, 2013, and 2019.

Case IV-1

Anheuser-Busch Inc. v. Budejovicky Budvar N.P.

Court of Appeal—Civil Division

February 07, 2000, [2000] EWCA Civ 30

Judgment

Lord Justice Peter Gibson

This dispute is the third round of the continuing conflict in the English courts between the American brewer, Anheuser-Busch Inc. ("AB"), and the Czech brewer, Budejovicky Budvar N.P. ("BB"), over the use and registration of the mark BUDWEISER and related marks in relation to beer.

The mark is derived from the name of the town in Bohemia which was known, when the town was part of the Austro-Hungarian empire, by its German name Budweis but which is now called by its Czech name Ceske Budejovice in the Czech Republic. For hundreds of years beer has been brewed there. BB is the successor of a brewing enterprise established in 1895. Its brewery is in the town. AB established its brewing business in Missouri during the nineteenth century. In 1875 it adopted Budweiser as the trade name under which it sold its beer in the U.S.A. In so doing AB was inspired by the method of brewing adopted in Budweis, but its use of the name is simply as a trade mark with no signification of the geographical origin of the product.

In 1919 BB and another brewery in Budweis which exported beer to the U.S.A. objected to the registration in the U.S.A. of the BUDWEISER trademark, that objection being based on a claim that the Budweiser name signified a geographical origin. That dispute led to a compromise agreement by which BB acknowledged AB's right to use the mark in connection with its beers in the U.S.A. and all other extra-European countries while AB acknowledged BB's right to use the word Budweiser whether in Europe or in North America and other extra-European countries as descriptive of the geographical origin of beer brewed by it at Budweis. Neither that agreement nor a further agreement made in 1939 by AB and BB specified that either was entitled to use BUDWEISER as a trademark in the U.K.

Prior to 1919 BB had used the word Budweiser as descriptive of its beer's geographical origin but not as a trade name, the beer being marketed under trade names one of which was Budvar. That is a combination of the first three letters of Budweis (or Budejovice) and "var", the Czech word for "brew". Between 1920 and 1960 the labelling concentrated generally on the trade name, Budvar. In 1960 BB registered BUDWEISER as an international mark in Europe, and that word was then incorporated from 1960 to 1970 into export labels printed in German, French and English. In 1967 BB effected various registrations as appellations d'origine with the International Bureau for the protection of intellectual property, including Budweiser Bier and Budweis Beer.

After 1967 beer with labelling giving prominence to Budweiser (with Budvar in smaller lettering) was consigned to (amongst other countries) Great Britain. The label stated in English that the beer "was brewed and bottled by the Budweiser Budvar Brewery, Ceske Budejovice, Czechoslovakia". BB obtained its designation Budweiser Budvar in 1967. No serious attempt was made by BB to export its beer to the U.K. prior to 1969. BB had registered the name BUDVAR as a trade mark for beer, and in 1962 had registered BUDWEISER BUDBRÄU but disclaiming any exclusivity in the use of the word BUDWEISER. In 1971 the mark BUDWEISER BUDVAR was registered, again with a similar disclaimer. Prior to 1973 no significant quantity of BB's beer was sold in the U.K. and BB had no significant reputation here. Budweiser as a name associated with AB's beer became well-known to a substantial number of people in the U.K. as a result of visits to the U.S.A. and of advertisements in films and American magazines circulating here.

On August 1, 1979, AB commenced proceedings against BB, seeking an injunction to prevent BB from selling or dealing in any beer not being AB's beer by the name Budweiser or Bud and from passing off in any other manner. BB counterclaimed for similar relief against AB. Whitford J., in a decision reported under the name Anheuser-Busch v. Budejovicky Budvar [1984] F.S.R. 413, dismissed both the claim and the counterclaim. He held that neither AB nor BB was disentitled to use the name Budweiser since in 1979 there was a dual reputation and neither had achieved the reputation improperly.

The second round of litigation between the parties was triggered by BB applying in 1979 to register BUD as a trade mark in class 32 for beer. This was opposed by AB. The Assistant Registrar, Mr. Myall, held that the application was properly registrable under s12(2) and that the opposition failed. Following that decision, AB registered the same mark for its beer.

Four further applications for registration have occasioned this third round of litigation... The marks which AB and BB respectively seek to register are, of course, identical and so are the goods in respect of which registration is sought. It would not be lawful to register both these marks except in exercise of the power conferred by Section 12(2)...

In my judgment the decisive factor in this litigation is that the exercise of the judge's discretion under s12(2) cannot be impugned. It focused on the practical realities, at least in part consequent on the sensible application of the previous decisions of the Court of Appeal and Walton J. Customers for either product who genuinely appreciate that there are two products, and that they are different, and who favour the one over the other, are likely to make their orders by specifying or referring to American Bud, or Budweiser, or Czech Bud, or Budweiser. If they are ignorant of the difference, or the difference is immaterial to them, they will ask for Budweiser or Bud and be supplied with whichever product the vendor has in stock. If he happens to stock both, he may ask the customer to specify which, and may then, at any rate if business is slack, become involved in a discussion of the differing qualities of the two beers, and if in expansive mood, with a history lesson. As to the variety he may elect to stock, if he only has room for one, his preference will be for the brew which experience suggests that the majority of his customers prefer. I remain unpersuaded that any consequent problems following the registrations sought by both AB and BB would give rise to confusion or difficulty in the public mind which would be of more than minimal significance and in my judgment it is too late for anything practical now to be done, without simultaneously putting one or other product at a significant and unfair commercial disadvantage as against the other.

I agree that the appeals by both AB and BB should be dismissed.[①]

2.1.4 Trade Secrets

A trade secret is any type of valuable information that is not generally known and is subject to reasonable efforts by the owner to keep it confidential. Examples of trade secrets

① More details about the disputes between AB and BB may be found at https://lawcarenigeria.com/anheuser-busch-inc-v-budejovicky-budvar-n-p-2000-ewca-civ-30-7-february-2000/.

may include blueprints, customer lists, pricing information, and source code. Unlike other forms of intellectual property, trade secrets are protected by contract, tort and trade secrecy laws, rather than by particular statutory enactments.

The TRIPS Agreement requires the WTO members to protect what the Agreement calls "undisclosed information". That is, natural and legal persons must be given the legal means to prevent information from being disclosed to, acquired by, or used by others without their consent in a manner contrary to honest commercial practice. The information, however, must (1) be secret, (2) have commercial value because it is a secret, and (3) have been reasonably protected from disclosure by its owner (Article 39 of TRIPS Agreement). For example, the secret recipe of "11 herbs and spices" for Kentucky Fried Chicken (KFC) lies in a bank vault. Few people know the secret recipe, and they are contractually obligated to secrecy. In manufacture process, the ingredients are mixed by two different companies in two different locations and then combined elsewhere in a third, separate location. To mix the final formula, a computer processing system is used to blend the mixtures together and ensure that no one outside KFC has the complete recipe. Such a recipe can be recognized as trade secret or undisclosed information under TRIPS Agreement.

In most cases, the legal protection given to trade secrets comes about in connection with its use by assignee, licensee, or employee. That is, the owner of trade secrets may prevent an assignee, licensee, or employee from disclosing secret information to third parties by agreements. Such agreements may take the forms of confidential agreement, non-competition agreement or confidentiality provisions in the franchise agreement. For example, a franchise agreement covers the following clauses:

"Franchisee shall not at any time, without franchisor's prior written consent, copy, duplicate, record, or otherwise reproduce in any manner any part of the manuals, updates, supplements, or related materials, in whole or in part, or otherwise make the same available to any unauthorized person.

"The manuals at all times remain the sole property of franchisor; upon the expiration or termination, for any reason, of the franchise agreement, franchisee shall return to franchisor the manuals and all supplements thereto."

2.2 International Intellectual Property Organizations and Treaties

Intellectual property rights (IPR) traditionally have been matters of national concern. Individual nation states have developed IPR regimes reflecting their domestic needs and priorities. Lying at the heart of intellectual property protection are the laws of states having territorial application. However, in an effort to drive these national rules of application toward greater uniformity, states have subscribed to a variety of international organizations and international treaties. Among them two international organizations currently play an active role in defining intellectual property rights and administering the international treaties that govern those rights.

2.2.1 International Intellectual Property Organizations

◆ World Intellectual Property Organization

The World Intellectual Property Organization (WIPO) was set up in 1970, the mission of which is "to lead the development of a balanced and effective intellectual property system that enables innovation and creativity for the benefit of all". There are now more than 170 member states of this organization, including China. The WIPO's primary function is to administer a group of IPR treaties which put forth minimum standards for member states. All international IPR treaties, save TRIPS Agreement, are administered by WIPO. In order to address digital technology issues not dealt with in the TRIPS Agreement, WIPO established the WIPO Copyright Treaty (WCT) and WIPO Performance and Phonograms Treaty (WPPT) in 1996, oftentimes collectively referred to as the "WIPO Internet Treaties". Recent WIPO efforts have focused on patent law. In June 2000, WIPO signatories adopted the Patent Law Treaty (PLT), which called for harmonization of patent procedures. This agreement went into force on April 28, 2005.

One of WIPO's more important tasks is to facilitate the transfer of technology, especially to and among developing countries. Thus WIPO has established two permanent committees: Committee for Development Cooperation Related to Industrial Property and Committee for Development Cooperation Related to Copyrights and Neighboring Rights responsible for helping countries modernizing their national intellectual property laws.[①]

WIPO's other functions include assisting member states through training programs, legislative information, intellectual property institutional development, automation and office modernization efforts, and public awareness activities. WIPO's enforcement activities are more limited than those of the WTO. Through its Advisory Committee on Enforcement (ACE), WIPO cooperates with member states to promote international coordination on enforcement activities.

---

① For more information about the operation of WIPO, see http://www.wipo.int/.

◆ **Council for Trade-Related Aspects of Intellectual Property Rights**

The Council for Trade-Related Aspects of Intellectual Property Rights (TRIPS Council) was created in 1995 with the adoption of the *Agreement Establishing the World Trade Organization* (WTO Agreement). The Council is responsible for overseeing the TRIPS Agreement, which sets minimum standards on IPR protection and enforcement with which all WTO members must comply. In particular, the Council is responsible for monitoring WTO members' compliance with the TRIPS Agreement, for helping members consult with each other on trade-related aspects of intellectual property rights, and for assisting members in settling disputes. The Council consults with WIPO.

2.2.2 Intellectual Property Treaties

Most matters relating to international protection of intellectual property rights are regulated by multilateral treaties. Most of these treaties are administered by the World Intellectual Property Organization and the Council for Trade-Related Aspects of Intellectual Property Rights.

The principal comprehensive agreement establishing general intellectual property obligations for most countries of the world is the ***Agreement on Trade-Related Aspects of Intellectual Property Rights*** (**TRIPS Agreement**), which came into effect in 1995 with the adoption of the *Agreement Establishing the World Trade Organization* (WTO Agreement).

The goal of the TRIPS Agreement is to create a multilateral and comprehensive set of rights and obligations governing the international trade in intellectual property rights. To accomplish this goal, the Agreement establishes a common minimum of protection for intellectual property rights applicable within all the WTO members. This common minimum is given force in five ways.

(1) The WTO members are required to be parties to the following conventions: (a) the *International Convention for Protection of Industrial Property*, or Paris Convention, of 1883; (b) *Berne Convention for the Protection of Literary and Artistic Property* of 1887 as revised in 1971; (c) *International Convention for the Protection of Performers, Producers of Phonograms, and Broadcasting Organizations*, or Rome Convention, of 1961; and (d) the 1989 *Treaty on Intellectual Property in Respect of Integrated Circuits*.

(2) The TRIPS Agreement fills in the gaps in many of these conventions. For example, it specifies the minimum duration of patents, copyrights, and trademarks. The TRIPS Agreement sets the minimum duration of patents at 20 years, and sets the minimum time period for which copyrights may be granted at 50 years. The TRIPS Agreement

requires that members of the World Trade Organization protect trademarks for terms of at least seven years. Also, it provides for trademarks to be renewable indefinitely.

(3) Dispute settlement is now governed by the TRIPS Agreement.

(4) Transition periods are specified for when developed countries (1996), developing countries (2000), and the least developed countries (2006) must bring themselves fully into compliance with the TRIPS Agreement.

(5) The basic principles of the *General Agreement on Tariffs and Trade*—such as national treatment and transparency—are made applicable to the field of intellectual property rights.

The principal convention dealing with artistic property is the ***Berne Convention for the Protection of Literary and Artistic Property***, better known as the **Berne Convention**. It deals with the granting of copyrights among signatory nations. The signatory nations are bound by four principles. These are: (1) national treatment, which requires member states to afford the works of authors from other signatory states the same treatment as those of their own citizens, (2) unconditional protection and member states must provide protection without any formalities. All that an author needs to do is affix the symbol © and the year of authorship to provide copyright protection throughout the world, and the Convention will grant national treatment to copyright holder from other signatory states automatically from the moment of creation rather than the time of filing, (3) independent protection in the country of origin, which allows authors who are nationals of non-member states to obtain protection within the Berne Union by publishing their works in a member state, and (4) common rules, which are the establishment of minimum standards for granting copyrights which are common in all member states.

Other conventions which deal with artistic property are the *International Convention for the Protection of Performers, Producers of Phonograms, and Broadcasting Organizations* of 1961, better known as Rome Convention which protects artists from the making of unauthorized recordings and from the unauthorized use of authorized recordings, the Phonogram Piracy Agreement of 1971 which protects producers of phonograms from the unauthorized reproduction of their works, the Agreement on Satellite Transmissions of 1974 which outlaws unauthorized satellite transmissions, and the WIPO Copyright Treaty of 1996 which extends the provisions of the Berne Convention to computer programs and databases.

The first international intellectual property treaty and the principal convention dealing with industrial property is the ***International Convention for the Protection of Industrial***

Property, or the Paris Convention. The Paris Convention was originally adopted in 1883 by 11 states and has been revised for many times. The latest amendment was made in 1979. China became a signatory state to this convention on March 19, 1985. It establishes a union of states responsible for protecting industrial rights. Three basic principles are incorporated in the Convention: (1) national treatment which requires member states to give the same protection to the nationals of other states that it grants to its own nationals. In other words, the Paris Convention eliminated the potential discrimination against foreigners in obtaining patents and trademarks; (2) right of priority which gives applicants who have filed for protection in one member state a grace period of 12 months in which to file in another member state. The Convention provides that the date of an applicant's foreign application is deemed the same as the date of the applicant's original application on the same invention within 12 months; (3) common rules which set minimum standards for the creation of intellectual property right. But the Convention does not require any minimum substantive standard of industry property protection.

In 1970, the *Patent Cooperation Treaty* (PCT) supplemented the Paris Convention by establishing a centralized utility patent application process. The PCT application is filed on a standard form with the WIPO. The WIPO processes the common application and forwards it to the countries designated by the applicant.

Other industrial property treaties are the *Treaty on Intellectual Property in Respect of Integrated Circuits* of 1989, which is not currently in force, but which the TRIPS Agreement requires the WTO members to apply, the Agreement on Sources of Goods of 1891 which forbids the importation of goods bearing false or deception indications of their source, and the *Trademark Law Treaty* of 1994 which simplifies national trademark protection rules.

3 International Transfer of Intellectual Property

Intellectual property rights may be transferred from one country to another in various ways. In addition to an owner's personal use abroad, the owner may assign part or all of the rights, **license** another to work them, or establish a **franchise**, or a government may grant a **compulsory license** so that a third party may exploit the rights.

Licensing is most widely used in international transfer of intellectual property rights. **A license** is a non-exclusive revocable privilege that allows a licensee to use a licensor's property. It means an intellectual property rights owner (licensor) authorizes a use of such rights to a licensee, in exchange for an agreed payment, such as copying software or using a patented invention to manufacture products. That is, only the right of use, not the ownership of the intellectual property is transferred through licensing. A license is created by agreement, and usually the standard-form agreement will be adopted. Under the licensing agreement of intellectual property right, the licensor wishes to transfer the exploitation of the intellectual property right, gaining the most return from the limited duration period of protection and trying to keep its dominant position in the corresponding field of technology as well. It is the licensee, which will exploit the intellectual property right and may be required by the licensing agreement to undertake considerable expenditure and accept some unreasonable restrictive clauses.

3.1 Typical Terms in International Licensing Agreements

These purposes of the licensor and licensee may find their expression in terms under a licensing agreement. The following list of terms in a licensing agreement is typical but not exhaustive:

◆ **Parties**

The information of parties to the licensing agreement and accuracy is important for obvious reasons.

◆ **Recitals**

It establishes the intentions of the parties.

◆ **Definitions**

It is required for ease of negotiation, drafting and later interpretation.

◆ **Date**

Date of agreement and effective date of license, which may be the basis for calculating the duration of the license.

◆ **Grant**

The specific description of the intellectual property under license, often accompanied by annexes of drawings or images and the like.

◆ **Acknowledgement of Title**

Intellectual property belongs to the licensor, it remains so during and after the license and that licensee will not attempt to challenge that title.

◆ **Territory**

The geographic area, customer groups, or industries in which the license may operate.

◆ **Exclusivity**

The type of license—exclusive license, sole license or non-exclusive license.

◆ **Term**

The duration of the licensing agreement within the protection period of the intellectual property.

◆ **Renewal**

Whether the term of the licensing agreement is renewal and the way to renew.

◆ **Most-Favored Treatment**

Whether the licensee has the right to better terms as may be offered and granted to future licensees in other territories.

◆ **Royalties and Payments**

Lump sums, one-time payments, periodic royalties, or sliding royalties based on performance. Basis for calculation: sales, net accounting, exclusive of taxes, duties, freight, returns or rejected goods.

◆ **Accounts and Inspection**

Whether the licensor has the right to inspect the accounts or plants of the licensee.

• **Information Sharing**

Whether the licensor and licensee shall share any information of technical advance related to the intellectual property under the license.

◆ **Technical Assistance**

In the process of licensee exploiting the intellectual property right, whether the licensor is under the obligation to provide technical assistance and training.

◆ **Confidentiality**

Requirements for non-disclosure agreements with employees, assignees, and sublicensees. Time limits for non-disclosure beyond the term of license.

◆ **Rights to Sublicense**

Whether permitted or on approval.

◆ **Rights to Assignment**

Whether permitted or on approval.

◆ **Defense of the Licensed Intellectual Property**

Costs of litigation in defense of intellectual property, sharing of damages, right to settle claims or suits.

◆ **Termination**

By the licensor: on notice, on anniversary date, for cause, or where licensee in breach of a material obligation.

By licensee: on notice, on anniversary date, for cause, or on payment of penalty.

◆ **Choice of Law**

Forum selection, applicable procedure and substantive law.

◆ **Arbitration**

Whether available, selection of arbitration institution, composition of tribunal, and applicable arbitration rules.

◆ **Force Majeure**

List of events agreed to excuse nonperformance of the licensing agreement.

Among the typical terms under a licensing agreement, some restrictive clauses is worthy of special attention.

3.2 Restrictive Business Practices in International Licensing

Licensor and licensee will negotiate over matters including conditions and extent of use, compensation, and confidentiality. For example, Article 26 of *Regulations on Technology Import and Export Administration of the People's Republic of China* (2002, amended in 2019) provides that the licensor and licensee to a technology import contract shall be under the obligation, within the scope of confidentiality and time limit thereof as agreed in the contract, to keep the undisclosed part of the technology confidential. However, in the international licensing agreements the licensor usually will impose some restrictive conditions on the licensee, which unreasonably impair free competition and unfairly restrict the due exploration of the transferred intellectual property rights. These conditions or clauses are deemed to be illegal by most countries including China. Such clauses include but not limited to price-fixing, non-competition clauses, challenges to validity, tying clauses and grant-back provisions.

Price fixing clauses require a licensee to sell products at a price specified by the licensor, are almost uniformly condemned. It may specify either maximum or minimum prices. It may be restricted to the technology or goods being licensed, or it may cover other products as well. It may apply only to the price charged by the licensee, or it may extend to the prices charged by retailers who purchase the goods from a wholesaler-licensee. Almost all the countries prohibit all forms of price-fixing. One exception is Indian, which allows a licensor to specify the price at which a licensee may sell a product manufactured using the licensor's technology or to which the licensor's trademark has been affixed.[①]

A non-competition clause forbids a licensee from entering into agreements to acquire or distribute technologies or products that compete with those furnished or designated by the licensor. Direct prohibitions may include an understanding that the licensee is required not to manufacture or sell competing technologies, or that the licensee is required to terminate the use of particular technologies or terminate the manufacture and distribution of particular products. Indirect prohibitions may require the licensee not to cooperate with a competing business or not to pay higher royalties for competing products. In general, non-competition clauses are prohibited. A few countries may allow them under exceptional circumstances. For example, when the non-competition clauses are meant to prevent disclosure of confidential technical information, they are exempted in Germany.

A "no-challenge" or "no-contest" clause forbids a licensee from challenging the validity of the statutory right granted by the licensor. The purpose of these clauses is to ensure that a licensee will comply with the agreed restrictions and payment obligations. Most countries consider such a clause in a patent or copyright license to be a restrictive trade practice. Many developing countries, including China and Brazil expressly forbid the no-challenge clauses in their regulations on transfer of technologies. Most developed countries including the United States and the European Union, interpret their unfair competition laws as forbidding no-challenge clauses in patent, and copyright licenses by case decisions. The European Union also views the no-challenge clauses in trademark licenses as in violation of the unfair competition article of the EC Treaty. The United States, however, holds that no-contest clauses in trademark licenses do not violate either trademark laws or antitrust legislation. Article 24 of *Regulations on Technology Import and Export Administration of the People's Republic of China* (2002) provides that the licensor to a technology import contract shall ensure that he is the legitimate owner of the technology supplied or one who has the right to assign or license the technology. From this provision, we may infer that such no-challenge or no-contest clause will be deemed illegal under the laws of China.

Tying clauses are provisions that require a licensee to acquire or use, separately from the technology wanted, additional goods or designated personnel either from the licensor or from a source named by the licensor. Examples of the additional goods include

---

① See Ray August, *International Business Law: Texts, Cases and Readings*, Higher Education Press, 2002, p.523.

raw materials, intermediate products, machines, or additional technology. Such clauses are prohibited in almost every country. This prohibition, however, is subject to several common exceptions. The most common exception is to allow tie-in clauses when they are necessary to protect quality standards or the goodwill of a trademark, which is established in the laws of Australia, India, U.K., and the United States. A few countries such as Australia and the U. K. allow tying clauses if the license is not charged an excessive price, or if the licensee is free to terminate the tie-in arrangements at any time.

A grant-back provision requires a patent or trade secrets recipient to transfer back to the supplier any improvements, inventions, or special trade secrets that it acquires while using the technology. Such a provision may be unilateral or reciprocal, exclusive or non-exclusive. A unilateral grant-back provision usually requires the licensee to transfer back new knowledge, while the reciprocal provision requires both to do so. Sometimes a reciprocity agreement will require both parties to exchange their developments, but sometimes only one party will be required to transfer new knowledge, while the other is required merely to pay adequate compensation. An exclusive grant-back provision will usually require the licensee to transfer any rights in the new development to the other party. A non-exclusive provision, sometimes also called a sharing provision, would allow the parties to share these rights.

Most countries prohibit grant-back provisions that unilaterally require the licensee to transfer exclusive rights to the licensor. One exception is the United States which permits such a provision so long as it has no anti-competitive effect, where the evidence shows that the grant-back provision did not unduly restrain trade or suppress industry development. However, if grant-back provisions are reciprocal and non-exclusive in the meaning of exchange technologies, laws in countries such as Brazil, Germany, Japan and Mexico expressly permit it. The relevant laws in China prohibit the grant-back provisions in the international licensing agreements from distinguishing between reciprocal ones and unilateral ones. Within the term of validity of a contract for technology import, an achievement made in improving the technology concerned belongs to the party making the improvement.

Besides the above restrictive provisions in the international licensing agreements, there are also other forms of restrictions including "restrictions that apply after the expiration of intellectual property rights". Payment obligations or restrictions based on statutory rights, which are to apply after the rights expire, are condemned worldwide. That is, countries generally hold that payment obligations or restrictions based on statutory rights must be terminated when the statutory right expires. The problem mainly exist in package licensing, which is the transfer of multiple statutory intellectual rights often including several patents and trademarks, under a single license. Generally if the licensing agreement was voluntarily concluded by both parties and payments do not extend beyond that of the last-to-expire statuary right, the agreement will be enforceable. If the licensee was at an economic disadvantage and entered into the licensing agreement on a take-it-or-leave-it basis, it will commonly be found to be illegal. This rule has been established in the United States through cases. However, the relevant laws of China prohibit any restriction that applies after the expiration of intellectual property rights.

3.3 Rules Regulating the Anti-competitive Aspects of International Licensing

International licensing of intellectual property is subject to two conflicting sets of legal rules. On one hand are the statutory rules creating intellectual property monopolies. On the other hand are unfair competition laws. In balancing these two rules, most countries have adopted rules to regulate the anti-competitive aspects of the intellectual property licensing in their regulations for transfer of technologies or competition laws. The international law also approves such regulations on intellectual property licensing. Article 40 of the TRIPS Agreement provides: "Nothing shall prevent members from specifying in their national legislation licensing practices or conditions that may in particular cases constitute an abuse of intellectual property rights having an adverse effect on competition in the relevant market. As provided above, a member may adopt, consistently with the other provisions of this Agreement, appropriate measures to prevent or control such policies, which may include, for example, exclusive grant-back conditions, conditions preventing challenges to validity, and coercive package licensing, in the light of the relevant laws and regulations of that member."

Such unfair competition rules are found in unfair competition legislation, such as the United States *Sherman Antitrust Act* or the European Union's *European Community Treaty*. These rules declare illegal any agreement or arrangement that adversely affects competition within the national state or, in the case of the EU, within the common market or any conduct that tends to monopolize trade. However, these rules, at the same time, declare some exemptions of licensing agreements. The EU Commission, for example, may do so either through block grants that apply to a particular category of agreements or on a case-by-case basis when the overall effect of a license "contributes to improving the production or distribution of goods, or to promoting technical or economic progress, while allowing consumers a fair share of the resulting benefit".① The U.S. courts arrive at the same end by applying a "rule of reason". Thus except for certain agreements, such as horizontal price fixing, which the courts regard as illegal, the courts will consider what overall impact a particular agreement will have on competition before declaring it invalid.

According to the *Foreign Trade Law of the People's Republic of China* (2004),② in the international licensing agreement, if the intellectual property right owner is involved in any one of such practices as preventing the licensee form challenging the validity of the intellectual property right in the licensing contract, conducting coercive package licensing or incorporating exclusive grant-back conditions in the licensing contract, which impairs the fair competition order of foreign trade, the Ministry of Commerce of the People's Republic of China may take measures as necessary to eliminate such impairment. And China prohibits the transfer of technologies relating to fissionable materials or the materials from which they are derived as well as the import or export relating to arms, ammunition and implements for war.

3.4 Compulsory Licenses

A compulsory license is to work a patent or use a copyright without the consent of the owner but based on a license that is issued by a government. Compulsory licenses are common in most countries of the world, especially in developing countries. They arise when the owner of the intellectual property, in particular patents or copyrights, refuses or is unable to work the property in a particular country within a certain period of time. In such a case, a third party may apply for a compulsory license, which will be issued by the government without the consent of the owner.

The *International Convention for the Protection of Industrial Property* (the Paris Convention) recognizes the right of countries to impose compulsory licenses on patents with certain limitations. It states:

(1) Members may legislate measures providing for the grant of compulsory licenses to prevent abuses of the exclusive rights conferred by the patent, for example, for failure to work.

(2) Forfeiture of the patent will not be provided for except where the grant of compulsory licenses is not sufficient to prevent abuses. Forfeiture or revocation of a

---

① See Articles 81, 82 and 83 of the EC Treaty.

② This Law has been amended in 2016.

patent will not be instituted before the expiration of three years from the grant of the first compulsory license.

(3) A compulsory license may not be applied for on the ground of failure to work or insufficient working before the expiration of three years from the date of application for the patent, or four years from the date of the grant of the patent whichever period expires last. It shall be refused if the patentee justifies his inaction by legislate reasons. Such compulsory license shall be non-exclusive and shall not be transferable even in the form of the grant of a sublicense.

Two types of compulsory licensing apply to copyrights. A statutory copyright license authorizes third parties to use a copyrighted work in exchange for a fee, which is fixed by the legislation or by a public or private agency authorized to fix. A compulsory copyright license compels a copyright owner to grant a license, but it allows the owner to negotiate the terms of the license. The *Berne Convention for the Protection of Literary and Artistic Works* recognizes the right of countries to impose compulsory licenses for broadcasting and recording. This right, however, is limited by the provision that compulsory licenses may "not in any circumstances be prejudicial to the moral rights of the author, nor to his right to obtain equitable remuneration which, in the absence of agreement, shall be fixed by the competent authority".

4 Regulation of International Franchising

Franchising constitutes a rapidly expanding form of doing business abroad. Now it even becomes a business model in which many different owners share a single brand name. A parent company allows the franchisee to use the company's strategies and trademarks; in exchange, the franchisee pays an initial fee and royalties based on revenues. The parent company also provides the franchisee with support, including advertising and training, as part of the franchising agreement. For the franchisor, the franchise is a faster, cheaper form of expansion than building "chain stores" to distribute goods and avoid investment and liability over a chain. For the franchisee, the franchisor's success is the success of the franchisees. The franchisee is said to have a greater incentive than a direct employee because he or she has a direct stake in the business. Thus hundreds of multinational companies have developed tens of thousands of foreign franchises, e.g. McDonald's may be one of the most successful ones. 70 different industries use the franchising business model, and according to the International Franchising Association the sector earns more than $1.5 trillion in revenues each year.

Under the intellectual property law, **franchise** is a specialized license in which the licensor (franchiser) permits the licensee (franchisee) to work the licensor's intellectual property under the supervision and control of a franchiser. A license allows a licensee to use an intellectual property, usually a trademark, for the licensee's own purposes. Depending on the licensing agreement between them, the licensee may use the intellectual property as a component of its own products, it may sell the products derived from it under the licensor's name or under its own name. Sometimes the licensee may even sell the intellectual property or the products derived from it in direct competition to the licensor. However, a franchisee has more limited rights. The key difference is that a franchisee is regarded as a unit or element of the franchiser's business.

Three types of franchise have evolved since the beginning of the twentieth century: distributorships, chain-style businesses, and manufacturing or processing plant. A **distributorship franchise** exists when a manufacturer licenses a dealer to sell its products. The automobile dealership is an example. A **chain-style franchise** is an arrangement in which a franchise operates under a franchiser's trade name and is identified as a part of the franchiser's business chain. Most of the foreign fast-food restaurants are operated in this way. A **manufacturing or processing plant franchise** exists when a franchiser provides the franchisee with the formula or the essential ingredients to make a popular product. The franchisee then wholesales or retails the product according to the standards established by the franchiser. Examples of this kind are Coca-Cola and other soft-drink firms.

Although the franchisee has more limited rights than a licensee, the regulations governing international franchising agreements are the same as those governing licenses. Competition laws will greatly affect the legal issue arising out of the franchising agreement. For example, the EU has invalidated franchisers' "quality assurance" provisions when they are deemed unduly restrictive of the franchisee's ability to compete. Tied-purchase clauses that require the franchisee to buy certain goods from the franchiser are sometimes difficult to justify on quality control grounds. And geographic exclusivity provision will not be permitted if it unduly restricts competition within the host country.

Most franchisers have standard contracts, which are used in their home markets and have them revised and adapted to international franchising without significantly altering the franchiser's successful business formula. Under an international franchising agreement franchise fees and royalties must be specified, the provision of services, training and control by the franchiser are detailed, the term and area of the franchise, accounting procedures agreed on, business standards and advertising selected, insurance obtained, taxes and other liabilities allocated, dispute settlement procedures should be decided. At the heart of all international franchising agreements lies a trademark licensing clause conveying the local trademark rights of the franchiser to the franchisee in return for royalty payment. The following case illustrates some legal problems in franchising.

Case IV-2

Dayan v. McDonald's Corp.

466 N.E. 2d 958 (1984)

Backgrounds and Facts

Dayan, the Plaintiff, received an exclusive franchise to operate McDonald's restaurants in Paris in 1971. The franchise agreement required that the franchise should meet all quality, service, and cleanliness (QSC) standards set by McDonald's. And the franchise agreement stated the rational for maintaining QSC standards was that: "A departure of restaurants anywhere in the world from these standards impedes the successful operation of restaurants throughout the world, and injures the value of McDonald's patents, trademarks and property." Dayan agreed to maintain these standards and also agreed not to vary from QSC standards without prior written approval. After several years of QSC standards violations by Dayan, McDonald's sought to terminate the franchise and Dayan brought this action to enjoin the termination. The lower court found that good cause existed for the termination and Dayan appealed.

Presiding Justice Buckley

Dayan argued that McDonald's was obliged to provide him with the operational assistance necessary to enable him to meet the QSC standards. He verbally asked Sollars (a McDonald's manager) for a French-speaking operations person to work in Paris for six months. Sollars testified that he told Dayan it would be difficult to find someone with such appropriate background but that McDonald's could immediately send him an English-speaking operations man. The idea was summarily rejected by Dayan as unworkable even though Sollars had informed Dayan that sending operations person who did not speak the language to a foreign country was very common and very successful in McDonald's international system. Nonetheless, Sollars agreed to attempt to locate a qualified person as requested by Dayan. Through Sollars' efforts, Dayan was put in contact with Michael Maycock, an operations person speaking French. Dayan testified that he hired Michael Maycock sometime in October 1977 and placed him in charge of the training, quality control and equipments.

As the trial court correctly realized: "It does not take a McDonald's-trained French-speaking operations person to know that grease dripping from the vents must be stopped and not merely collected in a cup hung from the ceiling, that dogs are not permitted to defecate where food is stored, that insecticide is not blended with chicken breading; that past-dated products should be discarded."

The finding that Dayan refused non-French-speaking operational assistance and that McDonald's fulfilled Dayan's limited request for a French-speaking operational employee is well supported by the record. Accordingly, we find McDonald's fulfilled its contractual obligation to provide a requested operational assistance to Dayan.

In view of the foregoing reasons, the judgment of the trial court denying plaintiff's request for a permanent injunction and McDonald's properly terminated the franchise agreement is affirmed.

Decision

Judgment was affirmed for McDonald's. McDonald's had fulfilled all of its responsibility under the agreement to assist the plaintiff in complying with the provisions of the license. The plaintiff had violated the provisions of the agreement by not complying with the QSC standards. The plaintiff is permitted to continue operation of his restaurants, but without use of McDonald's trademarks or name.

Chapter Summary

Trade in services has become the most dynamic segment of world trade. In an era of global value chains, goods and services are increasingly traded together. In this Chapter, fundamentals of intellectual property rights including patents, copyrights, trademarks and trade secrets are discussed. These private rights are created by the domestic laws, however, the international treaties on the intellectual property rights provide rules and guidelines for its uniform definition and protection. The *Agreement on Trade-Related Aspects of Intellectual Property Rights* (TRIPS Agreement) has fixed minimums for levels of protection and enforcement of intellectual property obligations for all the WTO members.[①] *The International Convention for Protection of Industrial Property*, *Berne Convention for the Protection of Literary and Artistic Property*, *International Convention for the Protection of Performers, Producers of Phonograms, and Broadcasting Organizations* and *Treaty on Intellectual Property in Respect of Integrated Circuits* will continue to be in force and provide international protection for intellectual property rights.

The licensing and franchising of intellectual property provide owners of the intellectual property a way to increase the turns yielded by the property, and offer the licensee or franchisee the opportunity to acquire advanced technologies. The logic of efficiency and accelerating technical advances that underlie licensing makes it a rapidly expanding and highly profitable form of doing business. Licensor and licensee will negotiate over matters including conditions and extent of use, royalties, and confidentiality etc. But in the international context, the negotiations between licensor and licensee are more complicated. Licensor may, relying on its strong bargaining power, impose restrictive provisions such as grant-back provisions and non-competition clauses to limit the use of the property and the competition in trade. Such provisions are prohibited in the legislation on technology transfer and competition of many countries, although such prohibitions are varying in degree in developed countries and developing countries. Besides, in order to prevent the abuse of intellectual property rights, compulsory licenses are recognized in most countries of the world. However, the *International Convention for the Protection of Industrial Property*, while recognizing the right of signatory countries to legalize compulsory licenses, imposes compulsory licenses with certain limitations.

Exercises

I. True or False Statements

1. The intellectual property rights can be created by the international treaties such as the Paris Convention and the Berne Convention.

2. Under the *Copyright Law of the People's Republic of China*, oral works will not be

---

① TRIPS Agreement has represented a major change in economic and development policy in developing countries. Although its long-run influence on the WTO members of developing countries is not so clear, it is certain that the costs of these countries associated with increased patent protection and the consequent payment of royalties will become great.

protected by copyrights.

3. The TRIPS Agreement sets the uniform time period for which copyrights shall be protected at 50 years.

4. The inventions the purpose of which is contrary to the public policy or public interests will not be granted patents in China.

5. The Berne Convention allows members to establish certain formalities such as the requirement that the word copyright or its abbreviation appears on the work as a prerequisite to granting protection.

6. After the TRIPS Agreement came into effect, the Berne Convention and the Paris Convention have ceased to be effective.

7. National treatment shall be followed in the protection of the foreign intellectual property rights among the WTO members.

8. The laws of China prohibit such clauses in international licensing agreement as preventing the licensee from challenging the validity of the intellectual property right, conducting coercive package licensing or stating exclusive grant-back conditions.

9. If the state has granted compulsory license on a patent to a third party, then the third party need not pay the patentee a royalty.

10. A franchise is a specialized license and the franchisee has more limited rights in using the intellectual property right.

II. Chapter Questions

1. What are the requirements for an invention to be granted a patent?

2. How do you understand the pecuniary rights and moral rights of a copyright's owner?

3. In a broad sense, how many kinds of trademarks? Give an example of each kind.

4. What are the legal requirements for the information to be regarded as trade secret?

5. In your eyes, what is the purpose of TRIPS Agreement in the field of intellectual property? Can you tell the influence of this Agreement on China?

6. In the international licensing agreements the licensee usually will impose some unfair restrictive provisions on the licensee. Name and explain two of them.

7. In what laws of a country may you find the prohibition of some restrictive provisions in the international licensing agreements?

8. In your point of view, what may be the reason or reasons justifying compulsory license?

9. What are the limitations for a state granting compulsory licenses under the Paris Convention? Are these limitations binding on China?

10. Explain the differences between a franchise and a license in the transfer of intellectual property.

III. Case Problems

Ferrero SpA v. Meng Te Sha Company

The Supreme People's Court of China (2006), April 7, 2008

The Supreme People's Court of China upheld an appellate decision that the sale of chocolates in similar packaging to that of Ferrero Rocher branded chocolates breached Chinese Anti-Unfair Competition Law.①

Facts

Ferrero has sold its Ferrero Rocher chocolates in China since 1984. Initially, the packaging carried not only the Ferrero Rocher brand but the Chinese characters "金莎" (pronounced "Jin Sha"). Ferrero advertised Ferrero Rocher products not only in Mainland of China but also in Hong Kong SAR and Taiwan region. Although it has owned the registered trademark for Jin Sha in Taiwan region and Hong Kong SAR since 1990 and 1993, respectively, it could not register in Mainland of China. This is because the Chinese company Meng Te Sha (MTS) held the Chinese registration for Jin Sha, having bought it from another company in 2002. In that year, MTS started manufacturing and selling chocolates under the brand name Trésor Doré Jin Sha in very similar packaging to that of Ferrero Rocher chocolates, but the price is relatively cheaper.

Lower Courts' Decisions

Ferrero sued MTS in the Tianjin No. 2 Intermediate People's Court for unfair competition in 2004 for use of packaging with decorative features confusingly similar to those used in the Ferrero Rocher packaging, but lost this action in February 2005. The court found that MTS had sold its product in many parts of China before Ferrero had done so, and that the Trésor Doré Jin Sha chocolates were more famous than those of Ferrero Rocher. It concluded that confusion was unlikely, particularly because the trademarks on

---

① Excerpt from Benjamin Qiu, *Ferrero Wins Unfair Competition Case in China*, 4 Journal of Intellectual Property Law and Practice 158 (2009).

the products were different and the products targeted different groups of consumers, based on the locations of sales.

Ferrero appealed and in January 2006, the Tianjin Higher People's Court (the "Higher Court") concluded that MTS had breached Anti-Unfair Competition Law. The Higher Court found that Ferrero Rocher, on the basis of its reputation not only in China but also in other countries, had been famous in China since 1984. MTS then petitioned the Supreme People's Court of China for a review of the Higher Court's decision and succeeded in obtaining a stay of the enforcement of the decision.

The Supreme People's Court's Decision

The Supreme People's Court upheld the Higher Court's decision that MTS violated the Anti-Unfair Competition Law and discussed four main issues.

1. Was Ferrero Rocher famous in China before MTS sold its products? The court held that it was, due to Ferrero's marketing efforts in China. The court rejected the Higher Court's reliance on Ferrero Rocher's global reputation but noted that fame acquired in other countries can increase fame in China.

2. Is the Ferrero Rocher packaging distinctive? The court held that, although individual elements (including the transparent plastic box and the foil wrapping) may not be distinctive, the packaging as a whole is clearly distinctive.

3. Is the public likely to confuse the MTS packaging with the Ferrero Rocher packaging? The court held that although there are differences, including different trademarks, the packaging is confusingly similar and thus violates the Chinese Anti-Unfair Competition Law.

4. Would damages of RMB 700,000 (approximately $100,000) be appropriate? The court held that, because Ferrero had not provided any information on MTS' profits from the sales of Trésor Doré Jin Sha chocolates, the amount should be reduced to RMB 500,000. This is the maximum statutory damages for trademark infringement. The court reasoned that it could refer to the Trademark Law in determining damages.

Questions:

1. Did Ferrero SpA own the registered trademark for Jin Sha in Mainland of China?

2. Why did Ferrero SpA bring legal claims for unfair competition instead of trademark infringement?

3. What legal issues did the Supreme People's Court of China analyze in its decision?

4. Regarding to trademark protection, how do you understand the relationship between trademark law and anti-unfair competition law?

IV. Reading Material

A Sample of License Agreement

This License Agreement (this "Agreement") is made effective as of [date] (the "Effective Date") between [Publisher, Address of Publisher, City of Publisher, State of Publisher, Country of Publisher Postal Code of Publisher] ("Licensor") and [Licensee, Address of Licensee, City of Licensee, State of Licensee, Country of Licensee Postal Code of Licensee] ("Licensee").

In consideration of the mutual promises contained herein and other good and valuable consideration, the receipt and sufficiency of which is hereby acknowledged, the parties agree as follows:

Ⅰ. Content of Licensed Materials; Grant of License

The materials that are the subject of this Agreement shall consist of [electronic information published or otherwise made available by Licensor] (hereinafter referred to as the "Licensed Materials").

Licensee and its Authorized Users acknowledge that the copyright and title to the Licensed Materials and any trademarks or service marks relating thereto remain with Licensor and/or its suppliers. Neither Licensee nor its Authorized Users shall have right, title or interest in the Licensed Materials except as expressly set forth in this Agreement.

Licensor hereby grants to Licensee non-exclusive use of the Licensed Materials and the right to provide the Licensed Materials to Authorized Users in accordance with this Agreement.

Ⅱ. Delivery/Access of Licensed Materials to Licensee

Licensor will provide the Licensed Materials to the Licensee in the following manner:

{Include all that apply; delete those that do not:}

Network Access. The Licensed Materials will be stored at one or more Licensor locations in digital form accessible by telecommunications links between such locations and authorized networks of Licensee.

Physical Media. Copies of the Licensed Materials will be provided to the Licensee on physical media (e.g., Digital Video Disk, CD-ROM, digital tape) for use on Licensee's network and workstations.

File Transfer. Copies of the Licensed Materials will be provided to the Licensee through electronic transfer (by means of File Transfer Protocol or otherwise).

Ⅲ. Fees

Licensee shall make payment to Licensor for use of the Licensed Materials pursuant to the terms set forth in Appendix A, attached hereto.

{Note: Pricing can follow any one of a number of models, including a fee per use of the Licensed Materials, a fee based on the number of Authorized Users, a periodic subscription fee or a fee based on the number of Full-Time Equivalent (FTE) students, faculty, employees or persons served by the License.}

Ⅳ. Authorized Use of Licensed Materials

Authorized Users. "Authorized Users" are:

Persons Affiliated with Licensee. Full and part time students and employees (including faculty, staff, affiliated researchers and independent contractors) of Licensee and the institution of which it is a part, regardless of the physical location of such persons.

Walk-ins. Patrons not affiliated with Licensee who are physically present at Licensee's site(s) ("walk-ins").

Authorized Uses. Licensee and Authorized Users may make all use of the Licensed Materials as is consistent with the Fair Use Provisions of United States and international law. Nothing in this Agreement is intended to limit in any way whatsoever Licensee's or any Authorized User's rights under the Fair Use Provisions of United States or international law to use the Licensed Materials.

The Licensed Materials may be used for purposes of research, education or other non-commercial use as follows:

Display. Licensee and Authorized Users shall have the right to electronically display the Licensed Materials.

Digitally Copy. Licensee and Authorized Users may download and digitally copy a reasonable portion of the Licensed Materials.

Print Copy. Licensee and Authorized Users may print a reasonable portion of the Licensed Materials.

Recover Copying Costs. Licensee may charge a reasonable fee to cover costs of copying or printing portions of Licensed Materials for Authorized Users.

Archival/Backup Copy. Upon request of Licensee, Licensee may receive from

Licensor and/or create one (1) copy of the entire set of Licensed Materials to be maintained as a backup or archival copy during the term of this Agreement or as required to exercise Licensee's rights under Section XIII, "Perpetual License", of this Agreement.

Course Packs. Licensee and Authorized Users may use a reasonable portion of the Licensed Materials in the preparation of Course Packs or other educational materials.

Electronic Reserve. Licensee and Authorized Users may use a reasonable portion of the Licensed Materials for use in connection with specific courses of instruction offered by Licensee and/or its parent institution.

Databases. If the Licensed Materials are a database, compilation, or collection of information, Authorized Users shall be permitted to extract or use information contained in the database for educational, scientific, or research purposes, including extraction and manipulation of information for the purpose of illustration, explanation, example, comment, criticism, teaching, research, or analysis.

Electronic Links. Licensee may provide electronic links to the Licensed Materials from Licensee's web page(s), and is encouraged to do so in ways that will increase the usefulness of the Licensed Materials to Authorized Users. Licensor staff will assist Licensee upon request in creating such links effectively. Licensee may make changes in the appearance of such links and/or in statements accompanying such links as reasonably requested by Licensor.

Caching. Licensee and Authorized Users may make such local digital copies of the Licensed Materials as are necessary to ensure efficient use by Authorized Users by appropriate browser or other software.

Indices. Licensee may use the Licensed Materials in connection with the preparation of or access to integrated indices to the Licensed Materials, including author, article, abstract and keyword indices.

Scholarly Sharing. Authorized Users may transmit to a third party colleague in hard copy or electronically, minimal, insubstantial amounts of the Licensed Materials for personal use or scholarly, educational, or scientific research or professional use but in no case for re-sale. In addition, Authorized Users have the right to use, with appropriate credit, figures, tables and brief excerpts from the Licensed Materials in the Authorized User's own scientific, scholarly and educational works.

Interlibrary Loan. Licensee may fulfill requests from other institutions, a practice commonly called Interlibrary Loan. Licensee agrees to fulfill such requests in compliance with Section 108 of the United States Copyright Law (17 USC §108, "Limitations on exclusive rights: Reproduction by libraries and archives") and clause 3 of the Guidelines for the Proviso of Subsection 108(g)(2) prepared by the National Commission on New Technological Uses of Copyrighted Works.

V. Access by and Authentication of Authorized Users

Licensee and its Authorized Users shall be granted access to the Licensed Materials pursuant to the following:

{Include all that apply; delete those that do not:}

IP Addresses. Authorized Users shall be identified and authenticated by the use of Internet Protocol ("IP") addresses provided by Licensee to Licensor.

Passwords. Authorized Users shall be identified and authenticated by the use of usernames and passwords assigned by Licensee. Licensee shall be responsible for issuing and terminating passwords, verifying the status of Authorized Users, providing lists of valid passwords to Licensor and updating such lists on a regular basis.

Public-keys/Certificates. Authorized Users shall be identified and authenticated by means of public-key and X.509 certificates.

Developing Protocols. Authorized Users shall be identified and authenticated by such means and protocols as may be developed during the term of this Agreement.

VI. Specific Restrictions on Use of Licensed Materials

Unauthorized Use. Licensee shall not knowingly permit anyone other than Authorized Users to use the Licensed Materials.

Modification of Licensed Materials. Licensee shall not modify or create a derivative work of the Licensed Materials without the prior written permission of Licensor.

Removal of Copyright Notice. Licensee may not remove, obscure or modify any copyright or other notices included in the Licensed Materials.

Commercial Purposes. Other than as specifically permitted in this Agreement, Licensee may not use the Licensed Materials for commercial purposes, including but not limited to the sale of the Licensed Materials or bulk reproduction or distribution of the Licensed Materials in any form.

VII. Licensor Performance Obligations

Availability of Licensed Materials. Within [time period], Licensor shall make the Licensed Materials available to Licensee and Authorized Users.

Documentation. Licensor will provide and maintain help files and other appropriate user documentation.

Support. Licensor will offer activation or installation support, including assisting with the implementation of any Licensor software. Licensor will offer reasonable levels of continuing support to assist Licensee and Authorized Users in use of the Licensed Materials. Licensor will make its personnel available by email, phone or fax during [time period] for feedback, problem-solving, or general questions.

Training. Licensor will provide appropriate training to Licensee staff relating to the use of the Licensed Materials and any Licensor software.

Quality of Service. Licensor shall use reasonable efforts to ensure that the Licensor's server or servers have sufficient capacity and rate of connectivity to provide the Licensee and its Authorized Users with a quality of service comparable to current standards in the online information provision industry in the Licensee's locale.

Licensor shall use reasonable efforts to provide continuous service [time period] with an average of [percentage] up-time per month. The [percentage] down-time includes periodic unavailability due to maintenance of the server(s), the installation or testing of software, the loading of additional Licensed Materials as they become available, and downtime related to the failure of equipment or services outside the control of Licensor, including but not limited to public or private telecommunications services or internet nodes or facilities. Scheduled down-time will be performed at a time to minimize inconvenience to Licensee and its Authorized Users.

If the Licensed Materials fail to operate in conformance with the terms of this Agreement, Licensee shall immediately notify Licensor, and Licensor shall promptly use reasonable efforts to restore access to the Licensed Materials as soon as possible. In the event that Licensor fails to repair the non-conformity in a reasonable time, Licensor shall reimburse Licensee in an amount that the non-conformity is proportional to the total Fees owed by Licensee under this Agreement.

Notification of Modifications of Licensed Materials. Licensee understands that from time to time the Licensed Materials may be added to, modified, or deleted from by Licensor and/or that portions of the Licensed Materials may migrate to other formats. Licensor shall give prompt notice of any such changes to Licensee. Failure by Licensor to provide such reasonable notice shall be grounds for immediate termination of the Agreement by Licensee. If any modifications render the Licensed Materials less useful to the Licensee or its Authorized Users, the Licensee may treat such modifications as a material breach subject to the Early Termination provisions of this Agreement below.

Completeness of Content. Where applicable, Licensor will inform Licensee of instances where online content differs from the print versions of the Licensed Materials.

Where applicable, Licensor shall use reasonable efforts to ensure that the online content is at least as complete as print versions of the Licensed Materials, represents complete, accurate and timely replications of the corresponding content contained within the print versions of such Materials, and will cooperate with Licensee to identify and correct errors or omissions.

Continued Training. Licensor will provide regular system and project updates to Licensee as they become available. Licensor will provide additional training to Licensee staff made necessary by any updates or modifications to the Licensed Materials or any Licensor software.

Notice of "Click-Through" License Terms or Other Means of Passive Assent. In the event that Licensor requires Authorized Users to agree to terms relating to the use of the Licensed Materials before permitting Authorized Users to gain access to the Licensed Materials (commonly referred to as "click-through" licenses), or otherwise attempts to impose such terms on Authorized Users through mere use or viewing of the Authorized Matierals, Licensor shall provide Licensee with notice of and an opportunity to comment on such terms prior to their implementation. In no event shall such terms materially differ from the provisions of this Agreement. In the event of any conflict between such terms and this Agreement, the terms of this Agreement shall prevail.

Compliance with Americans with Disabilities Act. Licensor shall comply with the Americans with Disabilities Act (ADA), by supporting assistive software or devices such as large print interfaces, voice-activated input, and alternate keyboard or pointer interfaces in a manner consistent with the Web Accessibility Initiative Web Content Accessibility Guidelines, which may be found at http://www.w3.org/WAI/GL/#Publications.

Withdrawal of Licensed Materials. Licensor reserves the right to withdraw from the Licensed Materials any item or part of an item for which it no longer retains the right to publish, or which it has reasonable grounds to believe infringes copyright or is defamatory, obscene, unlawful or otherwise objectionable. Licensor shall give written notice to the Licensee of such withdrawal no later than [time period] following the removal of any item pursuant to this section. If any such withdrawal renders the Licensed Materials less useful to Licensee or its Authorized Users, Licensor shall reimburse Licensee in an amount that the withdrawal is proportional to the total Fees owed by Licensee under this Agreement.

Usage Data. Licensor shall provide to Licensee statistics regarding the usage of the Licensed Materials by Licensee and/or its Authorized Users in conformance with the Guidelines for the Statistical Measures of Usage of Web-Based Indexed, Abstracted, and Full Text Resources (November 1998), adopted and approved by the International Consortium of Library Consortia.

Ⅷ. Licensee Performance Obligations

Provision of Notice of License Terms to Authorized Users. Licensee shall make reasonable efforts to provide Authorized Users with appropriate notice of the terms and conditions under which access to the Licensed Materials is granted under this Agreement including, in particular, any limitations on access or use of the Licensed Materials as set forth in this Agreement.

Protection from Unauthorized Use. Licensee shall make reasonable efforts to protect the Licensed Materials from any use that is not permitted under this Agreement. In the event of any unauthorized use of the Licensed Materials by an Authorized User, (a) Licensor may terminate such Authorized User's access to the Licensed Materials, (b) Licensor may terminate the access of the Internet Protocol ("IP") address(es) from which such unauthorized use occurred, and/or (c) Licensee shall terminate such Authorized User's access to the Licensed Materials upon Licensor's request. Licensor shall take none of the steps described in this paragraph without first providing reasonable notice to Licensee (in no event less than [time period]) and cooperating with the Licensee to avoid recurrence of any unauthorized use.

Maintaining Confidentiality of Access Passwords. Where access to the Licensed Materials is to be controlled by use of passwords, Licensee shall issue log-on identification numbers and passwords to each Authorized User and use reasonable efforts to ensure that Authorized Users do not divulge their numbers and passwords to any third party. Licensee shall also maintain the confidentiality of any institutional passwords provided by Licensor.

Ⅸ. Mutual Performance Obligations

Confidentiality of User Data. Licensor and Licensee agree to maintain the confidentiality of any data relating to the usage of the Licensed Materials by Licensee and its Authorized Users. Such data may be used solely for purposes directly related to the Licensed Materials and may only be provided to third parties in aggregate form. Raw usage data, including but not limited to information relating to the identity of specific users and/or uses, shall not be provided to any third party.

Implementation of Developing Security Protocols. Licensee and Licensor shall cooperate in the implementation of security and control protocols and procedures as they are developed during the term of this Agreement.

Ⅹ. Term

This Agreement shall continue in effect for [length of time] commencing on the Effective Date.

Ⅺ. Renewal

This agreement shall be renewable at the end of the current term for a successive [length of time] term unless either party gives written notice of its intention not to renew [time period] before expiration of the current term.

Ⅻ. Early Termination

In the event that either party believes that the other materially has breached any obligations under this Agreement, or if Licensor believes that Licensee has exceeded the scope of the License, such party shall so notify the breaching party in writing. The breaching party shall have [time period] from the receipt of notice to cure the alleged breach and to notify the non-breaching party in writing that cure has been effected. If the breach is not cured within the [time period], the non-breaching party shall have the right to terminate the Agreement without further notice.

Upon Termination of this Agreement for cause online access to the Licensed Materials by Licensee and Authorized Users shall be terminated. Authorized copies of Licensed Materials may be retained by Licensee or Authorized Users and used subject to the terms of this Agreement.

In the event of early termination permitted by this Agreement, Licensee shall be entitled to a refund of any fees or pro-rata portion thereof paid by Licensee for any remaining period of the Agreement from the date of termination.

XIII. Perpetual License

Except for termination for cause, Licensor hereby grants to Licensee a nonexclusive, royalty-free, perpetual license to use any Licensed Materials that were accessible during the term of this Agreement. Such use shall be in accordance with the provisions of this

Agreement, which provisions shall survive any termination of this Agreement. The means by which Licensee shall have access to such Licensed Materials shall be in a manner and form substantially equivalent to the means by which access is provided under this Agreement.

XIV. Warranties

Subject to the Limitations set forth elsewhere in this Agreement:

Licensor warrants that it has the right to license the rights granted under this Agreement to use Licensed Materials, that it has obtained any and all necessary permissions from third parties to license the Licensed Materials, and that use of the Licensed Materials by Authorized Users in accordance with the terms of this Agreement shall not infringe the copyright of any third party. The Licensor shall indemnify and hold Licensee and Authorized Users harmless for any losses, claims, damages, awards, penalties, or injuries incurred, including reasonable attorney's fees, which arise from any claim by any third party of an alleged infringement of copyright or any other property right arising out of the use of the Licensed Materials by the Licensee or any Authorized User in accordance with the terms of this Agreement. This indemnity shall survive the termination of this agreement. NO LIMITATION OF LIABILITY SET FORTH ELSEWHERE IN THIS AGREEMENT IS APPLICABLE TO THIS INDEMNIFICATION.

Licensor warrants that the physical medium, if any, on which the Licensed Materials is provided to Licensee will be free from defects for a period of [time period] from delivery.

XV. Limitations on Warranties

Notwithstanding anything else in this Agreement:

Neither party shall be liable for any indirect, special, incidental, punitive or consequential damages, including but not limited to loss of data, business interruption, or loss of profits, arising out of the use of or the inability to use the Licensed Materials.

Licensor makes no representation or warranty, and expressly disclaims any liability with respect to the content of any Licensed Materials, including but not limited to errors or omissions contained therein, libel, infringement of rights of publicity, privacy, trademark rights, moral rights, or the disclosure of confidential information.

Except for the express warranties stated herein, the Licensed Materials are provided on an "as is" basis, and Licensor disclaims any and all other warranties, conditions, or representations (express, implied, oral or written), relating to the Licensed Materials or any part thereof, including, without limitation, any and all implied warranties of quality, performance, merchantability or fitness for a particular purpose. Licensor makes no warranties respecting any harm that may be caused by the transmission of a computer virus, worm, time bomb, logic bomb or other such computer program. Licensor further expressly disclaims any warranty or representation to Authorized Users, or to any third party.

XVI. **Indemnities**

Each party shall indemnify and hold the other harmless for any losses, claims, damages, awards, penalties, or injuries incurred by any third party, including reasonable attorney's fees, which arise from any alleged breach of such indemnifying party's representations and warranties made under this Agreement, provided that the indemnifying party is promptly notified of any such claims. The indemnifying party shall have the sole right to defend such claims at its own expense. The other party shall provide, at the indemnifying party's expense, such assistance in investigating and defending such claims as the indemnifying party may reasonably request. This indemnity shall survive the termination of this Agreement.

XVII. **Assignment and Transfer**

Neither party may assign, directly or indirectly, all or part of its rights or obligations under this Agreement without the prior written consent of the other party, which consent shall not be unreasonably withheld or delayed.

XVIII. **Governing Law**

This Agreement shall be interpreted and construed according to, and governed by, the laws of [Jurisdiction Convenient to All Parties], excluding any such laws that might direct the application of the laws of another jurisdiction. The federal or state courts located in [Jurisdiction Convenient to All Parties] shall have jurisdiction to hear any dispute under this Agreement.

XIX. **Dispute Resolution**

In the event any dispute or controversy arising out of or relating to this Agreement, the parties agree to exercise their best efforts to resolve the dispute as soon as possible.

The parties shall, without delay, continue to perform their respective obligations under this Agreement which are not affected by the dispute.

{Include all that apply; delete those that do not:}

Mediation. In the event that the parties can not by exercise of their best efforts resolve the dispute, they shall submit the dispute to Mediation. The parties shall, without delay, continue to perform their respective obligations under this Agreement which are not affected by the dispute. The invoking party shall give to the other party written notice of its decision to do so, including a description of the issues subject to the dispute and a proposed resolution thereof. Designated representatives of both parties shall attempt to resolve the dispute within [time period] after such notice. If those designated representatives cannot resolve the dispute, the parties shall meet at a mutually agreeable location and describe the dispute and their respective proposals for resolution to responsible executives of the disputing parties, who shall act in good faith to resolve the dispute. If the dispute is not resolved within [time period] after such meeting, the dispute shall be submitted to binding arbitration in accordance with the Arbitration provision of this Agreement.

Arbitration. Any controversies or disputes arising out of or relating to this Agreement shall be resolved by binding arbitration in accordance with the then current Commercial Arbitration Rules of the American Arbitration Association. The parties shall endeavor to select a mutually acceptable arbitrator knowledgeable about issues relating to the subject matter of this Agreement. In the event the parties are unable to agree to such a selection, each party will select an arbitrator and the arbitrators in turn shall select a third arbitrator. The arbitration shall take place at a location that is reasonably centrally located between the parties, or otherwise mutually agreed upon by the parties.

All documents, materials, and information in the possession of each party that are in any way relevant to the claim(s) or dispute(s) shall be made available to the other party for review and copying no later than [time period] after the notice of arbitration is served.

The arbitrator(s) shall not have the authority, power, or right to alter, change, amend, modify, add, or subtract from any provision of this Agreement or to award punitive damages. The arbitrator shall have the power to issue mandatory orders and restraining orders in connection with the arbitration. The award rendered by the arbitrator shall be final and binding on the parties, and judgment may be entered thereon in any court having jurisdiction. The agreement to arbitration shall be specifically enforceable under prevailing arbitration law. During the continuance of any arbitration proceeding, the parties shall continue to perform their respective obligations under this Agreement.

XX. Force Majeure

Neither party shall be liable in damages nor has the right to terminate this Agreement for any delay or default in performing hereunder if such delay or default is caused by conditions beyond its control including, but not limited to Acts of God, Government restrictions (including the denial or cancellation of any export or other necessary license), wars, insurrections and/or any other cause beyond the reasonable control of the party whose performance is affected.

XXI. Entire Agreement

This Agreement constitutes the entire agreement of the parties and supersedes all prior communications, understandings and agreements relating to the subject matter hereof, whether oral or written.

XXII. Amendment

No modification or claimed waiver of any provision of this Agreement shall be valid except by written amendment signed by authorized representatives of Licensor and Licensee.

XXIII. Severability

If any provision or provisions of this Agreement shall be held to be invalid, illegal, unenforceable or in conflict with the law of any jurisdiction, the validity, legality and enforceability of the remaining provisions shall not in any way be affected or impaired thereby.

XXIV. Waiver of Contractual Right

Waiver of any provision herein shall not be deemed a waiver of any other provision herein, nor shall waiver of any breach of this Agreement be construed as a continuing waiver of other breaches of the same or other provisions of this Agreement.

XXV. Notices

All notices given pursuant to this Agreement shall be in writing and may be hand delivered, or shall be deemed received within [time period] after mailing if sent by registered or certified mail, return receipt requested. If any notice is sent by facsimile, confirmation copies must be sent by mail or hand delivery to the specified address. Either party may from time to time change its Notice Address by written notice to the other party.

If to Licensor:
[Licensor
Address of Licensor
City of Licensor
State of Licensor
Country of Licensor
Postal Code of Licensor]
If to Licensee:
[Licensee
Address of Licensee
City of Licensee
State of Licensee
Country of Licensee
Postal Code of Licensee]

IN WITNESS WHEREOF, the parties have executed this Agreement by their respective, duly authorized representatives as of the date first above written.

LICENSOR:
BY: ______________________________ DATE: ____________________
Signature of Authorized Signatory of Publisher
Print Name:
Title:
Address:
Telephone No.:
E-mail:
LICENSEE:
BY: ______________________________ DATE: ____________________
Signature of Authorized Signatory of Licensee
Print Name:
Title:
Address:
Telephone No.:
E-mail:

Part V Law of International Commercial Disputes Resolution

Learning Objectives
(1) Getting to know the advantages and disadvantages of different methods of international commercial dispute settlement
(2) Finding out the factors that influence the choice of methods of international commercial dispute settlement
(3) Having a good command of international commercial arbitration including the arbitration institutions, arbitration clauses, arbitration procedure and enforcement of arbitral awards
(4) Having an understanding of jurisdiction, choosing the governing law, proving foreign law and enforcing foreign judgment in settlement of international commercial disputes through litigation
(5) Having a good command of the international conventions and model laws on international commercial arbitration, mediation and litigation

An inevitable consequence of increased trade is increased number of disputes requiring resolution. Many of the same questions that are relevant to settle a domestic commercial dispute are equally relevant to an international commercial dispute, but they become infinitely complex. In international commercial transactions, the parties usually live and work oceans away. They look, speak and act differently from each other. The domestic laws of their jurisdictions governing such commercial transactions may be divergent and unfamiliar to each other. In one word, the business transactions that span continents and cultures raise many complicated legal and tactical problems.

This Chapter presents several alternatives for international commercial dispute resolution, including **Alternative Dispute Resolution**, **arbitration**, and **litigation**. These methods may be used individually or in a combined way.

1 Methods of International Commercial Dispute Settlement

Alternative Dispute Resolution (ADR) offers an amicable method of dispute resolution through voluntary consultation. It has become popular for its flexible procedure, and the least harm to the long-term business relationships between parties. However, the agreement for dispute resolution reached through ADR is not legally binding. If any of the party refuses to fulfill the above agreement, such dispute may still have to resort to other methods, that is, arbitration or litigation. To some degree, ADR may be regarded as the "screening procedure" for arbitration or litigation. ADR is usually thought to cover all the methods of dispute resolution but arbitration and litigation, although some argue it should also include the method of arbitration.①

◆ **Negotiation**

As its name implies, negotiation is the process of reaching an agreement by the parties through oral or written discussion. Despite its simplicity, negotiation is an important tool in the process of dispute settlement, and undoubtedly the one most commonly relied on. It is used not merely to resolve disputes but to prevent them from arising in the first place and to lay the groundwork for other forms of dispute settlement. Negotiation is carried out voluntarily between the parties without the involvement of any third party. It is much flexible in the procedure and form. One obvious advantage of negotiation is time-saving and money-saving. However, the potential shortcoming is that the agreement reached through negotiation highly depends on the bargaining power of the parties, which may put the economically weaker party in a disadvantaged position. Moreover, if negotiation fails, the parties may still have to resolve their disputes through other methods.

◆ **Mediation**

Mediation is a **voluntary**, **non-binding**, **and conciliation** process. The parties agree on an impartial third party (**mediator**) who helps them amicably reach a solution. The mediator may be an individual or an institution. It is **private** and there are no public court records. The mediator will see each party privately and listen to their respective viewpoints, trying to ensure that each party understands the other's point of view and helping them to achieve a compromise solution. A mediator cannot compel the parties to arrive at a settlement and the final decision to settle rests with the parties themselves. The parties reserve all the rights to resort to binding arbitration or litigation.

Mediation is a method of resolving disputes originating from the oriental countries. Now it has won increasing popularity as a way of settling international commercial

---

① See Richard Schaffer, Filiberto Agusti, et al., *International Business Law and Its Environment,* 8th ed., Cengage Learning, 2012, p.76.

disputes between the private parties in other parts of the world.

Adopted in December 2018, the *United Nations Convention on International Settlement Agreements Resulting from Mediation*, also known as the Singapore Convention on Mediation, applies to international settlement agreements resulting from mediation. The Singapore Convention on Mediation is an instrument for the facilitation of international trade and the promotion of mediation as an alternative and effective method of resolving commercial disputes. It establishes a harmonized legal framework for the right to invoke settlement agreements as well as for their enforcement. Being a binding international instrument, it is expected to bring certainty and stability to the international framework on mediation.

◆ Mini-trial

Mini-trial is often used to resolve the disputes between corporations. The dispute will be submitted to a mini-trial panel which is composed of a third party (Chairman) and a senior member of management from each of the parties in dispute. The parties meet to agree the basic rules of the process including the number of documents to be disclosed, the time for each party to prepare the brief and the date to present the case. On the appointed date for hearing, each party will make a presentation of the case. Following the presentations, the management representatives of each party will meet by themselves in an effort to reach a settlement. If no settlement can be made, the Chairman may put forward his/her proposal for resolution of the disputes. The proceedings are confidential and may not be referred to in any subsequent litigation. The mini-trial does not result in a formal decision but is a vehicle for the parties to arrive at a solution through a structured settlement process. It is used most effectively when complex issues are at stake and the parties wish to maintain an amicable relationship.

◆ Arbitration

Arbitration is a more formalized process. It implies that the parties agree to submit a dispute for settlement to **private persons**, which results in a **binding** award that will **be enforced by courts** of law in many countries.The parties must agree to arbitration, but once they do, they may not withdraw. Arbitration has two dimensions: contractual and judicial. On one hand, arbitration is based on the agreement between parties. No Arbitration is possible without such agreement. On the other hand, the arbitrator exercises a judicial task. Arbitration is based on arbitration law laying down the rules for arbitration procedure and the legal effects of the award. The court can enforce a correct award or annul an incorrect award.

A distinction is usually made between national arbitration and international arbitration. For **national arbitration**, all elements (parties, dispute, place of arbitration) are located within one legal system. In case of **international arbitration**, these elements have gone beyond one legal system. Strictly speaking, how to understand "international commercial arbitration" may not result in a uniform answer in all countries. According to Article 1.3 of *UNCITRAL Model Law on International Commercial Arbitration (1985)*, an arbitration "is **international** if: (a) the parties to an arbitration agreement have, at the time of the conclusion of that agreement, their **places of business** in different States; or (b) one of the following places is situated outside the State in which the parties have their places of business: (i) **the place of arbitration** if determined in, or pursuant to, the arbitration agreement; (ii) any place where a substantial part of the obligations of the commercial relationship is to be **performed** or the place with which the subject-matter of the dispute is **most closely connected**; or (c) the parties have expressly agreed that **the subject-matter** of the arbitration agreement relates to more than one country".① As for the term "commercial", *UNCITRAL Model Law on International Commercial Arbitration (1985)* gives the following interpretation: "**commercial**" should be given a wide interpretation so as to cover matters arising from all relationships of a commercial nature, whether contractual or not. Relationships of a commercial nature include, but are not limited to, the following transactions: any trade transaction for the supply or exchange of goods or services; distribution agreement; commercial representation or agency; factoring; leasing.② According to UNCITRAL, the international commercial arbitration is given a wide interpretation: if any of the elements of a commercial dispute including the party's place of business, the place of arbitration, the place of performance, the place with which the dispute is most closely connected and the subject matter connect with more than one legal system, it will be regarded as an international commercial arbitration.

There are two distinct types of commercial arbitration: ad hoc and institutional. **Ad hoc arbitration** involves selection by the parties of the arbitrators and rules governing the arbitration. The classic formula involves each side choosing one arbitrator who in turn chooses a third arbitrator. The ad hoc arbitration panel selects its procedural rules (such as the UNCITRAL Arbitration Rules). Ad hoc arbitration can be agreed upon in

---

① The bold words herein are marked by the author.

② You may find the full text of *UNCITRAL Model Law on International Commercial Arbitration (1985)* at http://uncitral.un.org.

advance or, quite literally, selected ad hoc as dispute arises. **Institutional arbitration** involves selection of a specific arbitration center, often accompanied by its own rules of arbitration. There are numerous competing centers of arbitration, each busy marketing its appeal to the world trade community. Some centers are long-standing and busy, such as ICC International Court of Arbitration, while other centers are recent in time and still struggling for clients such as the Commercial Arbitration and Mediation Center for the Americas (CAMCA). Some of the leading private arbitration organizations for arbitration of commercial disputes are as following:

- China International Economic and Trade Arbitration Commission;
- China International Maritime Arbitration Commission;
- American Arbitration Association;
- Court of Arbitration of the International Chamber of Commerce;
- London Court of International Arbitration;
- Arbitration Institute of the Stockholm Chamber of Commerce;
- St. Petersburg International Commercial Arbitration Court;
- Hong Kong International Arbitration Centre and the Hong Kong Mediation Centre;
- Singapore International Arbitration Centre;
- Japan Commercial Arbitration Association;
- World Intellectual Property Organization (WIPO) Arbitration and Mediation Center.

Ad hoc arbitration presupposes a certain amount of goodwill and flexibility between the parties. It can be speedy and less costly than institutional arbitration. The latter, on the other hand, offers ease of incorporation in an international business agreement, supervisory services, a stable group of experienced arbitrators and a fixed fee schedule. Award from well established arbitration centers are more likely to be recognized in the courts if enforcement is needed.

2 Settlement of International Commercial Disputes Through Arbitration

2.1 Advantages and Disadvantages of International Commercial Arbitration

Being informal. The arbitration proceedings are less formal than court proceedings. Arbitrators do not wear gowns. Advocates of the parties do not plead from the bench like barristers in court. On the contrary, arbitrators, parties and lawyers often sit around one big conference table. The statements in arbitration are usually alternated in with open discussions, with the parties contributing and putting their arguments forward. Indeed, the arbitrators often make all efforts to maintain an informal climate.

The informal atmosphere enhances the chance of an amicable settlement. After each party has put across their arguments, supported with documents, there is a better understanding of each other's legal position, which may lead to an amicable settlement of their dispute. In some cases the parties will then request the arbitrators to make an agreed arbitral award along the lines of their amicable settlement.

Being speedy. It may take several months or even years to bring the case through court proceedings. With the chance of an appeal by the losing party, the court settlement of the dispute may be further considerably delayed. It is obvious that this delay is damaging trade where quick access to money due is desired.

In arbitration there is in principle only **a first instance procedure** and therefore no time should be lost in appeal procedures. The informality of arbitration proceedings also enhances the speed of settlement. A hearing is generally more quickly arranged in arbitration proceedings. If the arbitrators make it clear to the parties in an earlier stage that they understand the essence of their dispute, the parties do not need to spend more time repeating their arguments but can direct their attention to the points which are still unclear to the arbitrators, thus saving time.

Although occasionally time is lost in the appointment of arbitrators because the opposing party is intent on delaying the arbitration in bad faith and therefore does not appoint an arbitrator, such loss of time can be avoided when the claimant is not deceived by this conduct and requests the arbitration institution to appoint the arbitrator.

Being professional. International commercial disputes can be very complicated. Anyone entrusted to find a solution ought to be sufficiently familiar with the technical and commercial background of the dispute. Some disputes require extensive technical knowledge, so it is impossible and unrealistic for a judge who has to adjudicate all kinds of disputes to be an all-round technical expert. Disputes are sometimes rooted in a particular commercial sphere and can therefore only be solved in the light of practices of that environment. Outsiders, like judges, are less familiar with these practices. The judge may of course consider the appointment of an expert, but the intervention of the expert takes time and costs money. It can therefore be better to give the expert the task of adjudicating in the dispute directly, that is, to appoint him as an arbitrator. The wish to have disputes settled by professionals explains the success of the commodity arbitration in the different sectors.

Being confidential. The proceedings of the court are public with a few of exceptions. This public nature of the court is not always welcome: a competitor may hear the arguments in court and draw confidential information from this; newspapers may give the dispute unnecessary publicity, etc. Businessmen who need a confidential settlement may opt for arbitration because arbitration is not public: only the parties and their advocates have access to the meetings, the arbitrator are bound to secrecy and the award can only be published with the content of the parties.

Being neutral. One of the parties is often not willing to submit to the jurisdiction of a court in the country of the other party for fearing of being at a disadvantage. Arbitration permits the resolution of the case in a third "neutral" country, rather than in the country of one of the parties. The parties are generally free to choose the place of arbitration that is mutually convenient. For example, a dispute between a Canadian company and a Russian company might be arbitrated in Beijing or Paris. Moreover, the arbitrators may be chosen by the parties from a roster of impartial commercial professionals and legal professionals, who may also be from a third country. And the case may be resolved by using the impartial arbitration rules of the arbitral tribunal, rather than the procedure buried in the statutes of the country of one party.

Costs. Some argue arbitration fees are far less than litigation, as are attorney fees. But such a conclusion is not true in every case. Arbitration costs are more likely to be more than the costs of court proceedings. Arbitration is usually more expensive since parties generally have to pay the arbitrators for their services. Arbitrators can be paid on time basis: they are compensated for the time spent on the arbitration. This is the most important criterion in Anglo-American arbitration. Sometimes the importance of the dispute determines the remuneration: for example, in ICC International Court of Arbitration, the arbitrators are to a large extent paid according to the monetary value of the claim. For a $100,000 claim, the arbitration cost would be closer to 13%.

Yet, the relatively high costs of arbitration proceedings are partly compensated by the speed and informality of the proceedings, which in turn reduce the attorney's fees. Moreover, the parties can defend their case without an attorney.

Judicial confirmation. Arbitration only works efficiently when the arbitrators have actually solved a dispute. It is a fact that arbitral awards are generally fulfilled voluntarily. According to reports, 90% of the ICC International Court of Arbitration awards are honored by the losing party without any problems. However, there is always a risk that the losing party refuses to abide or apply for nullity of the arbitral award. In that case a court procedure must decide on the enforcement or the annulment of the award. Generally, such enforcement or the annulment proceedings have a limited scope and courts only examine the procedure problems for making the award. For instance, the scope is limited to the extent that whether there exists an invalid arbitration agreement, whether the arbitrator awards more than asked for (an *ultra petita* award), whether the rights of the defense are violated or whether an award is contrary to the public policy.

2.2 Arbitration Clauses in International Commercial Arbitration

The arbitration process requires at the outset an arbitration agreement or an arbitration clause in the contract for goods or services by the parties that they will resolve any disputes that arise between them by arbitration. It is important to note this need not be the only way that parties to an international contract may have recourse to arbitration, as they may agree, for example, to arbitration after a dispute arises between them. However, to remove much of the uncertainty and difficulty in the event of dispute, it is highly recommended the parties to agree to arbitration at an earlier stage when no dispute has yet arisen.

◆ Form of Arbitration Clauses

The arbitration clause or arbitration agreement is generally included in a contract signed by both parties. Sometimes an exchange of letters, telexes, faxes or electronic form will suffice. According to Article 16 of *Arbitration Law of the People's Republic of China* (1994) and Article 1 of *Judicial Interpretation on the Application of Arbitration Law of the People's Republic of the China* (2006), the arbitration agreement may take the form of written contract, letters, telexes, faxes, electronic data exchange or electronic mail.

◆ Validity of Arbitration Clauses

Generally, different arbitration laws have their own requirements for the validity of an arbitration agreement. Chinese Arbitration Law, for instance, requires that the dispute submitted to arbitration shall not exceed the scope of arbitration stipulated by the law, parties to the arbitration agreement have full competence, and the arbitration agreement shall not be reached through duress [Article 17 of *Arbitration Law of the People's Republic of China* (1994)]. In international commercial arbitration, the validity of arbitration agreement is in the first place determined by the applicable law of this agreement. Article 16 of *Judicial Interpretation on the Application of Arbitration Law of the People's*

Republic of China (2006) stipulates, the validity of arbitration agreement in international commercial arbitration is governed by the law chosen by the parties; in case that the parties do not choose the governing law but choose a seat of arbitration, the law of the seat of arbitration is applicable; where no governing law or a seat of arbitration is chosen, the *lex fori* shall apply.

A valid arbitration agreement/arbitration clause will exclude the jurisdiction of the court over the dispute to the extent covered by the arbitration agreement or arbitration clause. Now it is generally accepted. But in the early development of the international arbitration, this is not so clear. Read the following case: *Scherk v. Alberto-Culver Co.*

Case V-1

Scherk v. Alberto-Culver Co.

417 U.S. 506 (1974)

Background and Facts

Alberto-Culver Co. (respondent), an American manufacturer based in Illinois, in order to expand its overseas operations, purchased from Scherk (petitioner), a German citizen, three enterprises owned by him and organized under the laws of Germany and Liechtenstein, together with all trademark rights of these enterprises. The sales contract, which was negotiated in the United States, England, and Germany, signed in Austria, and closed in Switzerland, contained express warranties by the petitioner that the trademarks were unencumbered and a clause providing that **"any controversy or claim [that] shall arise out of this agreement or the breach thereof" would be referred to arbitration before the International Chamber of Commerce in Paris, France, and that Illinois laws would govern the agreement and its interpretation and performance**. Subsequently, after allegedly discovering that the trademarks were subject to substantial encumbrances, respondent offered to rescind the contract, but when petitioner refused, respondent brought suit in District Court for damages and other relief, contending that petitioner's fraudulent representations concerning the trademark rights violated s 10(b) of the *Securities Exchange Act of 1934*. Petitioner moved to dismiss the action or alternatively to stay the action pending arbitration, but the District Court denied the motion to dismiss and arbitration was enjoined. The Court of Appeals affirmed.

Justice Stewart

The United States Arbitration Act, now 9 U.S.C. 1 et seq., reversing centuries of judicial hostility to arbitration agreements, was designed to allow parties to avoid "the costliness and delays of litigation", and to place arbitration agreements "upon the same footing as other contracts". Accordingly, the Act provides that an arbitration agreement is here involved "shall be valid, irrevocable, and enforceable, save upon such grounds as exist at law or in equity for the revocation of any contract". (9 U.S.C. 2)

In *Wilko v. Swan* this Court acknowledged that the Act reflects a legislative recognition of the "desirability of arbitration as an alternative to the complications of litigation".

Alberto-Culver's contract to purchase the business entities belonging to Scherk was a truly international agreement. Alberto-Culver is an American corporation with its principal place of business and the vast bulk of its activity in this country, while Scherk is a citizen of Germany whose companies were organized under the laws of Germany and Liechtenstein. The negotiations leading to the signing of the contract in Austria and to the closing in Switzerland took place in the United States, England, and Germany, and involved consultations with legal and trademark experts from each of those countries and from Liechtenstein. Finally, and most significantly, the subject matter of the contract concerned the sale of business enterprises organized under the laws of and primarily situated in European countries, whose activities were largely, if not entirely, directed to European markets.

Such a contract involves considerations and policies significantly different from those found controlling in Wilko. In Wilko, quite apart from the arbitration provision, there was no question but that the laws of the United States generally, and the federal securities laws in particular, would govern disputes arising out of the stock-purchase agreement. The parties, the negotiations, and the subject matter of the contract were all situated in this country, and no credible claim could have been entertained that any international conflict-of-laws problems would arise. In this case, by contrast, in the absence of the arbitration provision considerable uncertainty existed at the time of the agreement, and still exists, concerning the law applicable to the resolution of disputes arising out of the contract.

Such uncertainty will almost inevitably exist with respect to any contract touching two or more countries, each with its own substantive laws and conflict-of-laws rules.

A contractual provision specifying in advance the forum in which disputes shall be litigated and the law to be applied is, therefore, an almost indispensable precondition to achievement of the orderliness and predictability essential to any international business transaction. Furthermore, such a provision obviates the danger that a dispute under the agreement might be submitted to a forum hostile to the interests of one of the parties or unfamiliar with the problem area involved.

A parochial refusal by the courts of one country to enforce an international arbitration agreement would not only frustrate these purposes, but would invite unseemly and mutually destructive jockeying by the parties to secure tactical litigation advantages. In the present case, for example, it is not inconceivable that if Scherk had anticipated that Alberto-Culver would be able in this country to enjoin resort to arbitration he might have sought an order in France or some other country enjoining Alberto-Culver from proceeding with its litigation in the United States. Whatever recognition the courts of this country might ultimately have granted to the order of the foreign court, the dicey atmosphere of such a legal no-man's-land would surely damage the fabric of international commerce and trade, and imperil the willingness and ability of businessmen to enter into international commercial agreements...

For all these reasons we hold that the agreement of the parties in this case to arbitrate any dispute arising out of their international commercial transaction is to be respected and enforced by the federal courts in accordance with the explicit provisions of the Arbitration Act.

Decision

The judgment of the Court of Appeals is reversed and the case is remanded to that court.

Dispute resolution in international commercial transactions runs the gamut from friendly negotiation to litigation. In between lies the international commercial arbitration, a binding alternative to litigation. The volume of international commercial arbitration has grown enormously in recent decades around the world. Contracting parties often agree that potential disputes concerning the contract will be settled through arbitration. Thus a clear understanding of the arbitration is necessary.

However, it may be that one party claims that the contract which contains the arbitration clause, is invalid as a whole for a reason unrelated to the arbitration clause.

The arbitration clause then is protected against the alleged invalidity of the contract as a whole, because the nullity of the contract does not necessarily result in the invalidity of the arbitration clause (the so-called "**autonomy of the arbitration clause**").

◆ **Drafting Arbitration Clauses**

The arbitration clause/agreement is not only the basis for arbitration, it often gives the arbitration shape as well. An arbitration clause must be carefully structured and worded. Generally speaking, the parties may arrange everything in the arbitration clause through mutual agreement on the condition that such arrangements are not contrary to the applicable law. Arbitration laws of different countries determine the least specific elements of an arbitration clause. Article 16 of *Arbitration Law of the People's Republic of China* (1994) requires an arbitration clause shall cover: **intention of the parties to submit the dispute to arbitration, disputes covered by the jurisdiction of the arbitrators** and **the selection of an arbitral institution**. For example, an arbitration clause states "disputes arising from the performance of a contract shall be submitted to arbitration" may have excluded disputes on other issues such as contract interpretation and nullity to be heard by the arbitration institution.

If the drafters of a contract do not have the necessary expertise, they had better incorporate one of the available ready-made arbitration clauses. Many arbitration institutions offer suitable draft arbitration clauses. They may possibly offer sufficient inspiration for the drafting of an appropriate arbitration clause. Hereafter follows the arbitration clauses recommended by ICC and UNCITRAL for submission of disputes to arbitration by the respective institutions.

The arbitration clause of the ICC reads:

"All disputes arising in connection with the present contract shall be finally settled under the Rules of Conciliation and Arbitration of International Chamber of Commerce by one or more arbitrators appointed in accordance with the said Rules."

The arbitration clause of the UNCITRAL reads:

"Any dispute, controversy or claim arising out of or relating to this contract, or the breach, termination or invalidity thereof, shall be settled by arbitration in accordance with the UNCITRAL Arbitration Rules as at present in force."

They are concise ones. And sometimes parties may wish to consider adding:

"The number of arbitrators shall be ... (one or three); the place of arbitration shall be ... (city or country) and the language(s) to be used in the arbitral proceedings shall be ..."

2.3 Arbitration Procedure in International Commercial Arbitration

The arbitration procedure is relatively straightforward. In its simplest form, the parties begin the process by the selection of an arbitrator or arbitrators. If they have agreed upon a place for arbitration to take place, the location is decided; otherwise the arbitrator or tribunal may fix the location. The parties then exchange statements of claim and defense and any further statements, including any pleas as to the jurisdiction of the arbitral tribunal. The next step in the process is hearing itself, where the arbitrator or arbitral tribunal will hear the evidence of the parties, any expert testimony, and final arguments. The arbitrator or arbitral tribunal will then deliberate and issue an award. Generally if the parties have selected an arbitration institution, rules of the arbitration institution shall apply to the process of arbitration, unless the parties agree to be bound by other arbitration rules. For example, UNCITRAL rules cover the appointing authority, notice requirements, representation of the parties, challenges of arbitrators, evidence, hearings, statements of claims and defenses, pleas to the arbitrator's jurisdiction, provisional remedies, experts, default, rule waivers, the form and effect of the award, applicable law, settlement, interpretation of the award and costs. *Arbitration Rules of China International Economic and Trade Arbitration Commission* (2015) cover similar items of matters.

◆ Appointment of Arbitrators

An arbitral tribunal consists of one or three arbitrators. When only one arbitrator has to adjudicate on a dispute the parties usually have no difficulty over this appointment. In case of three arbitrators, each of the party, within 15 days upon receiving the notice of arbitration, appoints an arbitrator and a third arbitrator is then appointed jointly by the parties or by the arbitration institution based on the authorization of the parties. The third arbitrator is the presiding arbitrator. The nominated arbitration institution is also competent to appoint an arbitrator if one of the parties refuses to cooperate. For example, Article 27 of *Arbitration Rules of China International Economic and Trade Arbitration Commission* (2015) provides: within 15 days from the date of receipt of the Notice of Arbitration, the Claimant and the Respondent shall each nominate, or entrust the Chairman of CIETAC to appoint, an arbitrator, failing which the arbitrator shall be appointed by the Chairman of CIETAC; within 15 days from the date of the Respondent's receipt of the Notice of Arbitration, the parties shall jointly nominate, or entrust the Chairman of CIETAC to appoint, the third arbitrator, who shall act as the presiding arbitrator; the parties may each recommend one to five arbitrators as candidates for the presiding arbitrator and shall each submit a list of recommended candidates within the time period specified in the preceding paragraph. Where there is only one common candidate on the lists, such candidate shall be the presiding arbitrator jointly nominated by the parties. Where there is more than one common candidate on the lists, the Chairman of CIETAC shall choose the presiding arbitrator from among the common candidates having regard to the circumstances of the case, and he/she shall act as the presiding arbitrator jointly nominated by the parties. Where there is no common candidate on the lists, the presiding arbitrator shall be appointed by the Chairman of CIETAC; where the parties have failed to jointly nominate the presiding arbitrator according to the above provisions, the presiding arbitrator shall be appointed by the Chairman of CIETAC. The arbitrator appointed by one party cannot consider himself as an agent of that party: he must have an independent and impartial view. If this independence and impartiality are compromised the arbitrator must refuse or hand back the appointment. Arbitrators must, in any event, disclose to the parties all instances, such as conflict of interests, financial ties, personal ties, etc. that could jeopardize their independence and impartiality. And the parties are entitled to challenge the independence and impartiality of arbitrators with cause.

◆ **Arbitration Proceedings**

Parties have a wide range of options for the setting up of arbitration proceedings. If they do not make use of these options, it is up to the arbitration institution to direct the arbitration proceedings. *Arbitration Rules of China International Economic and Trade Arbitration Commission* (2015) require a fundamental condition for the arbitration procedure that every party is entitled to an equal and fair trial. A breach of the fundamental rule of the right to an equal and fair trial results in the award set aside by the court of China.

The parties state the claims and defenses, submit evidence and debate. The arbitrators can order an expert assessment, a local visit, hear parties or witnesses and decide which evidence will be considered sufficient proof. If one of the parties does not cooperate without legal reasons the arbitrators have jurisdiction to make an award by default. The arbitrators are required to make their award within six months, and at the due request of arbitrators the Director of China International Economic and Trade Arbitration Commission may grant an extension.

2.4 Enforcement of Foreign Arbitral Awards: New York Convention

The enforcement of an international commercial arbitration award is obviously of critical importance to the winner in the award. Parties are deemed to be bound by the arbitral award unless the award has been annulled. As for the international commercial arbitration, often the losing party gives effect to the arbitral award voluntarily. Because there is frequently social and commercial pressure from the commercial sector to abide by the arbitral award: an enterprise known for defaulting on arbitral awards loses credibility. However, the arbitral award can be enforced where necessary through a court order. Necessarily, this requires a mechanism by which the award of a private adjudicator becomes enforceable by public authorities—the award must be recognized and enforced by states. The award is enforceable where the losing party has assets located or where that party resides. To overcome the problems of enforcing an international arbitral award in another country than that of the seat, an important international treaty has been adopted—the *United Nations Convention on the Recognition and Enforcement of Foreign Arbitral Awards* [New York Convention (1958)]. This convention, up to now being in force between over 160 states, improves the enforcement of international commercial arbitration awards considerably. The New York Convention (1958) has been praised to be "the single most important pillar on which the edifice of international arbitration rests."①

The New York Convention (1958) **applies to the recognition and enforcement of arbitral awards, which are rendered in another territory of state**. Such arbitral awards are intended to settle the disputes between private parties not states. The New York Convention (1958) commits the courts in each contracting states to recognize and enforce (under local procedure rules) the awards of arbitral tribunals under arbitration clauses and arbitration agreements, which are valid and capable of being performed. Among contracting states of the New York Convention (1958), the party seeking enforcement of an arbitral award only needs to submit the arbitration agreement and the award to a court of the forum state. The burden of proof rests on the defendant to show that the award cannot be enforced by the court. The New York Convention (1958) sets forth the limited grounds under which recognition and enforcement of arbitral awards may be refused:

(1) Incapacity of a party to the agreement containing the arbitration clause or the invalidity of the arbitration agreement under the law applicable to a party to the agreement;

(2) Lack of proper notice of arbitration proceedings, the appointment of arbitrators or other reasons denying an adequate opportunity to present a defense;

(3) Failure of the arbitral award to restrict itself to the terms of the submission to

① Alan Redfern & Martin Hunter, *Law and Practice of International Commercial Arbitration*, Sweet & Maxwell, 1991, p.457.

arbitration, or decision of matters not within the scope of that submission;

(4) Composition of the arbitral institution not according to the arbitration agreement or applicable law; and

(5) Non-finality of the arbitral award under applicable law.

In addition to these grounds for refusal, **recognition or enforcement of arbitral awards may also be refused if it would be contrary to the public policy** of the country in which enforcement is sought; or **if the subject matter of the dispute cannot be settled by arbitration under the law of that country**. To some degree, the connotation of public policy is not so clear. Generally it is thought to be the most basic and material morality and public interests. Courts in the United States have taken the position that the "public policy limitation on the New York Convention (1958) is to be construed narrowly and to be applied only where enforcement would violate the forum state's most basic notions of morality and justice."①

The People's Republic of China (China) has adopted the New York Convention (1958) on December 2, 1986, while two reservations to the New York Convention (1958) were made:

(1) China will apply the New York Convention (1958) to the recognition and enforcement of arbitral awards rendered in the territory of another contracting state only on the basis of reciprocity; and

(2) China will apply the New York Convention (1958) only to the disputes arising from the contractual and non-contractual commercial relationships defined by the laws of China.

The New York Convention (1958), subject to the above reservations, became legally effective in China on April 22, 1987. That is, China will apply the New York Convention (1958) to the recognition and enforcement of arbitral awards rendered in the territory of another contracting state. And China will apply the New York Convention (1958) to disputes arising from commercial relationships defined by the laws of China.

As for the mutual recognition and enforcement of arbitral awards between Hong Kong SAR and the Mainland of China, it deserves special attention. After July 1, 1997, the New York Convention (1958) still applies to Hong Kong SAR. That is, the arbitral awards rendered in Hong Kong SAR can be recognized and enforced by other contracting parties to the New York Convention (1958). However, arbitral awards rendered in Hong

① See Fotochrome, Inc. *v.* Copal Co., Ltd., 517 F. 2d 512 (2d Cir. 1975).

Kong SAR shall not be recognized and enforced in the Mainland of China pursuant to the New York Convention (1958), since Hong Kong is a SAR under the sovereignty of the People's Republic of China. In order to facilitate the mutual recognition and enforcement of arbitral awards between Hong Kong SAR and the Mainland of China, the *Arrangement on the Mutual Enforcement of Arbitral Awards Between Hong Kong SAR and Mainland of China* was issued by the Supreme People's Court of China, which has come into effect since February 1, 2000. Most of the provisions on the enforcement of arbitral awards in this Arrangement are much similar to those in the New York Convention (1958).

3 Settlement of International Commercial Disputes Through Litigation

Litigation is the last resort in attempting to settle a dispute including international commercial one. The complexity of settling international disputes through litigation mainly lies in the divergences of different legal systems and the lack of uncertainty in the jurisdiction and enforcement of judgment. For example, the role of judge may be very different. In some countries the judges is an impartial arbiter of fairness and procedure, while in other countries he may examine witnesses and take an active role in the search of the truth.

To facilitate the settlement of international commercial disputes through litigation, the China International Commercial Court (CICC) has been established by the Supreme People's Court of China (SPC) to deal with international commercial disputes. The CICC has two branches: the First International Commercial Court is situated in Shenzhen, Guangdong Province, and the Second International Commercial Court in Xi'an, Shaanxi Province. The CICC's objective is to try international commercial cases fairly and timely in accordance with law, protect the lawful rights and interests of the Chinese and foreign parties equally, and create a stable, fair, transparent, and convenient rule of law international business environment. Cases tried by the CICC shall be heard by a collegial panel consisting of three or more judges. The judgments and rulings made by the CICC are final and binding on the parties. CICC accepts the following cases:

(1) First instance international commercial cases in which the parties have chosen the jurisdiction of SPC in accordance with Article 34 of *Civil Procedure Law of the People's Republic of China*, with an amount in dispute of at least RMB 300,000,000;

(2) First instance international commercial cases under the jurisdiction of a higher

people's court of which nonetheless the higher people's court considers that the cases should be tried by SPC and have obtained the relevant permission;

(3) First instance international commercial cases that have a significant nationwide impact;

(4) Cases where the parties apply for confirmation of the validity of the arbitration agreement or for setting aside the arbitral award, which are subject to Article 14, Para. 2, of the *Provisions of the Supreme People's Court on Several Issues Regarding the Establishment of the International Commercial Court*; and

(5) Other international commercial cases that SPC deems necessary to be tried by CICC. Parties to an international commercial case may apply for online case filing by clicking the "Litigation Service" button on the "One-Stop" International Commercial Dispute Resolution Platform, which can be accessed via the CICC official website (cicc.court.gov.cn).①

3.1 Jurisdiction

Jurisdiction is one of the key concepts of jurisprudence and the power of a court to hear and decide a case. A court that has jurisdiction is said to be a "competent" court. Jurisdiction is the starting point for a suit and the legal basis for a court to hear the case. For settling an international dispute through litigation, deciding the proper jurisdiction over the dispute is on the first place. Several principles have been developed to establish the jurisdiction over international suits. **In personam jurisdiction** (jurisdiction over the person) refers to the courts' power of one sovereign state over an individual or a legal entity of its nationality or domicile in the state. Under **in rem jurisdiction** (jurisdiction over the thing), the courts of one state have the power to determine the disputes arising from property located within the territory thereof. **Subject matter jurisdiction** refers to the court's authority to hear a certain type of legal matter, such as tort cases or breach of contract. **Territorial jurisdiction** is a jurisdictional responsibility that is established by geography, which is widely adopted by nations. Territorial jurisdiction is the primary consideration when determining which court will hear a case. A court cannot assert subject-matter or personal jurisdiction if it does not also have territorial jurisdiction. At the international law, it is a well-established principle that every state possesses exclusive

① More information about the China International Commercial Court (CICC) can be found at http://cicc.court.gov.cn/.

sovereignty and jurisdiction over persons and property within its territory, and no state can exercise direct jurisdiction and authority over persons and property outside its territory. Thus the jurisdiction over the person is limited to people physically present in the court's territory. However, as the international commerce expanded, the concept was broadened by the U.S. Supreme Court to allow jurisdiction over persons who were not present within the court's geographical territory. In decisions dealing with both interstate and international commerce, a state court may exercise jurisdiction over persons located outside the state's territory, but only if the defendant had "minimum contacts" with the forum state and "such that the maintenance of the suit does not offend traditional notions of fair play and substantial justice."[①] But for the factors of "minimum contacts", the courts have answered the question on a case-by-case basis. For example, did the defendant have an office in the territory of the forum? Did it advertise or otherwise solicit business there? Did it ship goods there? Did it enter into a contract there, or was the contract to be performed there? There is no uniform answer. Later, the U.S. courts began to apply the minimum contacts test in the international context, which has provoked substantial criticism.

Civil Procedure Law of the People's Republic of China provides its jurisdiction over international civil suits (including international commercial suits) as follows:

(1) A contractual dispute or a dispute arising from other interests of property may be heard by the forum where the contract is entered into, the contract is performed, the subject matter is located, the executable property is located, the tort is committed, or the representation agency domiciles, in case that the defendant does not have a domicile in the territory of China.

(2) Without prejudice to the exclusive jurisdiction and hierarchy jurisdiction of courts of China, parties to a contractual dispute or a dispute arising from other interests of property may, by written agreement, choose a forum from those bearing an actual connection with the dispute under the laws of China.

(3) The disputes arising out of performing the Chinese-foreign contractual joint venture agreement, Chinese-foreign equity joint venture agreement, Chinese-foreign agreement for exploration and development of natural resources shall **exclusively** fall within the jurisdiction of courts of China.

(4) The act that the defendant does not challenge the jurisdiction of the court and reply to the complaint shall be deemed to have approved such jurisdiction.

---

① See International Shoe Co. *v*. Washington, 326 U.S.C. 310 (1945).

Cross-border litigation inherently provides for the possibility of the law of at least two nations. And laws in different states often compete in jurisdiction. Therefore these undoubtedly will give rise to conflicts of jurisdiction on the international commercial disputes.

Business people negotiating international business transactions can avoid much of the uncertainty over jurisdiction by including a **forum selection clause** in their contracts. A forum selection clause is a provision in a contract that fixes in advance the jurisdiction in which any disputes will be arbitrated or litigated. It provides certainty because the parties know where a dispute will be resolved. One of the major advantages of these clauses is that they eliminate the last-minute attempt by lawyers to go "forum shopping" by filing suits in jurisdictions that offer the best law for their case. The last chance for forum shopping may very well be during contract negotiations. This allows both parties to agree on a forum, perhaps the courts of a certain country, which they find acceptable. Of course, negitiation on a forum selection clause will be suject to the bargaining power of the parties in the reality. It is often that the party to the contract with the greatest bargaining power calls for disputes to be resolved in the courts of the country where it is located. Forum selection clauses are generally accepted as valid provided that the forum chosen has some reasonable connection to the transaction.

3.2 Choosing the Governing Law

Laws in most countries will allow parties to a commercial contract to have some control over choosing the governing law by incorporating choice of law clauses in their contracts. **Choice of law clauses**, also known as governing law clauses, are a provision in contracts determining which laws apply to the adjudication if a question or dispute arises. As a general rule, the choice of law clauses will be upheld as long as there is **a reasonable relationship between the transaction and the jurisdiction chosen**. Choice of law clauses are generally accepted valid and will be applied to solve the dispute unless otherwise proven. *The Law of the Application of Law for Foreign-Related Civil Relations of the People's Republic of China* provides that the parties may expressly choose the law applicable to foreign-related civil relations (Article 3). However, where the laws of the People's Republic of China have mandatory provisions on foreign-related civil relations, such mandatory provisions shall directly apply (Article 4), and where the application of foreign laws will harm the social and public interests of the People's Republic of China, the laws of the People's Republic of China shall apply (Article 5).

A choice of law clause can gives the parties more certainty of how a dispute will be handled and helps to reduce the lengh of time for solving the dispute. Different governing law will have a significant impact on how the dispute turns out. Of course, negotiations on a choice of law clause will also be subject to the bargaining power of the parties in the reality. Though the specific language may vary, parties to contracts should make sure the wording of choice of clauses is thorough and detailed, avoiding ambiguity.

3.3 Proving Foreign Law

If the court hearing an international commercial dispute determines that it should apply foreign law to the case, how does it know what that law is? In U.S. the federal courts will follow the *Federal Rules of Civil Procedure*. Rule 44.1 states that: A party who intends to raise an issue concerning the law of a foreign country shall give notice by pleadings or other reasonable written notice. The court, in determining foreign law, may consider any relevant material or source, including testimony, whether or not submitted by a party or admissible under the *Federal Rules of Evidence*. Accordingly, judges may conduct their own research of foreign law, they may request briefs provided by the parties, or they may rely on the testimony of foreign lawyers in or out of court.

In China, the Supreme People's Court's Interpretation on Implementing General Rules of Civil Law (1988) has provided the general rules for proving foreign law: the applicable foreign law may be proved by the means that (1) the parties concerned provide; (2) the central organ of the foreign state with which China has concluded such judicial aid agreement provide; (3) Chinese embassy and consulate in the foreign state provide; (4) the legal experts (home or abroad) provide. Where exhausting all the above means only fails to prove the foreign law, the laws of the People's Republic of China will apply. *The Law of the Application of Law for Foreign-Related Civil Relations of the People's Republic of China* provides that the foreign laws applicable to foreign-related civil relations shall be ascertained by the people's courts, arbitration institutions or administrative organs. If a party chooses to apply the law of a foreign country, it shall provide the law of that country. If it fails to prove foreign laws or there are no applicable provisions in the laws of that country, the laws of the People's Republic of China shall apply (Article 10). Further, Judicial Interpretation on the Application of Law in Foreign-Related Civil Relations of PRC (I) provides that if the court fails to obtain the foreign law through reasonable channels such as those provided by the parties, the channels provided by the international treaties that are binding on the People's Republic of China, and the channels provided by Chinese and foreign legal experts, it may be deemed that the foreign laws cannot be proven. Where providing the foreign law is the obligation of one party to the dispute, a party shall provide the foreign law. If the party fails to provide such foreign laws without justified reasons within a reasonable time limit specified by the court, it may be deemed that the foreign law cannot be proven.

Proof of foreign law often requires obtaining translations. If there is a published version of the foreign statutes, it is likely to have been translated objectively and thus will be accepted by the court. Where the parties have to translate the foreign statutes, they may do so with a choice of words favoring their case. The court may have to choose between two versions.

3.4 Recognizing and Enforcing Foreign Judgment

Unlike the recognition and enforcement of foreign arbitral awards, there is no such a widely accepted international convention as the New York Convention (1958) governing the recognition and enforcement of foreign judgment. Each legal system has its own enforcement rules for foreign judgment. Therefore, generally it is more difficult to enforce a foreign judgment. In practice it is often sensible to take legal action in the country where the defendant has assets in order to facilitate the enforcement of a judgment in that country, since a judgment can be enforced in the country where it was passed without additional proceedings.

Convention on the Recognition and Enforcement of Foreign Judgments in Civil or Commercial Matters, adopted on July 2, 2019 by the Hague Conference on Private International Law, aims to promote efficiency by facilitating a uniform set of core rules for the recognition and enforcement of international judgments. The Convention imposes an obligation on contracting states to ensure judgments given by a court of a contracting state is recognized and enforced in another contracting state. The Convention broadly applies to commercial and civil matters. However, there are distinct areas of civil and commercial law which are excluded from the scope of the Convention, such as insolvency, defamation and intellectual property. Additionally, the Convention does not apply to arbitrations and arbitration related proceedings. The Convention outlines a relatively simple procedure to apply to have a foreign judgment recognized and enforced. The party seeking the enforcement has to provide a complete and certified copy of the judgment. The remainder of the enforcement procedure is left to the law of the state in which judgment is to be enforced. Recognition and enforcement of an eligible judgment may only be refused on the grounds specified in the Convention. Such grounds are specified in Article 7 of the Convention:

"1. Recognition or enforcement may be refused if —

(a) the document which instituted the proceedings or an equivalent document, including a statement of the essential elements of the claim —

(i) was not notified to the defendant in sufficient time and in such a way as to enable them to arrange for their defence, unless the defendant entered an appearance and presented their case without contesting notification in the court of origin, provided that the law of the State of origin permitted notification to be contested; or

(ii) was notified to the defendant in the requested State in a manner that is incompatible with fundamental principles of the requested State concerning service of documents;

(b) the judgment was obtained by fraud;

(c) recognition or enforcement would be manifestly incompatible with the public policy of the requested State, including situations where the specific proceedings leading to the judgment were incompatible with fundamental principles of procedural fairness of that State and situations involving infringements of security or sovereignty of that State;

(d) the proceedings in the court of origin were contrary to an agreement, or a designation in a trust instrument, under which the dispute in question was to be determined in a court of a State other than the State of origin;

(e) the judgment is inconsistent with a judgment given by a court of the requested State in a dispute between the same parties; or

(f) the judgment is inconsistent with an earlier judgment given by a court of another State between the same parties on the same subject matter, provided that the earlier judgment fulfils the conditions necessary for its recognition in the requested State.

"2. Recognition or enforcement may be postponed or refused if proceedings between the same parties on the same subject matter are pending before a court of the requested State, where —

(a) the court of the requested State was seised before the court of origin; and

(b) there is a close connection between the dispute and the requested State."

A refusal under this Paragraph does not prevent a subsequent application for recognition or enforcement of the judgment.

Under *Civil Procedure Law of the People's Republic of China*, where a legally effective judgment or written order rendered by a foreign court requires recognition and enforcement by a people's court of the People's Republic of China, the party may directly apply to the intermediate people's court with jurisdiction or the foreign court may apply for the recognition and enforcement pursuant to the international treaties concluded or acceded to by the foreign state and the People's Republic of China or on the basis of reciprocity. After review, the people's court, if reaching the conclusion that the foreign judgment does not contradict the basic principles of the laws of the People's Republic of China nor violates state sovereignty, security and public interests, will recognize the judgment and enforce it in accordance with relevant provisions of *Civil Procedure Law of the People's Republic of China.* Where the application for recognition and enforcement contradicts the basic principles of laws of the People's Republic of China or violates state sovereignty, security and public interests, the people's court will deny the recognition and enforcement.

Chapter Summary

During the course of international commercial transactions, disputes are not welcome but seemingly unavoidable. The disputes will do harm to the long-term business relationships between parties. And when disputes become combative, it can be money costing, time consuming, and physically and mentally exhausting for all parties. However, there is the real possibility that one or both of the parties will have to resolve the dispute between them through methods of resolution. ADR such as negotiation, mediation or mini-trial usually provides a faster and cheaper alternative to litigation. Arbitration is a more formalized process. The parties to the dispute must agree to arbitration by agreeing upon an arbitration clause or agreement. Arbitration will result in a binding award that will be enforced by courts in many countries under the New York Convention (1958). Litigation is the final step in attempting to resolve a dispute. One of the key concepts in litigation is jurisdiction. No court can enter a judgment against a natural person or a legal entity unless the court has the jurisdiction over them. Different principles of juridiction are established and interpreted in different countries. To reduce the uncertainty in the jurisdiction and governing law to the case, the parties to an international business transaction may negotiate a forum selection clause and a choice of law clause in their contract. A forum selection clause is a provision in a contract that provides in advance the court in which any disputes will be litigated. A choice of law clause is a contract provision that stipulates which country's law will apply to solve any disputes arising from the contract. As a general rule, the foreign judgment will be enforced according to the international treaties between nations or on the basis of reciprocity.

When negotiating international transactions, the prudent businessperson should hope for the best and always plan for the worst. Planning for disputes in advance, such as by inserting a well-draft arbitration clause or a choice of law clause in the contract, is a proper method of minimizing risk in transactions. The importance of the contract cannot be overstated because if and when a dispute arises, the terms of the contract provide the basis for dispute resolution.

Exercises

I. True or False Statements

1. To resolve an international commercial dispute, the parties must firstly submit it to arbitration.

2. If the party did not obtain a satisfactory award through mediation, he/she may continue to bring the same dispute to a court with jurisdiction for resolution.

3. According to the laws of China, an arbitration clause taking the form of e-mail is deemed to be invalid.

4. If the contract, which contains the arbitration clause, is invalid as a whole for a reason unrelated to the arbitration clause, the arbitration clause then is invalid and parties cannot resort to arbitration.

5. A court in China may refuse to enforce a foreign arbitral award rendered by American Arbitration Association on the basis that the award contradicts the public policy of China.

6. An arbitration agreement must be made before a dispute arises between the parties.

7. In an agreement for exploration and development of natural resources in China concluded between a Chinese company and an American corporation, the parties may choose the U.S. law to govern the disputes arising out of the performance of this agreement.

8. China will not apply the New York Convention (1958) to the recognition and enforcement of arbitral awards rendered in the territory of a non-contracting state.

9. A dispute arising out of inheritance between a Chinese citizen and a Canadian citizen can be submitted to China International Economic and Trade Commission for arbitration.

10. A contracting state of the New York Convention (1958) can refuse to recognize

and enforce a foreign arbitral award rendered in another contracting state on the ground that the arbitrators took bribery.

II. Chapter Questions

1. How many methods of dispute resolution in international commercial transactions? Please give the list.

2. How do you understand the relationship between ADR and arbitration?

3. What is the essential difference between mediation and arbitration?

4. What are the advantages and disadvantages of resolving international commercial disputes by arbitration?

5. Suppose two parties of a sales contract agree to submit any dispute arising from performance of the contract to China International Economic and Trade Arbitration Commission. Try to draft the arbitration clause for them.

6. How would a choice of law clause in the contract help to address some of a party's concern?

7. What the differnce between the forum selection clause and the choice of law clause?

8. In accordance with the New York Convention (1958), what are the grounds under which recognition and enforcement of foreign arbitral awards may be refused?

9. Will a Chinese court enforce a Mexico judgment dealing with a loan agreement on a promissory note if the note contradicts the relevant provisions in Negotiable Instruments Law of China? Suppose there is no treaty in this aspect but reciprocity between China and Mexico.

10. How many ways can the court prove the applicable foreign law when hearing an international commercial dispute under the laws of China?

III. Reading Material

The UNCITRAL Arbitration Rules provide a comprehensive set of procedural rules upon which parties may agree for the conduct of arbitration. The Rules cover all aspects of the arbitral process, providing a model arbitration clause, setting out procedural rules regarding the appointment of arbitrators and the conduct of arbitral proceedings, and establishing rules in relation to the form, effect and interpretation of the award. Thus the Rules are widely used in ad hoc arbitrations as well as institutional arbitrations.

The original UNCITRAL Arbitration Rules were adopted in 1976 and have been used for the settlement of a broad range of disputes, including disputes between private commercial parties, investor-state disputes, state-to-state disputes. In 2006, the UNCITRAL decided that the Rules should be revised in order to meet changes in arbitral practice over the last 30 years. The revision is aimed at enhancing the efficiency of arbitration under the Rules and does not alter the original structure of the text, its spirit or drafting style.

The UNCITRAL Arbitration Rules, as revised, have been effective since August 15, 2010. A number of innovative features contained in the Rules aim to enhance procedural efficiency, including revised procedures for the replacement of an arbitrator, the requirement for reasonableness of costs, and a review mechanism regarding the costs of arbitration. They also include more detailed provisions on interim measures.

The following is an excerpt of the UNCITRAL Arbitration Rules. Read and compare them with China International Economic and Trade Arbitration Commission Arbitration Rules (2015).

CHAPTER III. COMPOSITION OF ARBITRAL TRIBUNAL

Article 10. Number of arbitrators

(1) The parties are free to determine the number of arbitrators.

(2) Failing such determination, the number of arbitrators shall be three.

Article 11. Appointment of arbitrators

(1) No person shall be precluded by reason of his nationality from acting as an arbitrator, unless otherwise agreed by the parties.

(2) The parties are free to agree on a procedure of appointing the arbitrator or arbitrators, subject to the provisions of paragraphs (4) and (5) of this article.

(3) Failing such agreement,

(a) in an arbitration with three arbitrators, each party shall appoint one arbitrator, and the two arbitrators thus appointed shall appoint the third arbitrator; if a party fails to appoint the arbitrator within thirty days of receipt of a request to do so from the other party, or if the two arbitrators fail to agree on the third arbitrator within thirty days of their appointment, the appointment shall be made, upon request of a party, by the court or other authority specified in article 6;

(b) in an arbitration with a sole arbitrator, if the parties are unable to agree on the arbitrator, he shall be appointed, upon request of a party, by the court or other authority specified in article 6.

(4) Where, under an appointment procedure agreed upon by the parties,

(a) a party fails to act as required under such procedure, or

(b) the parties, or two arbitrators, are unable to reach an agreement expected of them under such procedure, or

(c) a third party, including an institution, fails to perform any function entrusted to it under such procedure, any party may request the court or other authority specified in article 6 to take the necessary measure, unless the agreement on the appointment procedure provides other means for securing the appointment.

(5) A decision on a matter entrusted by paragraph (3) or (4) of this article to the court or other authority specified in article 6 shall be subject to no appeal. The court or other authority, in appointing an arbitrator, shall have due regard to any qualifications required of the arbitrator by the agreement of the parties and to such considerations as are likely to secure the appointment of an independent and impartial arbitrator and, in the case of a sole or third arbitrator, shall take into account as well the advisability of appointing an arbitrator of a nationality other than those of the parties.

Article 12. Grounds for challenge

(1) When a person is approached in connection with his possible appointment as an arbitrator, he shall disclose any circumstances likely to give rise to justifiable doubts as to his impartiality or independence. An arbitrator, from the time of his appointment and throughout the arbitral proceedings, shall without delay disclose any such circumstances to the parties unless they have already been informed of them by him.

(2) An arbitrator may be challenged only if circumstances exist that give rise to justifiable doubts as to his impartiality or independence, or if he does not possess qualifications agreed to by the parties. A party may challenge an arbitrator appointed by him, or in whose appointment he has participated, only for reasons of which he becomes aware after the appointment has been made.

Article 13. Challenge procedure

(1) The parties are free to agree on a procedure for challenging an arbitrator, subject to the provisions of paragraph (3) of this article.

(2) Failing such agreement, a party who intends to challenge an arbitrator shall, within fifteen days after becoming aware of the constitution of the arbitral tribunal or after becoming aware of any circumstance referred to in article 12(2), send a written statement of the reasons for the challenge to the arbitral tribunal. Unless the challenged arbitrator withdraws from his office or the other party agrees to the challenge, the arbitral tribunal

shall decide on the challenge.

(3) If a challenge under any procedure agreed upon by the parties or under the procedure of paragraph (2) of this article is not successful, the challenging party may request, within thirty days after having received notice of the decision rejecting the challenge, the court or other authority specified in article 6 to decide on the challenge, which decision shall be subject to no appeal; while such a request is pending, the arbitral tribunal, including the challenged arbitrator, may continue the arbitral proceedings and make an award.

Article 14. Failure or impossibility to act

(1) If an arbitrator becomes de jure or de facto unable to perform his functions or for other reasons fails to act without undue delay, his mandate terminates if he withdraws from his office or if the parties agree on the termination. Otherwise, if a controversy remains concerning any of these grounds, any party may request the court or other authority specified in article 6 to decide on the termination of the mandate, which decision shall be subject to no appeal.

(2) If, under this article or article 13(2), an arbitrator withdraws from his office or a party agrees to the termination of the mandate of an arbitrator, this does not imply acceptance of the validity of any ground referred to in this article or article 12(2).

List of Legal Terms

Part I

absolute advantage	绝对优势
Association of Southeast Asian Nations (ASEAN)	东南亚国家联盟（东盟）
civil law system	民法法系（大陆法系）
common law system	普通法系
comparative advantage	比较优势
competitive advantage	竞争优势
Convention on the Recognition and Enforcement of Foreign Arbitral Awards (New York Convention 1958)	《承认及执行外国仲裁裁决公约》（《纽约公约》）
deglobalization	逆全球化
equity	衡平法
export control	出口管制
export license	出口许可
fiqh	伊斯兰教法理学
foreign aid/assistance	对外援助
French Civil Code of 1804	1804 年《法国民法典》
General Agreement on Tariffs and Trade 1947 (GATT 1947)	1947 年《关税与贸易总协定》
General Agreement on Trade in Services (GATS)	《服务贸易总协定》
General Assembly	（联合国）大会
German Civil Code of 1896	1896 年《德国民法典》
good faith	善意
inheritance law	继承法

inter alia	除其他事项以外
intergovernmental organizations (IGOs)	政府间国际组织
international business law	国际商法
International Chamber of Commerce	国际商会
International Committee of the Red Cross	国际红十字会
International Court of Justice	国际法院
international criminal law	国际刑法
international humanitarian law	国际人道法
International Institute for the Unification of Private Law (UNIDROIT)	国际统一私法协会
international law	国际法
Islamic law	伊斯兰法
Judicature Acts of 1873 and 1875	（英国）《司法组织法》
know-how	专业技术
Koran	《古兰经》
law of obligations	债法
law of persons	人法
model law	示范法
multilateral trade negotiations	多边贸易谈判
nongovernmental organizations (NGOs)	非政府组织
non-tariff barriers	非关税壁垒
nuclear proliferation	核扩散
pacta sunt servanda	有约必守
precedent	判例
private international law	国际私法
protectionism of trade	贸易保护主义
public international law	国际公法
quotas	配额
Security Council	（联合国）安全理事会
sharia	伊斯兰教法
soft law	软法
specialization	（生产）专门化
Statute of the International Court of Justice	《国际法院规约》
sunna	伊斯兰教教规

supranational powers	超国家权力
tariff barriers	关税壁垒
The Final Act Embodying the Results of the Uruguay Round of Multilateral Trade Negotiation	《乌拉圭回合多边贸易谈判成果最终文件》
the principle of most-favored-nation treatment	最惠国待遇原则
the principle of national treatment	国民待遇原则
trade liberalization	贸易自由化
Trade Policy Review Mechanism (TPRM)	贸易政策审查机制
Understanding on Rules and Procedures Governing the Settlement of Disputes (DSU)	《关于争端解决规则与程序的谅解》
United Nations Charter	《联合国宪章》
United Nations Commission on International Trade Law (UNCITRAL)	联合国国际贸易法委员会
United Nations Conference on Trade and Development (UNCTAD)	联合国贸易和发展会议
World Trade Organization (WTO)	世界贸易组织

Part II

Civil Code of the People's Republic of China	《中华人民共和国民法典》
contracting states	缔约国
convention	公约
Hague Rules	《海牙规则》
International Bank for Reconstruction and Development (IBRD or World Bank)	国际复兴开发银行（世界银行）
International Monetary Fund (IMF)	国际货币基金组织
International Rules for the Interpretation of Trade Terms (Incoterms)	《国际贸易术语解释通则》
international trade customs and usages	国际贸易惯例
lex mercatoria (law merchant)	商人法
Montreal Convention	《蒙特利尔公约》
Principles of International Commercial Contract	《国际商事合同通则》
Sale of Goods Act	（英国）《货物买卖法》

sources of law (*fonts juris*)	法律渊源
sovereign	主权国家
treaty	条约
UNCITRAL Model Law on International Commercial Arbitration	《联合国国际贸易法委员会国际商事仲裁示范法》
Uniform Commercial Code (UCC)	（美国）《统一商法典》
United Nations Convention on Contracts for the International Sale of Goods (CISG)	《联合国国际货物销售合同公约》
Uruguay Round of Multilateral Trade Negotiations	乌拉圭回合多边贸易谈判

Part III

Chapter 1

acceptance	承诺
agency contract	委托合同
anticipatory breach	预期违约
avoidance of contract	解除合同
battle of forms	格式之争
bilateral contract	双务合同
breach of contract	违约（违反合同）
brokerage contract	居间合同
choice of law clause	法律选择条款
consideration	对价（约因）
construction contract	建筑合同
contract formation	合同的成立
Contract Law of the People's Republic of China	《中华人民共和国合同法》
counteroffer	反要约
damages for lost profits	可得利益损失
duress	胁迫
employment contract	雇佣合同
excused performance	（违约）免责事由
favor contractus	支持合同（原则）
firm offer	不可撤销的要约

force majeure	不可抗力
foreseeability rule	可预见规则
fraud	欺诈
freedom to contract	缔约自由
fundamental breach	根本违约
General Principles of the Civil Law of the People's Republic of China	《中华人民共和国民法通则》
grace period	（履行合同的）宽限期
greatly unconscionable	显失公平的（合同）
Guaranty Law of the People's Republic of China	《中华人民共和国担保法》
impediment	阻碍性事件
infringement of intellectual property rights	侵害知识产权
invitation to offer	要约邀请
legal capacity	法律行为能力
legal detriment	法律上的不利
mailbox rule	投邮原则
material mistake	重大误解
memorandum	备忘录
minor	未成年人
mirror image rule	镜像原则
mistake	误解
mitigation of damages	损害赔偿之减轻
mutual consent/assent	合意
negligence	过失
negotiable instrument	票据
non-conforming goods	与合同要求不符的货物
offer	要约
offeree	受要约人
offeror	要约人
oral contract	口头合同
passing of risk	风险转移
place of business	营业地
preempt to	优先于
price reduction	降价

promissory estoppel	禁止反言
public policy	公共政策
quasi-contract	准合同
real property	不动产
receipt rule	到达原则
remedies for breach of contract	违约救济措施
Restatement (Second) of Contracts of the United States	《美国合同法（第二次）重述》
revocation of an offer	撤销要约
revocation/repudiation/rescission/cancellation	解除 / 撤销
safekeeping contract	保管合同
sales contract	买卖合同
specific performance	实际履行
subject matter	标的物
suspension of performance	中止履行
title to the goods	货物的所有权
valid contract	有效合同
voidable contract	可撤销合同
void contract	无效合同
warehousing contract	仓储合同
will	遗嘱
withdrawal of an offer	撤回要约
written contract	书面合同

Chapter 2

act of god	天灾
act or omission of the shipper	托运人的作为或不作为
actual total losses	实际全损
Agreement on the International Goods Transport by Rail (SMGS)	《国际铁路货运协定》
Agreement on the International Passenger Transport by Rail (SMPS)	《国际铁路客运协定》
air waybill	航空货运单

all risks coverage	一切险
Baltic and International Maritime Conference (BIMCO)	波罗的海国际航运公会
bill of lading	提单
Carriage of Goods by Sea Act (COGSA)	（美国）《海洋货物运输法》
Chamber of Shipping Australian Grain Charter (Austral)	《澳大利亚谷物租船合同》（奥斯特拉尔）
charterparty	租船合同
clean bill of lading	清洁提单
common carrier	公共承运人
constructive total losses	推定全损
Convention concerning International Carriage by Rail (COTIF)	《国际铁路运输公约》
Convention for the Unification of Certain Rules for International Carriage by Air (Warsaw Convention 1929)	《关于统一国际航空运输若干规则的公约》（《华沙公约》）
Convention for the Unification of Certain Rules for International Carriage by Air (Montreal Convention 1999)	《统一国际航空运输某些规则公约》（《蒙特利尔公约》）
Convention on the Contract for the International Carriage of Goods by Road (CMR)	《国际货物公路运输合同公约》（《公路货运公约》）
cool chamber	冷藏室
dead freight	空舱费
demurrage	滞期费
documentary sale	跟单销售
draft	汇票
due diligence	适度谨慎
electronic bill of lading	电子提单
endorsement	背书
free of particular average (FPA)	平安险（单独海损不赔）
freight forwarder	货运代理人
general average	共同海损
general average contribution	共同海损分摊
Hague–Visby Rules	《海牙－维斯比规则》

Hamburg Rules	《汉堡规则》
Harter Act	（美国）《哈特法》
Himalaya Clause	喜马拉雅条款 / 规则
hold	船舱
insurance certificate	保险凭证（简式保险单）
insurance policy	保险单
Intergovernmental Organisation for International Carriage by Rail (OTIF)	国际铁路运输组织
legal seizure	法定扣押
marine cargo insurance	海洋货物运输保险
Maritime Law of the People's Republic of China	《中华人民共和国海商法》
Multimodal Transport of Goods	多式货物联运
notice of abandonment	委付通知
on board (loaded) bills of lading	已装船提单
open cargo policy	预约 / 开口货物运输保险单
order bill of lading	指示提单
Organization for Cooperation Between Railways (OSJD)	国际铁路合作组织
particular average	单独海损
perils clause	基本险
quarantine restriction	检疫限制
received-for-shipment bills of lading	待装船提单
refrigerating chamber	冷冻室
Regulations on Liability Limits of Air Carriers in Domestic Carriage by Air	《国内航空运输承运人赔偿责任限额规定》
riots and civil commotions	暴动与民变
SDR (Special Drawing Right)	特别提款权
specially to cover clause	附加险
straight bill of lading	不可转让提单
tackle to tackle	钩至钩
time charterparty	定期租船合同
trade terms	贸易术语
Uniform General Charter (Gencon)	《统一杂货租船合同》（《金康合同》）

voyage charterparty	航次租船合同
York–Antwerp Rules	《约克－安特卫普规则》

Chapter 3

advising bank	通知行
applicant (the account party)	（信用证）申请人
bearer draft	无记名汇票
beneficiary	（信用证）受益人
bill of exchange	汇票
Bills of Exchange Act of 1882	（英国）1882 年《汇票法》
blank endorsement	空白背书
certificate of origin	（货物）原产地证书
commercial invoice	商业发票
check	支票
clean collection	光票托收
confirming bank	保兑行
demand draft (D/D)	即期汇票
disclaimer	拒绝承担法定责任
documentary collection	跟单托收
documents against acceptance	承兑交单
documents against payment	付款交单
drawee	（票据）受票人
drawer	（票据）出票人
fictitious payee rule	虚构受款人规则
forged endorsement	伪造背书
fraud exception	欺诈例外
French Commercial Code of 1807	1807 年《法国商法典》
Geneva Conventions on the Unification of the Law Relating to Bills of Exchange (ULB)	《关于统一汇票法日内瓦公约》
Geneva Conventions on the Unification of the Law Relating to Checks (ULC)	《关于统一支票法日内瓦公约》

holder	持票人
holder in bad faith	恶意持票人
holder in due course	正当持票人
impostor rule	假冒受款人规则
International Standard Banking Practice for the Examination of Documents under Documentary Credits（ISBP）	《跟单信用证单据审查国际标准银行惯例》
issuing bank	发证行
letter of credit	信用证
Negotiable Instruments Law of the People's Republic of China	《中华人民共和国票据法》
negotiation	转让
nominated bank	指定行
notice procedures for the dishonor	拒付通知程序
order bill of exchange	指示汇票
presentment	提示（票据）
principle of independence	（信用证）独立原则
promissory note	本票
protest	拒付证书
qualified endorsement	附条件背书
restrictive endorsement	限制性背书
rule of strict compliance	严格相符原则
sight bill of exchange	即期汇票
special endorsement	特别背书
standby letter of credit	备用信用证
telegraphic transfer (T/T)	电汇
time bill of exchange	远期汇票
Uniform Customs and Practices for Documentary Credits (UCP 600)	《跟单信用证统一惯例》
Uniform Rules for Collections (URC 522)	《跟单托收统一规则》
waiver of the discrepancies	放弃不符点声明书

Part IV

Berne Convention for the Protection of Literary and Artistic Property	《保护文学与艺术作品伯尔尼公约》
certification mark	认证商标
challenge to validity	质疑（所转让知识产权的）有效性
Code of Conduct on the Transfer of Technology	《技术转让行为守则》
collective mark	集体商标
compulsory license	强制许可
confidential agreement	保密协议
copyright	著作权（版权）
Copyright Law of the People's Republic of China	《中华人民共和国著作权法》
Council for Trade-Related Aspects of Intellectual Property Rights	与贸易有关知识产权理事会
exclusive license	排他许可
exhaustion of rights doctrine	权利用尽原则
franchise	特许经营权
franchising agreement	特许经营协议
grant-back provision	回授条款
industrial property	工业产权
industrial utility	工业实用新型
International Convention for the Protection of Industrial Property (Paris Convention)	《保护工业产权国际公约》（《巴黎公约》）
International Convention for the Protection of Performers, Producers of Phonograms, and Broadcasting Organizations (Rome Convention)	《保护表演者、录音制品制作者和广播组织国际公约》（《罗马公约》）
international licensing agreement	国际许可协议
license	许可；许可证
lump sum	总包（价格）
moral rights	精神权利

neighboring rights	邻接权
no-challenge clause	禁止质疑条款
non-competition clause	禁止竞争条款
novelty	新颖性
one-time payment	一次付清
originality	原创性
package licensing	一揽子许可
Patent Law of the People's Republic of China	《中华人民共和国专利法》
pecuniary right	财产权利
price fixing clause	定价条款
Regulations on Technology Import and Export Administration of the People's Republic of China	《中华人民共和国技术进出口管理条例》
restrictive business practices	限制性商业惯例
right of distribution	分销权
right of performance	表演权
right of priority	优先权
right of reproduction	复制权
royalties	知识产权使用费；版税
service mark	服务商标
Sherman Antitrust Act	（美国）《谢尔曼反托拉斯法》
sliding royalties	滑动提成法
sole license	独家许可
The Agreement on Trade-Related Aspects of Intellectual Property Rights	《与贸易有关的知识产权协定》
trade name	商号
trade secret	商业秘密
Treaty on Intellectual Property in Respect of Integrated Circuits	《集成电路知识产权条约》
tying clause	搭售条款
utility patent	实用新型专利
World Intellectual Property Organization (WIPO)	世界知识产权组织

Part V

ad hoc arbitration	临时仲裁
Alternative Dispute Resolution (ADR)	替代性（选择性）争端解决机制
American Arbitration Association	美国仲裁协会
amicable	友好的
annul	宣告无效；废止
arbitration	仲裁
arbitration award	仲裁裁决
Arbitration Law of the People's Republic of China	《中华人民共和国仲裁法》
arbitration proceedings	仲裁程序
Arbitration Rules of China International Economic and Trade Arbitration Commission	《中国国际经济贸易仲裁委员会仲裁规则》
autonomy of the arbitration clause	仲裁条款的独立性
burden of proof	举证责任
China International Economic and Trade Arbitration Commission	中国国际经济贸易仲裁委员会
China Maritime Arbitration Commission	中国海事仲裁委员会
Civil Procedure Law of the People's Republic of China	《中华人民共和国民事诉讼法》
Convention on the Recognition and Enforcement of Foreign Judgments in Civil or Commercial Matters	《承认及执行外国民商事判决公约》
finality of the arbitral award	仲裁裁决的终局性
forum selection clause	审判地选择条款
in personam jurisdiction	属人管辖权
in rem jurisdiction	属物管辖权
institutional arbitration	机构仲裁
Japan Commercial Arbitration Association	日本商事仲裁协会
lex fori	审判地法
litigation	诉讼
London Court of International Arbitration	伦敦国际仲裁院
mediation	调解

minimum contacts test	最低限度联系标准
mini-trial	诉讼外公断
proving foreign law	外国法查明
settlement of international commercial disputes	国际商事争端的解决
Singapore International Arbitration Centre	新加坡国际仲裁中心
St. Petersburg International Commercial Arbitration Court	圣彼得堡国际商事仲裁院
subject matter jurisdiction	事项管辖权
territorial jurisdiction	领土管辖权
ultra petita award	超越当事人请求范围的仲裁裁决
United Nations Convention on International Settlement Agreements Resulting from Mediation （Singapore Convention on Mediation）	《联合国关于调解所产生的国际和解协议公约》（《新加坡调解公约》）
WIPO Arbitration and Mediation Center	世界知识产权组织仲裁与调解中心

References

[1] Arcy, Leo D', Murray, Carole & Cleave, Barbara, *Schmitthoff's Export Trade: The Laws and Practice of International Trade*, 10th ed., Sweet & Maxwell, 2000.

[2] Augusti, Ray, *International Business Law: Text, Cases, and Readings*, 6th ed., Pearson Education Ltd., 2013.

[3] Baron, David P., *Business Law and the Legal Environment*, 7th ed., Prentice Hall, 2013.

[4] Baumer, David L. & Poindexter, J. C., *Legal Environment of Business in the Information Age*, The McGraw-Hill Companies, Inc., 2003.

[5] Brown, Gordon W. & Sukys, Paul A., *Business Law: With UCC Applications*, 11th ed., The McGraw-Hill Companies, Inc., 2006.

[6] Chow, Daniel C. K. & Schoenbaum, Thomas J., *International Business Transactions: Problems, Cases, and Materials*, 4th ed., Wolters Kluwer, 2020.

[7] DiMatteo, Larry A., *International Business Law and the Legal Environment: A Transactional Approach*, 4th ed., Routledge, 2020.

[8] Emanuel, Steven L., *Contracts*, Citic Publishing House, 2003.

[9] Fawcett, James, *International Economic Conflicts: Prevention and Resolution*, Europa Publications Limited, 1977.

[10] Fletcher, Ian, Mistelis, Loukas & Cremona, Marise, *Foundations and Perspectives of International Trade Law*, Sweet & Maxwell, 2001.

[11] Folsom, Ralph, Alstine, Michael Van & Ramsey, Michael, *International Business Transactions in a Nutshell*, 11th ed., West Academic Publishing, 2020.

[12] Garner, Bryan A., *Black's Law Dictionary*, 9th ed., West Publishing Co., 2009.

[13] Jackson, John H., Davey, William J. & Sykes, Alan O., *Legal Problems of International Economic Relations: Cases, Materials and Text*, 6th ed., West Publishing Co., 2013.

[14] Lowenfeld, Andreas F., *International Economic Law*, Oxford University Press, 2008.

[15] Matsushita, Mitsuo, Schoenbaum, Thomas J. & Mavroidis, Petros C., *The World Trade Organization: Law, Practice and Policy*, 2nd ed., Oxford University Press, 2006.

[16] Miller, Roger Leroy, Jentz, Gaylord A. & Cross, Frank B., *West's Business Law: A Case Study Approach*, West Legal Studies in Business, 2003.

[17] Miller, Roger Leroy, Jentz, Gaylord A. & Cross, Frank B., *West's Business Law: An Extended Case Study Approach*, 2nd ed., Cengage Learning, 2006.

[18] Schaffer, Richard, Agusti, Filiberto, et al., *International Business Law and Its Environment*, 8th ed., Cengage Learning, 2012.

[19] Seidl-Hohenveldern, Ignaz, *International Economic Law*, 3rd ed., Kluwer Law International, 1999.

[20] Willes, John H. & Willes, John A., *International Business Law: Environments and Transactions*, The McGraw-Hill Companies, Inc., 2005.

[21] Han Yonghong, *International Business Law*, 2nd ed., University of International Business and Economics Press, 2018.

[22] Jiang Zuoli, *International Business Law*, 3rd ed., Law Press·China, 2013.

[23] Qu Guangqing, *International Business Law*, 2nd ed., Northeast University of Finance Publishing House, 2008.

[24] Ren Rongming & Hou Xingzheng, *International Business Law*, Tsinghua University Publishing House, 2004.

[25] Wang Chuanli, *International Economic Law*, 5th ed., Law Press·China, 2019.

[26] Zhang Xuesen, *International Business Law*, Fudan University Publishing House, 2008.

[27] Zuo Haicong, *International Business Law*, Law Press·China, 2008.